The Women's Lectionary

The Women's Lectionary

Preaching the Women of the Bible throughout the Year

Ashley M. Wilcox

WESTMINSTER
JOHN KNOX PRESS
LOUISVILLE · KENTUCKY

First edition
Published by Westminster John Knox Press
Louisville, Kentucky

21 22 23 24 25 26 27 28 29 30—10 9 8 7 6 5 4 3 2 1

Book design by Sharon Adams
Cover design by Mary Ann Smith
Cover illustration: Madonna assumption—Sanctissima . . . *Brintle, Patricia /*
Private Collection / © *Patricia Brintle / Bridgeman Images*

Library of Congress Cataloging-in-Publication Data

Names: Wilcox, Ashley M., author.
Title: The women's lectionary : preaching the women of the Bible throughout the year / Ashley M. Wilcox.
Description: First edition. | Louisville, Kentucky : Westminster John Knox Press, [2021] | Includes index. | Summary: "Focusing on passages about women in the Bible and feminine imagery of God, The Women's Lectionary reimagines the liturgical calendar of preaching for one year"— Provided by publisher.
Identifiers: LCCN 2021012085 (print) | LCCN 2021012086 (ebook) | ISBN 9780664266196 (paperback) | ISBN 9781646980062 (ebook)
Subjects: LCSH: Bible—Biography—Sermons. | Women in the Bible—Sermons. | Femininity of God—Biblical teaching. | Lectionaries.
Classification: LCC BS575 .W5337 2021 (print) | LCC BS575 (ebook) | DDC 220.92082—dc23
LC record available at https://lccn.loc.gov/2021012085
LC ebook record available at https://lccn.loc.gov/2021012086

Most Westminster John Knox Press books are available at special quantity discounts when purchased in bulk by corporations, organizations, and special-interest groups. For more information, please e-mail SpecialSales@wjkbooks.com.

To Jada, Joshua, and AdaMarie

Contents

Acknowledgments

I have so many people to thank, but without three in particular, this book would not exist. First, my partner, Troy Winfrey, became my first reader and offered a generous listening ear. Thank you for keeping the home fires burning and for suggesting that I write a lectionary in the first place. Thanks to Ted Smith for advice and encouragement when this was just an idea, for trusting me with students, and for keeping me honest. And thanks to Anna Hull for letting me use your beautiful home as a quiet place to pray and write: you are on every page of this book.

Thanks to everyone who helped with the book proposal, particularly Brent Bill, Erica Schoon, and Layton E. Williams. I am so grateful to everyone at Westminster John Knox Press, especially my editor Jessica Miller Kelley, for her advocacy and incisive questions; David Garber, for his copy edits; and Natalie Smith, for publicity. Many thanks to my agent, Laura Blake Peterson, for her good humor and creative problem solving, and to everyone at Curtis Brown. Thanks to Mia Blankensop and Jen Graham for helping me navigate the world of publishing. Thanks to Shannon Mayfield for engaging conversations and gifts at key moments. I am grateful for the spiritual support of my anchoring committee and my spiritual director, Tavye Morgan. Thanks to Rachel Guaraldi for our spiritual friendship and monthly video calls.

I feel fortunate to be part of communities of care both in person and online, including the folks at Freedom Friends Church, Church of Mary Magdalene, Friendship Friends Meeting, Clairmont Oaks, *Friends Journal*, Young Clergy Women International, the Speaking of Writing group, and Queer Christian Twitter. Thanks to everyone at Candler School of Theology, especially John Blevins, Susan Hylen, Luke Timothy Johnson, Joel LeMon, Steffen Lösel, Jan Love, Carol Newsom, Karen Schieb, Ellen Shepard, Andrea White, and the P501 teaching team and students. I feel blessed by the community of ministers who let me work alongside them and who offer support and encouragement, including Betsy Blake, Amanda Crice, Wess Daniels, Tricia Hersey, Julie Hliboki, Quest Hunter, Brett Isernhagen, Emily Provance, Christina

Repoley, Deborah Shaw, Karen Stephenson, Deborah Suess, Margaret Webb, and Lloyd Lee Wilson.

Thanks to Myles, Simon, Talia, and Emily Weaver Brown, for giving me a place to land after finishing my manuscript. Many thanks to my parents, Dawn and Paul Wilcox, and to Maggie Winfrey, for giving me so many of the resources I needed for this project; and to my siblings, Rachel, Lael, and James Chase Wilcox, for being such cool weirdos. Thank you to all my friends and family who have celebrated with me. And all my thanks to the Spirit, who speaks to and through us all.

Introduction

What if the church took one year to focus on the stories of women in the Bible? *The Women's Lectionary* reimagines the liturgical calendar of preaching for one year to focus on the passages about women in the Bible and feminine imagery of God. These texts include women who are daughters, wives, and mothers—and more than daughters, wives, and mothers. They are also strong female leaders, evil queens, and wicked stepmothers. They are disciples, troublemakers, and prophetesses. The feminine descriptions of God in the Bible are similarly varied: how does it change our understanding if God is described as feminine wisdom, as having wings, or as an angry mother bear? Preaching on these passages gives us a better comprehension of God and how God interacts with people.

This book provides a calendar for preaching each Sunday and on holy days for a year, using texts that may also appear in the Revised Common Lectionary (RCL), Year D, or other alternative lectionaries. (The calendar of readings on pages xxiii–xxvii emphasizes in bold those texts that are also in the RCL.) This calendar includes one text from the Hebrew Scriptures and one from the New Testament for each of these days. In addition, there is a commentary for each passage that provides exegesis of the text and context. The purpose of the commentaries is to be evocative, not comprehensive: my hope is to spark your imagination as you prepare your sermons.

ORIGINS AND INFLUENCES

Some may be wondering why a Quaker is writing a lectionary. That's a fair question. I am part of a tradition that, at least historically, completely disregards the liturgical calendar. In our traditional worship in the Religious Society of Friends, we sit in silence, waiting to hear the voice of God. We believe that God may lead anyone to speak, so we sit facing each other. We do not mark holy days because we believe that every day is sacred. For Friends who worship in the unprogrammed tradition, it does not matter what the occasion is—a holy day, a wedding, or a memorial—the order of worship is the same. We sit in silence, and people speak as led. So I do not seem like an obvious person to take on this project. And yet, I feel led by the Spirit to do so, and I will start by describing some of the influences that brought me here.

I was raised in the church, though not as a Quaker. My first experiences of church were as an infant. My parents attended the local Episcopal church in my hometown of Anchorage, Alaska. I was two months old when I played the baby Jesus in the Christmas pageant (by all accounts, I slept through the whole thing). When I was still a young child, my parents started attending a charismatic nondenominational church; this is the first church I remember. I recall singing, clapping, and being completely unable to speak in tongues. I attended Sonrise Christian School, a small, parent-driven private school in Anchorage, where most of the teachers came from Calvin College. I was involved in Calvinettes (now GEMS) and later the youth group. For most of my childhood, I was in a Christian bubble, with the good and bad that comes with being part of that kind of subculture.

Like many in my generation, I left the church of my childhood because the congregation where I attended was unwilling to affirm the worth and dignity of LGBTQ+ people. Alaska was one of the first states to pass a "defense of marriage" state constitutional amendment. I was in public high school by that point, and I could not reconcile the good I saw in my queer friends with the messages I heard on Sunday mornings in my church. Although I continued attending with my family until I left for college, I no longer considered myself a Christian.

At seventeen I left home to attend a blessedly secular public university in California—and experienced culture shock in more ways than I could name. Although I was in the same country, Santa Cruz was an entirely different world than the one in which I grew up. There I met people who did not go to church and were not conflicted about it, unlike my friends in Alaska. I did not attend church once while I was in Santa Cruz, nor did I seek out any of the religious activities available on campus. I felt free, and I had no intention of going back to church.

The exception was a year I spent studying abroad in Santiago, Chile. That was my first experience of living for an extended time in a predominantly Catholic country, and I found it fascinating. The entire city would shut down for Holy Week, and everyone I met was Catholic. It was a difficult year for me, in large part because a stranger sexually assaulted me halfway through the year. I felt lost, and I would spend Sunday mornings climbing to the top of the large hill near my apartment in Santiago, which had a statue of Mary at the peak. I would stay there, sitting with Mary, until I felt that I could walk back down. Occasionally I would attend mass. One of my roommates' mothers came to visit, and she asked me if I believed in God. I said that I did not know if I believed in God. Then she asked if I believed in Mary, and I assured her that I did. She said, "That's fine, then, as long as you believe in Mary!"

I found my way back to church when I was in law school a few years later. Law school was a strange place for me. I enjoyed the academic challenge, but I struggled to connect with my classmates. I did not like the competition and posturing that law school seemed to bring out in people. My roommate felt similarly, so we did what we had learned to do as children: find a church. We agreed that we could not go back to the denominations we had grown up in (Southern Baptist, in her case), so we tried all the others that we could find. We almost ended up picking an Episcopal church and attended services there several times.

Then I went to visit my aunt and uncle for Thanksgiving. My parents had told them that I was looking for a church, and they suggested that I try a Quaker gathering. They had attended a local Quaker church for several years, and they thought that it might be a good fit for me. When I got home, I looked online for a Quaker church and found Freedom Friends Church. I went with my roommate, and I immediately felt at home. Freedom Friends Church was a semi-programmed Quaker worship, with singing, prayers, and an extended period of silence. I loved all of it, and I kept going on my own after my roommate moved away. I felt that I had found a place where I could be myself, without others telling me how to be or what to believe. My church supported me when I came out as queer. I went deeper and deeper into the silence in worship.

I moved to Seattle for work and joined an unprogrammed Quaker meeting there. Unexpectedly, within my first year of working as a lawyer, I experienced an undeniable call to ministry. I began doing ministry and traveling among Friends, and I became well known for blogging and organizing Quaker events. What was even more strange, I felt called to preach. I would pray in the United Church of Christ church across the street from the court where I worked and envision myself in the pulpit. I felt led to attend a two-year program called The School of the Spirit, with residencies four times a year in North Carolina. People kept asking me if I planned to go to seminary, and I would say, "No, I already have a graduate degree." Then one night it became clear to me and my support committee that I was led to attend seminary. I planned to go to Candler School of Theology, a United Methodist seminary in Atlanta. Just months before I left, my church recorded me as a minister, the Quaker version of ordination.

At Candler, I studied with professors from many traditions, including Lutheran, Catholic, Presbyterian, and Baptist, as well as United Methodist. After graduation, I stayed connected to Candler as part of the teaching team for professor Ted Smith's Introduction to Preaching course, and I cofounded a church called Church of Mary Magdalene, where women preached. Church of Mary Magdalene came out of a dream I had of preaching for women, who moved their chairs up to hear what I had to say. This was my first experience with weekly preaching, and I enjoyed the challenge. About a year in, I said to my partner Troy that I was feeling torn between wanting to use the Revised Common Lectionary—with the community and resources that accompany it—and wanting to preach about women. Troy said, "Well, why don't you write your own lectionary?"

This idea captured my imagination, and I spent the next several days putting together a draft of a lectionary based on women in the Bible and feminine images of God. I met with Ted Smith to discuss the idea, and he encouraged me to write commentaries for each of the passages. I used this lectionary for a year at Church of Mary Magdalene, exegeting the texts to preach on them and then turning the sermons into commentaries. In addition to preaching at Church of Mary Magdalene, I preached once a month at a local retirement community vespers service. One evening after the service, a woman came up to thank me for my message; she said that she had never heard a sermon from Mary's perspective before. "The women are there in the Bible," she mused, "but no one ever talks about them!" Incrementally, the project grew.

In the course Introduction to Preaching, Ted Smith uses the metaphor of "hybrid vigor" to describe the class's teaching team. Each person on the teaching team has experience in at least two traditions. Many, like me, come from several different traditions. The idea behind hybrid vigor is that this mixing of traditions makes us stronger preachers: we bring the best of multiple denominations to our study and delivery of the message. I believe this to be true, based on my own experiences and having observed students preaching in the class for four years now. We can be deeply rooted in one tradition while appreciating and borrowing from others. As you read the commentaries, you will see the influence of each of the traditions I have encountered, and I am sure you will bring your own as well.

HOW TO USE THIS BOOK

The primary use for this book is for preachers, who can take a year (or two!) to focus on the stories of women in the Bible and feminine images of God. The texts follow the liturgical calendar, with texts for each Sunday and Christian holiday throughout the year. Sometimes the texts from the two Testaments are related to each other—particularly on holidays—but for the most part, they are not. I recommend picking one of the texts and focusing on that for your sermon; you may choose to include the other as a reading during the liturgy.

Each text has a commentary to accompany it. These commentaries are intended to provide some background on the text and stimulate your ideas as a jumping-off point for your own engagement with the text. I advise you to do your own exegesis on the text as well, working with other translations, sources, and commentaries. One of the reasons I have included many texts from the Revised Common Lectionary is because there are many resources available for working with those texts. The commentaries in this book represent just one voice among many: feel free to disagree with my analysis and conclusions!

One benefit of preaching from a lectionary is being part of a larger community using the same texts each week. I hope that people using this book will have conversations with others who are using *The Women's Lectionary*, both in person and online. You may also want to use this book for group Bible studies or your own personal devotions. If so, I recommend reading the biblical text in multiple modern versions and using the questions at the end of each commentary section for conversation or reflection. If you are posting about your use of this book, connect with others doing the same by using the hashtag #TheWomensLectionary.

If you are not able to do a full year of preaching from this lectionary, this book can serve as a supplement to preaching from the Revised Common Lectionary. Look for the texts that are drawn from the RCL and use the commentaries on those texts in your sermon preparation. Or organize texts from *The Women's Lectionary* into sermon series, either by using the suggested sermon series plans (starting on page xxix) or coming up with your own themes. These texts lend themselves to talking about topics such as feminine images of God, responses to sexual violence, motherhood, and women in leadership.

Notes of Care and Caution

GENDER

As I wrote this book, I felt tension between being a part of the queer community and talking about women. It can be hard to talk about women without falling into some version of gender essentialism or believing that women are a certain way simply because they are women. To counter this, my goal is to present many stories about women and feminine images of God side by side, to illustrate the complexity of femininity and womanhood. I hope that readers will also take an expansive definition of women to include trans women and femme nonbinary people. Categories necessarily create distance, but in my experience, focusing on one area tends to expand my thinking in other areas. I hope this is also the case for you.

RELATIONSHIP WITH JUDAISM

As Christian preachers, there is no way for us to avoid the fact that we are using another religion's scripture. The Hebrew Bible is a Jewish text. Christians have used it for millennia and interpreted it, but it is not originally ours. At some level, all of Christianity is cultural appropriation. Unfortunately, feminist scholars have contributed to anti-Judaism in harmful ways. Specifically, it can be easy to fall into the trap of making the Jews in the Gospels look bad so that Jesus appears to be a feminist in the way he treats women.[1]

There are better and worse ways to use the Hebrew Scriptures in Christian preaching, and I have tried to model some of these approaches in my commentaries. I am grateful for the work of Jewish scholars in guiding these approaches, especially Amy-Jill Levine. First, take the text on its own terms and avoid supersessionism, the belief that Christianity is the fulfillment of Jewish Scripture. Not everything is pointing toward Jesus. Second, listen to Jewish voices, especially when they are telling us that something we have said is

anti-Jewish or anti-Semitic. Third, be mindful of the history of Christian violence against Jews; approach this with humility. Finally, take care when using
Christian commentaries, which often repeat misinformation about Judaism.
We are blessed to have the record of Christian thought from millennia of
scholarship, but some of these works repeat anti-Jewish—or entirely inaccurate—information. We can preach without relying on dangerous shortcuts.
God is present in women and in the Bible without our being disingenuous.

PATRIARCHY

Anyone who attempts to preach from a feminist perspective must find a way
to critically engage patriarchy in the Bible. Patriarchy is unavoidable in our
sacred text. Many preachers today tend to gravitate to extremes: saying either
that patriarchy is God's will for ordering society or that patriarchy is an evil
that must be eradicated. In this book, I suggest an alternative approach: patriarchy is a coping strategy that no longer serves us.

Those who preach "crush the patriarchy" impose our current norms on
a premodern cultural phenomenon and ignore the ways that patriarchy has
solved problems historically, especially in (1) keeping young men from killing each other over women and (2) creating a system of protection for young
women. Women who fit within the patriarchal system had protection their
entire lives—first from their fathers, then their husbands, and finally their sons.

It is useful to acknowledge this because many of the biblical stories about
women are about those who fall outside the protection of patriarchy. This
includes all the women who pray to have sons as well as those whose husbands
die and leave them without support. It is a mistake to equate women in the
Bible who are praying for sons with our current understanding of infertility;
the women in the Bible prayed for a son in large part so that they would have
someone to protect them in their old age. Women who found themselves outside the bounds of patriarchy faced destitution and sometimes punishment (cf.
Tamar, Gen. 38).

Patriarchy was a solution that seemed to work for most people and for most
of the time. I find it useful to see patriarchy as a coping strategy because that
gives us a framework to appreciate it for what it was and see the ways it no longer
serves us. Like the coping strategies that we develop early in life, this is one that
worked for a long time. But there comes a point when we see the limitations of
our coping strategies and need to leave them behind so that we can live fully.

In addition, many people are attached to the idea of patriarchy. I believe,
however, that there are other, better strategies, ones that recognize the full
humanity of women. I find this useful as a preacher, because in preaching we

must examine the text in its original context and find ways to apply it to our contexts today. I reject the idea that patriarchy is God's will for the ordering of humanity. I know from Scripture that all people are created in the image of God, and I hope that in our preaching we can critically address the ways that patriarchy has been useful in the past but may harm us now.

VIOLENCE AGAINST WOMEN

As scholar Gale Yee notes, "We read all kinds of violence in the Hebrew Bible, and the violence against women is especially distressing. Why don't we hear about these stories in church?"[2] Every lectionary makes choices about what to include and what to leave out. Unfortunately, the Revised Common Lectionary often leaves out the stories of violence against women (it even makes strategic cuts to take out the troubling parts of passages, which often have to do with women, such as the text where the king accuses Haman of attempted rape in Esth. 7:7–8). In our culture today, we are in a time of reckoning: leaders in all fields need to face the ways that they have harassed, abused, disparaged, and dismissed women or been complicit in these actions. This is true in church as much as anywhere else, as we have seen in the #MeToo and #ChurchToo movements.

Too often, the church's response to stories of sexual assault and rape in the Bible has been to avoid them. Every sexual assault is different: there is no one way to experience or respond to that specific kind of trauma. In this book I want to honor these stories and the women who have experienced sexual violence. They did what they had to do to survive, and in some cases they did not survive. Some responded with righteous anger. Some accepted that this was part of daily life. Each of their experiences is valid.

Preachers have a responsibility to talk about the sexual violence in our sacred text. Members of the congregation have experienced rape and assault, and they deserve to know that stories like theirs are part of our sacred texts. Many preachers—of all genders—have experienced sexual violence, and they have found ways to process their trauma, individually and in community. For those who do not have personal experience with sexual violence, this is an opportunity to learn and grow, to empathize with those who have had these experiences, and to work toward justice for all. I hope that sharing these stories will help to deepen our conversations about sexual violence and will inspire Christians to work for justice for women in our sacred texts, our churches, and the world.

The Lectionary Chart

Texts in bold include passages from the Revised Common Lectionary.

ADVENT-CHRISTMAS-EPIPHANY		
First Sunday of Advent	Genesis 38:13–19, 24–27 (Tamar)	**Luke 1:26–38** (The Call of Mary)
Second Sunday of Advent	Joshua 2:1–21 (Rahab)	**Luke 1:39–45** (Mary Visits Elizabeth)
Third Sunday of Advent	**Ruth 3:1–18; 4:13–17** (Ruth)	**Luke 1:46–55** (Magnificat)
Fourth Sunday of Advent	**2 Samuel 11:1–15** (Bathsheba)	Luke 1:57–66 (Elizabeth Gives Birth)
Christmas	**Isaiah 42:5–9**, 14 (God Giving Birth)	**Luke 2:1–20** (Mary Gives Birth)
First Sunday of Christmas	**Isaiah 49:1–7** (Called in the Womb)	**Matthew 2:13–15, 19–23** (Mary's Family Goes to Nazareth)
Second Sunday of Christmas	**Isaiah 49:8–16** (Mothers Do Not Forget)	**Matthew 2:16–18** (Mothers' Babies Are Killed)
Epiphany	**Isaiah 43:1–7** (Bring Daughters)	**Matthew 2:1–12** (Mary Meets the Magi)
1st Sunday in Ordinary Time	**Psalm 131** (Mother with Weaned Child)	**Luke 2:22–38** (Anna Sees Jesus)

ADVENT-CHRISTMAS-EPIPHANY (cont.)		
2nd Sunday in Ordinary Time	**Isaiah 60:1–6** (Return to Zion)	**Luke 2:41–52** (Mary Loses Jesus in the Temple)
3rd Sunday in Ordinary Time	**Isaiah 62:1–5** (Zion as Bride)	**John 2:1–11** (Mary Attends the Wedding at Cana)
4th Sunday in Ordinary Time	**Jeremiah 29:1, 4–7** (Wives in Exile)	Matthew 12:33–37, 46–50 (Mary Waits for Jesus)
5th Sunday in Ordinary Time	**Lamentations 1:1–6** (Jerusalem as Widow)	**Mark 6:14–29** (Herodias)
6th Sunday in Ordinary Time	Ezekiel 16:1–22 (Unfaithful Wife)	**Mark 7:24–37** (The Syrophoenician Woman)
7th Sunday in Ordinary Time	Ezekiel 23:1–21 (Oholah and Oholibah)	**Luke 10:38–42** (Mary and Martha)
8th Sunday in Ordinary Time	**Hosea 1:2–10** (Gomer)	**Luke 20:27–38** (Marriage after Resurrection)
Transfiguration Sunday	**Hosea 11:1–11** (God as Parent)	**Mark 5:25–34** (Woman with Hemorrhages)

LENT–EASTER–PENTECOST		
Ash Wednesday	**Genesis 3:1–24** (Eve and Adam)	**Matthew 25:1–13** (The Ten Bridesmaids)
First Sunday of Lent	**Psalm 17:1–9** (Under God's Wings)	**Mark 12:38–44** (The Widow's Offering)
Second Sunday of Lent	**Isaiah 66:10–14** (God as Comforting Mother)	John 8:1–11 (The Woman Accused of Adultery)
Third Sunday of Lent	Judges 16:6–21 (Delilah)	**John 4:7–15** (The Woman at the Well)
Fourth Sunday of Lent	Job 28:1–20 (Wisdom)	**John 11:17–35** (Mary and Martha's Brother Raised)

LENT–EASTER–PENTECOST (cont.)		
Fifth Sunday of Lent	**Proverbs 1:20–33** (Wisdom Calls)	Luke 8:1–15 (Women Accompany Jesus)
Sixth Sunday of Lent	**Proverbs 8:1–4, 22–31** (Wisdom's Gifts)	**Matthew 27:11–23** (Pilate's Wife)
Maundy Thursday	**Proverbs 9:1–6** (Wisdom's Feast)	**Mark 14:1–9** (The Woman Anoints Jesus)
Good Friday	Deuteronomy 32:10–20 (God as Mother Eagle)	John 19:23–30 (The Women Watch)
Holy Saturday	Hosea 13:2–16 (God as Angry Mother Bear)	Luke 23:50–56 (The Women See the Tomb)
Resurrection Sunday	Song of Solomon 1:1–8 (Beloved)	**Mark 16:1–8** (The Women Go to the Tomb)
Resurrection Evening	**Song of Solomon 2:8–13** (Lover)	**John 20:11–18** (Mary Magdalene Sees Jesus)
Second Sunday of Easter	Esther 1:10–22 (Vashti)	**Matthew 28:1–10** (Mary Magdalene and Mary)
Third Sunday of Easter	Esther 2:1–18 (Women Taken / Esther Is Queen)	**Luke 24:13–24** (The Women Are Not Believed)
Fourth Sunday of Easter	Esther 5:1–8 (Esther's Banquet)	**Luke 7:11–17** (The Widow's Son Raised)
Fifth Sunday of Easter	**Esther 7:1–10; 9:20–22** (Esther)	Luke 13:10–17 (The Crippled Woman)
Sixth Sunday of Easter	**Job 1:1; 2:1–10** (Job's Wife)	Luke 13:31–35 (God as Mother Hen)
Ascension (Thursday)	**Psalm 123** (Maid and Mistress)	Luke 15:1–10 (The Woman Finds Her Coin)

LENT–EASTER–PENTECOST *(cont.)*		
Seventh Sunday of Easter	Proverbs 7:6–23 (Strange Woman)	**Luke 18:1–8** (The Widow and the Judge)
Pentecost Sunday	**Joel 2:23–32** (Daughters Shall Prophesy)	**Acts 1:14; 2:1–8, 14–18** (Women Pray and Prophesy)

SEASON AFTER PENTECOST		
Trinity Sunday	**Genesis 1:1–2:4** (Creator)	**John 7:37–39** (Holy Spirit)
9th Sunday in Ordinary Time	Genesis 2:4–9, 15–25 (Woman and Man)	Acts 5:1–11 (Sapphira)
10th Sunday in Ordinary Time	**Genesis 18:1–15** (Sarah Laughs)	**Acts 9:36–43** (Tabitha)
11th Sunday in Ordinary Time	Genesis 19:12–26 (Lot's Wife)	Acts 12:11–16 (Rhoda)
12th Sunday in Ordinary Time	Genesis 19:30–38 (Lot's Daughters)	Acts 16:11–19 (Lydia and the Enslaved Girl)
13th Sunday in Ordinary Time	**Genesis 21:8–21** (Sarah and Hagar)	Acts 18:1–4, 24–28 (Priscilla)
14th Sunday in Ordinary Time	Genesis 24:10–21 (Rebekah)	Acts 21:7–15 (Daughters Who Prophesy)
15th Sunday in Ordinary Time	**Genesis 25:21–28** (Rebekah Gives Birth)	Romans 16:1–7, 12–16 (Phoebe)
16th Sunday in Ordinary Time	**Genesis 29:15–28** (Rachel and Leah)	**1 Corinthians 1:10–18** (Chloe)
17th Sunday in Ordinary Time	Genesis 31:14–35 (Rachel Steals the Gods)	**1 Corinthians 7:25–40** (Unmarried and Widows)
18th Sunday in Ordinary Time	Genesis 34:1–29 (Dinah)	1 Corinthians 14:26–40 (Women Speaking)
19th Sunday in Ordinary Time	Genesis 39:1–20 (Potiphar's Wife)	**Mark 10:2–16** (Divorce)

20th Sunday in Ordinary Time	**Exodus 1:8–2:10** (Shiphrah and Puah)	Galatians 4:21–30 (Hagar and Sarah)
21st Sunday in Ordinary Time	Exodus 4:18–26 (Zipporah)	Ephesians 5:21–33 (Wives and Husbands)
22nd Sunday in Ordinary Time	**Exodus 15:1–11, 20–21** (Miriam)	**Philippians 4:1–9** (Euodia and Syntyche)
23rd Sunday in Ordinary Time	Numbers 27:1–11 (Mahlah, Noah, Hoglah, Milcah, and Tirzah)	Colossians 4:2–15 (Nympha)
24th Sunday in Ordinary Time	**Judges 4:1–7** (Deborah)	**1 Timothy 2:1–15** (Women Silent/Saved)
25th Sunday in Ordinary Time	Judges 4:12–22 (Jael)	1 Timothy 5:1–16 (Widows)
26th Sunday in Ordinary Time	Judges 11:29–40 (Jephthah's Daughter)	**2 Timothy 1:3–7** (Lois and Eunice)
27th Sunday in Ordinary Time	**Ruth 1:1–22** (Ruth and Naomi)	2 Timothy 3:1–7 (Silly Women)
28th Sunday in Ordinary Time	**1 Samuel 2:1–10** (Hannah)	2 Timothy 4:9–22 (Claudia and Prisca)
29th Sunday in Ordinary Time	1 Samuel 19:11–17 (Michal)	Titus 2:1–10 (Household Roles)
30th Sunday in Ordinary Time	1 Samuel 25:2–3, 18–31 (Abigail)	**Philemon 1–7** (Apphia)
All Saints' Day	**Proverbs 31:10–31** (Capable Wife)	**James 2:14–26** (Rahab)
31st Sunday in Ordinary Time	2 Samuel 13:1–21 (Tamar and Amnon)	Revelation 12:1–6, 13–17 (Woman and Earth)
32nd Sunday in Ordinary Time	1 Kings 10:1–13 (Queen of Sheba)	Revelation 17:1–6 (The Great Whore)
33rd Sunday in Ordinary Time	2 Kings 9:30–37 (Jezebel)	Revelation 2:18–29 (Jezebel)
Christ the King Sunday	2 Kings 22:3–20 (Huldah)	Revelation 19:4–9; 22:17 (Bride)

Sermon Series

Advent, Christmas, and Epiphany

First Sunday of Advent

GENESIS 38:13–19, 24–27

Tamar

The story of Tamar may be the least familiar of the four women listed in Jesus' genealogy in Matthew 1:1–17. Tamar's story falls in the middle of the Joseph narrative, immediately after Joseph's brothers sell him into slavery and before the passage about Potiphar's wife (another seductive foreign woman). This account is about Joseph's brother Judah and Judah's daughter-in-law, Tamar.

Tamar is a woman who has experienced a lot of loss. She loses two husbands and her home, and she is waiting for her husbands' third brother to be old enough to marry and give her sons. Her first husband, Er, was "wicked in the sight of the Lord, and the Lord put him to death" (Gen. 38:7). Her second husband, Onan, pulled out and "spilled his semen on the ground" instead of impregnating Tamar (38:9).[1] This was displeasing to the Lord, so God put him to death as well. According to the law of levirate marriage, Judah should give Tamar his third son, Shelah, to marry (cf. Deut. 25:5–10). But Judah is afraid that Shelah will die too, so he instead sends Tamar back to her father's house to wait until Shelah grows up.

This text illustrates the failure of patriarchy to protect women who fall outside the patriarchal structure. One of the benefits of a patriarchal system is that everyone knows who the head of the family is: the patriarch (in this case, Judah). In an ideal patriarchal system, a woman has protection throughout her life: first from her father, then her husband, and then her sons. However, Tamar is a woman outside of this protection.[2] After the deaths of her husbands, she is no longer a virgin, a wife, or a mother. She is a foreigner, making

3

her even more of an outsider. Tamar is stuck in limbo, waiting at her father's
house and unable to marry again or to have children.[3]

When Tamar discovers that Shelah has grown but Judah has not given
her to him in marriage, she takes the law into her own hands. She acts to
protect herself and the family line by going to the next closest male relative:
Judah. Tamar takes off her widow's garments and disguises herself in a veil.
Thus, Judah thinks that she is a prostitute and solicits her for sex (38:14–15).
Tamar negotiates for his signet and cord and his staff in exchange, and Judah
"[comes] in to" Tamar and impregnates her (38:18).

When Tamar takes Judah's signet, cord, and staff, she puts herself in Judah's
role as the head of the tribe and takes on his identity;[4] the Hebrew word for
"staff" also translates as "tribe." Symbolically, Tamar is now the head of the
tribe. Thus, this marginalized woman subverts the patriarchy to do what is
right and continue the family line, which leads to David and Jesus. When
Tamar later confronts Judah with the signet, cord, and staff, he recognizes
what she has done and says, "She is more in the right than I" (38:26). Jewish
tradition does not stigmatize Tamar for what she did, but instead praises her.[5]

Because this text probably is unfamiliar to many in the congregation, one
way for the preacher to approach it is to retell the story of Tamar, explaining her actions in the context of the law of levirate marriage. Without this
context, it may seem like Tamar is engaging in strange or unethical sexual
behavior. But with an understanding of why she makes these choices, the congregation can see that, through her courageous acts, Tamar saves the family
name. The sermon can also highlight how God works through this seemingly
powerless woman, who upends the power structure to save herself, her family,
her people, and all of us. Christians should remember her story.

- Have you heard the story of Tamar before? In what context?
- How does the law of levirate marriage protect women?
- How can churches celebrate Tamar and remember her story?

LUKE 1:26–38

The Call of Mary

This text begins with "In the sixth month" (Luke 1:26), which refers to the
sixth month of Elizabeth's pregnancy.[6] Thus the story of Mary's miraculous
pregnancy is bookended by Elizabeth's miraculous pregnancy. There are
other parallels between the two stories. For example, the conversation between
Mary and the angel Gabriel echoes and contrasts with the conversation that

Zechariah had with Gabriel. Zechariah's story may be more of what people might expect: an announcement to a priest in a temple (1:8).[7] Instead, this announcement is to a young woman in a small, rural village in Galilee.[8]

The angel says to Mary, "Greetings, favored one! The Lord is with you" (1:28). From this point on, the angel's conversation with Mary follows the prophetic call narrative. Traditionally, a prophet's call includes a divine confrontation, an introductory word, a commission, an objection, reassurance, and a sign; a classic version of this type of call occurs in Exodus, when God called Moses from the burning bush (Exod. 3:2–12). These parts of a prophetic call are present in Mary's story. There is a divine confrontation when the angel comes to Mary (Luke 1:26–27). The introductory word occurs when the angel says to Mary that she is "favored" and that the Lord is with her (1:28). Then there is a commission: "And now, you will conceive in your womb and bear a son, and you will name him Jesus" (1:31). Like Moses questioning God, Mary also objects: "How can this be, since I am a virgin?" (1:34). And God gives her a sign: Elizabeth's pregnancy. The angel says, "And now, your relative Elizabeth in her old age has also conceived a son; and this is the sixth month for her who was said to be barren" (1:36). Finally, Mary accepts this call: "Here I am, the servant of the Lord; let it be with me according to your word" (1:38).

Some commentators say that this is not a fully prophetic call.[9] They argue that it falls short of a full prophetic call because Mary is merely called to womanly things like childbirth and raising a child. However, there are many examples of God calling prophets to use their bodies as signs. Examples include God calling Isaiah to walk naked and barefoot for three years as a sign (Isa. 20:2–4), Ezekiel lying bound on the ground in ropes (Ezek. 4:4–8), and Jeremiah burying a waist sash and then digging it up to show that he could not wear it (Jer. 13:1–7). These are called sign acts, and they have two parts: (1) a nonverbal act followed by (2) a prophetic word. Both Mary and Elizabeth have a nonverbal act followed by a prophetic word. Their nonverbal acts are in their miraculous pregnancies, and then the Holy Spirit calls them to prophetic speech. When Mary goes to Elizabeth's house, Elizabeth is filled with the Holy Spirit and cries out, "Blessed are you among women, and blessed is the fruit of your womb" (Luke 1:42). And Mary responds with the Magnificat (1:46–55).

This is such a familiar story, one that is often taken out of context. By using the prophetic call narratives and the story of Elizabeth, preachers can place this story back into the context of the biblical narrative and the book of Luke. The angel appearing to Mary, while miraculous, is not unique in the Bible. Mary is one of a long line of people whom God has called to speak and act prophetically, and she immediately joins another prophetess when she visits her relative Elizabeth.

- How is Mary's interaction with the angel similar to the story of Zechariah and the angel? Why do they each respond differently to the angel's announcement?
- How is this text like prophetic call stories in the Hebrew Scriptures?
- Does it change your perspective on Mary and Elizabeth to see them as prophetesses?

Second Sunday of Advent

JOSHUA 2:1–21

Rahab

Rahab, the Canaanite woman at the center of this story, is the second woman listed in Matthew's genealogy leading to Jesus (Matt. 1:5). Some have characterized this passage as Rahab outsmarting the spies,[1] but really, Rahab outsmarts everyone. First, she outmaneuvers her own king and army. When the king of Jericho sends orders to her to bring out the men (Josh. 2:3), she tells just enough of the truth for it to be believable. Undaunted by the king's power, she says that the men were there, but she did not bother to learn where they were from, and they left before dark (2:4). Then she gives the king's men specific instructions on where to pursue them (2:5), making sure the gate shuts behind them (2:7).

Next, Rahab outsmarts the spies. She takes them up to her roof (2:6), where they are both hidden and visible. The flax that Rahab has drying on the roof hides them, but the roof is out in the open and potentially visible to others.[2] While she has them there, she negotiates with them for her family's life (2:12–13). The spies, who must be in a hurry to get away from the city, respond heartily with "Our life for yours!" (2:14). It is only after Rahab has secured their promise that she lowers them down by a rope, and then she gives them similarly specific instructions on which way to go to avoid their pursuers (2:15–16). The spies' response seems notably cooler once they have climbed down from the roof—repeatedly characterizing their promise as "this oath that you made us swear to you" (2:17, 20). They also add some requirements: that she have all her family in the house (2:18–19) and that she put a crimson cord in the window. Perhaps they regret agreeing to her terms so quickly.

Notably, Rahab does not just secure a promise to save herself. In fact, she mentions her family members specifically: "Spare my father and mother, my brothers and sisters, and all who belong to them, and deliver our lives from death" (2:13). She puts her family members and "all who belong to them" before herself. Rahab is not a solitary woman who is estranged from her family: she is close to them and makes sure that they will be spared. For the preacher, there is room in this message to include not just Rahab's biological family, but also her chosen family.

One could even argue that Rahab outsmarts God. Deuteronomy 7:2 explicitly says that when the Israelites conquer the land, they must "utterly destroy" the people there: "Make no covenant with them and show them no mercy."[3] But Rahab finds a way to make a covenant with these Israelite spies, and she is an essential part of their conquest of Jericho. If she had not hidden the spies, they would not have survived to return to Joshua. In addition, when the spies report back to Joshua, the report they give is directly from Rahab (Josh. 2:9, 24).

At the heart of this text, Rahab preaches. She gives what may be the longest prose speech by a woman in the Bible.[4] Rahab reminds the spies (and the readers) of what God has done for Israel: drying up the sea when they came out of Egypt and leading them to triumph in battle against other kings (2:10). She tells them that the people of Jericho "melt in fear" before them (2:9) and prophesies that God will give them the land. This foreign woman speaks the word of God to the people of God!

Most of the commentaries about Rahab focus on her profession. The reception history about her has sexualized her as a prostitute and speculated about whether the spies had sex with her. Others have argued that Rahab was not a sex worker but instead translate her occupation in verse 1 as "innkeeper."[5] The flax and the crimson cord also lead to the idea that Rahab worked with textiles.[6] Considering all the other things that Rahab does in this text—outwitting armies, protecting her family, and speaking truth about God—it is unfortunate that she has been reduced to "Rahab the prostitute."

- When you have heard the story of Rahab before, what parts of the story did the tellers focus on? What did they leave out?
- How can preachers hold the tension between this story and the command to utterly destroy the people of Canaan in Deuteronomy 7:2?
- Is Rahab's profession important? Why or why not?

LUKE 1:39–45

Mary Visits Elizabeth

Mary has just learned that she is pregnant, and she goes with haste to visit her relative Elizabeth (Luke 1:39). This text does not say why Mary is going to see Elizabeth, but it probably is to see the sign that the angel told her: that Elizabeth in her old age has conceived a son (1:36). The text also does not say how Mary feels about the message the angel gave her. She may have doubts about what has happened. In the moment, everything seemed so clear. Mary heard the angel and responded, "Let it be with me according to your word" (1:38). But afterward, Mary may wonder: Since she was the only one there when the angel appeared—maybe it was a dream? Mary takes a risk by going to Elizabeth's house. What if Elizabeth does not believe her? Or shames her for being pregnant before marriage? But Elizabeth is also pregnant through miraculous means: if anyone can understand what Mary might be feeling, it's Elizabeth.

Before Elizabeth even sees Mary, she cries out with prophetic speech. Elizabeth is a loud, joyful prophet. The Greek phrase means "megaphone,"[7] and some scholars suggest that this reflects the loud cries of giving birth. But Elizabeth is still three months away from childbirth. She cries out loudly because she is filled with the Holy Spirit—the feminine presence of God within her. Elizabeth recognizes the child leaping with joy in her womb as a sign from God.[8] The first thing Elizabeth says is that Mary is blessed (1:42). Elizabeth does not say that Mary *will be* blessed: she already *is* blessed. Elizabeth also says that the child in Mary's womb is blessed, but that comes second. This must be reassuring for Mary. Elizabeth has no way of knowing that Mary is pregnant other than a message from the Holy Spirit. Elizabeth confirms what the angel said to Mary, and the confirmation comes with a blessing.

Elizabeth is also the first person to name Jesus as Lord (1:43).[9] This will be echoed later when Jesus calls Mary Magdalene to be the first person to preach the gospel after his resurrection.[10] In both cases, women are the ones to speak the truth about who Jesus is and who he will be. Finally, Elizabeth says, "Blessed is she who believed that there would be a fulfillment of what was spoken to her by the Lord" (1:45). Mary is blessed because she believes. In Greek, the word "fulfilled" can also mean the consummation, perfection, or the event that verifies the promise. The baby that Mary carries is the fulfillment of the prophecies in the Hebrew Scriptures about a Savior who would come to save his people.[11]

Here, the fulfillment is bodily: both Elizabeth and Mary are filled with babies. These powerful women are called by God to have these sons, and they approach their births with fear and joy. Jesus' ministry will be embodied and about bodies: Mary will give birth to him, he will grow and heal the sick, and he will die and be resurrected. It is no accident that Elizabeth feels this message in her body. God's word is embodied, and it is through bodies that God's word is fulfilled. Preachers can celebrate with Elizabeth and Mary the ways that God has spoken to and through them, directly and through their bodies.

- Why does Mary go to visit Elizabeth? What do you think she is thinking and feeling on her way there?
- How is Elizabeth like the prophets in the Hebrew Scriptures?
- What are some other ways that God's word is embodied?

Third Sunday of Advent

RUTH 3:1–18; 4:13–17

Ruth

The harvest is ending, and Naomi knows that she and Ruth need more security. Until now, the women have relied on Ruth's daily gleanings, but that source of food will end with the harvest. So Naomi devises a plan for Ruth to marry Boaz.[1] Naomi's plan is risky: she is sending Ruth into a situation where she could be humiliated or even raped.[2] But these women know that Boaz is a good man. They know this because Ruth has been gleaning with the other young women who work for him (Ruth 2:8), and women talk to each other about whether a man is trustworthy.

This passage is filled with innuendo and sexual language, which may be one of the reasons the Revised Common Lectionary skips over Ruth 3:6–18. Naomi's goal is for Ruth to entice Boaz: she tells Ruth her to wash and anoint herself and put on her best clothes.[3] Naomi then instructs Ruth to go to the threshing floor, wait until Boaz has eaten and drunk and is lying down, and uncover Boaz's feet (a euphemism for genitalia).[4] When Ruth does this, Boaz is terrified: he wakes up startled and demands to know who she is.

Instead of waiting for Boaz to tell her what to do, as Naomi told her, she proposes! She tells Boaz to "spread your cloak over your servant" (3:9), a phrase that was symbolic of marriage in the Israelite tradition. She also invokes the levirate law by saying, "You are next-of-kin [to me]" (3:9). In effect, she is telling Boaz that, as the closest male relative, he must marry her, and their first son will be considered the offspring of her deceased husband (cf. Deut. 25:5–6). Ruth is asking Boaz to act as her "kinsman-redeemer," a

11

word that is used in the Bible for both this kind of relative and for God (e.g., Ps. 69:18).

It is unclear what happens between Ruth and Boaz that night. Boaz sends her away at first light to protect their reputations. But he does not send Ruth away empty-handed. When Boaz gives Ruth grain, he provides food for her and Naomi and gives Ruth the hope of being filled with a child. Then Boaz uses levirate law to his advantage. He knows that there is a closer relative who could serve as kinsman-redeemer, and Boaz goes to him and asks if he wants to buy a field from Naomi. According to levirate law, if a person falls into difficulty and sells a piece of property, the next-of-kin shall redeem what the relative has sold (Lev. 25:25). But in this case, the field would come with a widow—Ruth. When the closer relative realizes that Ruth's first child would inherit the field, he forfeits his claim,[5] leaving the field (and Ruth) to Boaz.

Ruth and Boaz marry, and one of the blessings of the people is the hope that their house will "be like the house of Perez, whom Tamar bore to Judah" (4:12). This links to another woman in Jesus' lineage and is a reminder that for these people, Tamar is a hero. Ruth has a son named Obed, who is part of Naomi's line under levirate law (he is considered the son of her son). Obed is the father of Jesse, who is the father of David, and the ancestor of Jesus.

Throughout this text, there are examples of people investing in each other. Ruth has followed Naomi to a strange land, and she trusts Naomi enough to put herself in a dangerous position on the threshing floor. Naomi knows that Boaz is a good man and that he will follow the law and take care of Ruth. Finally, Boaz recognizes the goodness in Ruth and Naomi, and he acts quickly to resolve the situation and marry Ruth. Each person chooses to turn toward another, and all of it builds toward God's plan.

- How have you heard the story of Ruth told before? Is the sexual language in this text surprising?
- How does it change the story to omit 3:6–18, as the Revised Common Lectionary does?
- What are some parallels between Ruth and Tamar?

LUKE 1:46–55

Magnificat

In response to Elizabeth's prophetic speech, Mary bursts into song. Like Elizabeth, Mary is filled with the Holy Spirit and speaks prophetically about who God is and what God has done. Mary's message takes the form of a psalm, which echoes many writings in the Hebrew Scriptures (cf. Ps. 34:1–3).[6] For most of the psalms, the gender of the psalmist is unknown; this text provides a psalm explicitly by a woman. Like many of the psalms, this song begins with praise. Mary cries out that her soul magnifies the Lord and her spirit rejoices in God (Luke 1:46–47).

Mary's song is an interesting place to substitute feminine pronouns for God. If God is without gender, Mary should be able to say, "She has looked with favor on the lowliness of her servant" (cf. 1:48). How do female pronouns change the sense of who God is? How does it change the meaning to hear, "Her mercy is for those who fear her"? Using feminine pronouns here is a reminder of a God who says, "Now I will cry out like a woman in labor, I will gasp and pant" (Isa. 42:14). This is the God who will comfort us as a mother comforts her child (Isa. 66:13) and hide us in the shadow of her wings (Ps. 17:8).

Mary is aware of all the generations before her and the generations to come. As many commentaries point out, Mary's song mirrors Hannah's song in form and content (1 Sam. 2:1–10).[7] When Mary recalls the promise that God made to her ancestors (Luke 1:55), she evokes the generations of women before her in Jesus' lineage in Matthew 1:1–17: Tamar, who took on the role of head of the tribe to continue the family line (Gen. 38:18–26); Rahab, who risked everything for a new world (Josh. 2:8–13); Ruth, who boldly asked a good man to marry her (Ruth 3:9); and Bathsheba, who rose from tragedy to power (1 Kgs. 2:20). All these women have played their part in leading to the fulfillment of God's promise.

When Mary says, "From now on all generations will call me blessed" (Luke 1:48), she is speaking of *this* moment. It is from this time forward that all will call her blessed, not the moment of Jesus' birth. The generations that will call her blessed include all the women who come after her. Anna, the prophet who waits at the temple to see the baby Jesus (2:36–37). Mary and Martha, the sisters who take care of Jesus' needs and listen to his teaching (10:38–42). Mary Magdalene, the first person whom Jesus calls to preach after his resurrection (John 20:17). And the women of the early church: Priscilla, Chloe, Lois, Eunice, Junia, and many more.

Mary's song is good news for the poor and bad news for the powerful. She says that God "has brought down the powerful" and "lifted up the lowly" (Luke 1:52); God "has filled the hungry" and "sent the rich away empty" (1:53). The God whom Mary knows turns the expectations of the world upside down. This is not something that will happen at some future date: Mary says that God has already done this.[8] Mary speaks into being a world in which oppressed people are free from systemic injustice.[9] These are not nice or gentle words. Mary prophetically announces social, political, and economic upheaval and a complete reversal of the power structure.

- How is Mary's song like the psalms?
- What stands out to you when you substitute feminine pronouns for God in this text?
- How does Mary connect the women of the Hebrew Scriptures to the women of the early church?

Fourth Sunday of Advent

2 SAMUEL 11:1–15

Bathsheba

Bathsheba is one of the most famous women in the Hebrew Scriptures, which is ironic because this text says so little about her. The only description is that she is bathing and very beautiful (2 Sam. 11:2). Her father and her husband are named (11:3); both are part of David's army.[1] But there is nothing here about Bathsheba's inner life, her hopes, or her desires. This lack of Bathsheba's point of view has made it possible for commentators to project many things onto her, particularly the idea that she is a seductress, though there is no indication in the text that she is. She is a beautiful woman and no more—an object that David desires.

Did David rape Bathsheba? The Hebrew is unclear. Where the NRSV says that David "sent messengers to get her," the Hebrew really means "to take her" (11:4). This is the same verb that Samuel used when he warned the elders that kings would "take" from the people (1 Sam. 8:10–18).[2] However, the text does not say that David uses force against Bathsheba, as in other instances of rape.[3] Whether Bathsheba consents or not, the fact remains that David is the most powerful man in the country, who sends his men to take her. Whatever her feelings about the matter, it is unlikely that Bathsheba would be able to refuse him.

Although Bathsheba speaks little in this text, her body speaks volumes. David is first stirred to lust when he sees her body, and he is unwilling to control that lust even after he learns that she is married (2 Sam. 11:3). Bathsheba menstruates and purifies herself after her period (11:4), demonstrating

15

that she has not become pregnant by her husband. After her encounter with David, she sends word to him directly, "I am pregnant" (11:5). David can no longer ignore or discard her body, and he cannot control her pregnancy. Bathsheba grieves for her husband after David has him killed (11:26). She carries David's child in her body, gives birth to a son, and then mourns him when he dies (12:24).

For David, Bathsheba's pregnancy is a problem to be solved. He first tries to solve it by tricking Uriah into having sex with Bathsheba, so that Uriah will think the baby is his (11:8). But Bathsheba's husband is more religiously observant than David, refusing to have sexual relations with a woman during battle (1 Sam. 21:4–5).[4] When it becomes clear that David's initial plan will not work, he turns to a deadlier solution to his problem: having Uriah killed in battle (2 Sam. 11:15). There is no indication that David speaks to Bathsheba about his plans or that he gives any thought to her at all. David later feels grief about what he has done, but he only goes to console Bathsheba after the death of her child (12:24). Bathsheba has lost so much: her husband, her home, and her child.

But this is not the end of the story for Bathsheba. David lies with her again, and she gives birth to a son, which David names Solomon (12:24). At the end of David's life, Bathsheba works with the prophet Nathan to ensure that Solomon will inherit the throne (1 Kgs. 1:11–37).[5] She later delivers a message that inspires Solomon to consolidate his power (2:13–25). Solomon rises to meet her, bows to her, and has a throne brought in for her to sit on his right (2:19). This woman, who has been seen as a problem, has become a powerful ruler alongside Solomon.

In a story about her, Bathsheba is rarely named. In the passage after this text, when Nathan confronts David, her name is never mentioned: she is instead called "the wife of Uriah the Hittite" (2 Sam. 12:10). Even in the genealogy of Jesus in Matthew, she is called "the wife of Uriah" (Matt. 1:6). This text gives preachers an opportunity to right this wrong: to say Bathsheba's name and to honor her memory. She is not merely a victim, but a woman who would not let the man who mistreated her forget her or what he did to her body.

- How would this story be different if it were told from Bathsheba's perspective?
- What would you like to know more about in this text?
- How can churches mourn with and honor women who have lost children?

LUKE 1:57–66

Elizabeth Gives Birth

In the first chapter of Luke, the story of Elizabeth and the birth of John is a frame for the story of Mary and the birth of Jesus. Before the angel Gabriel appears to Mary and announces that she will have a son (Luke 1:31), the angel appears to Zechariah and announces that his wife, Elizabeth, will bear him a son (1:13). And before Mary gives birth to Jesus in Bethlehem (2:7), Elizabeth gives birth to John (1:57). These parallel stories illustrate how God is at work in the world through these two women.

In addition to the parallels between Elizabeth and Mary, there are parallels between the story of Elizabeth and Zechariah and the stories about Sarah and Abraham in Genesis 17–21.[6] Elizabeth and Zechariah are both "righteous before God" (Luke 1:6), but they are childless and "getting on in years" (1:7). Zechariah is a priest, and Elizabeth is a descendant of Aaron (1:5). It is unusual for a woman's ancestor to be listed in the Bible, but this shows that both Zechariah and Elizabeth come from a priestly lineage.[7]

Although he is a priest, Zechariah has not learned from the story of Sarah and Abraham. When the angel Gabriel appears to him and says that his wife will bear a son whom they will name John, Zechariah echoes Sarah's laughter (Gen. 18:12) and asks how this can be so, since he and his wife are elderly (Luke 1:18). The angel responds that, because Zechariah does not believe him, he will be mute "until the day these things occur" (1:20). Then Elizabeth conceives, and she recognizes this as an act of God (1:24–25).

In this text, everything that the angel Gabriel foretells to Zechariah comes to be. The description of the birth of John is very brief (1:57), and Luke's emphasis is on the theological implications of this birth.[8] The neighbors do not come to celebrate with Elizabeth merely because she has given birth, but because God has shown great mercy to her by giving her a child (1:58). For these neighbors and relatives, this is a sign of God's power and favor.

Most of the text concerns the naming of the child. On the day of his circumcision, the neighbors and relatives want to name the baby Zechariah, after his father (1:59).[9] But Elizabeth says, "No; he is to be called John" (1:60).

Then the text makes a turn for the comic.[10] Zechariah is mute, not deaf, but the neighbors do not seem to understand this. Instead of merely asking him what the child's name should be, they begin motioning to him (1:62). Unfortunately, this is probably all too familiar for people with disabilities: those around them take one aspect of their disability and assume that it applies to other functions. Fortunately, Zechariah is able to clear up the confusion quickly by writing on a tablet that the child's name is John (1:63), which means "God has been gracious."[11]

As soon as Zechariah confirms what the angel has said to him, that his son would be named John, his tongue is freed (1:64). Zechariah begins praising God (1:67). The neighbors react with fear; in Luke this is a typical response to signs of God's presence; they go away to share the news and wonder what this child will become (1:65–66). Like Elizabeth when she visited Mary (1:41–42), Zechariah is filled with the Holy Spirit and is led to speak prophetically (1:67).

- What are the similarities and differences between the stories of Elizabeth and Mary in Luke 1–2?
- Why did God make Zechariah mute during Elizabeth's pregnancy? Was it a punishment, a sign, or both?
- Both Elizabeth and Zechariah are filled by the Holy Spirit to speak. How does the Holy Spirit speak through people?

Christmas

ISAIAH 42:5–9, 14

God Giving Birth

This text builds to a strongly feminine image of God: God crying out like a woman in labor.[1] The line "I will gasp and pant" (Isa. 42:14) brings to mind a woman in late stages of giving birth, when the baby is about to be born. A midwife once told me that she and her colleagues listen for when a mother in labor says, "I can't do this!" That is a signal that the baby is going to be born soon. Perhaps that is how God feels in the act of creation. What will God give birth to after this gasping and panting?

Although only 42:14 explicitly refers to birth, there is birth imagery throughout the text. God is the one who "created the heavens and stretched them out" (42:5), like a woman's body stretches to make way for new life. God also "gives breath to the people" (42:5), which is reminiscent of the first breath a baby draws after birth. How does our understanding of the creation story change if we think of it as a woman giving birth? Rather than a tidy, step-by-step creation, birth is a messy and painful process. God chooses birth as the way for new life to come into the world.

Birth imagery is not confined to the Hebrew Scriptures. The central figure in the New Testament, Jesus, came into the world through birth. Jesus could have come in any number of ways, but God chose for him to be born of Mary. Another important example of birth imagery in the New Testament is the conversation between Jesus and Nicodemus about being "born again" (John 3:1–10; 3:3 NRSV note). The idea of being born again has taken on a specific meaning in conservative Christianity in the United States, but the original imagery is still powerful. When a baby is born, the entire family changes. Maybe being born again is just as hard, messy, and painful as being born the first time, and God uses the pain of birth and rebirth to shape and mold God's people.

When God says, "I have called you in righteousness, I have taken you by the hand and kept you" (Isa. 42:6), the "you" is ambiguous. It is most likely the people of Israel, though it could be a servant that God is calling (and Christians tend to think the call is for Jesus).[2] The ambiguity in the text allows for all these interpretations. As in the creation stories, God speaks things into being in this passage: "See, the former things have come to pass, and new things I now declare; before they spring forth, I tell you of them" (42:9). As God declares new things, they spring forth.

The imagery of Israel as God's baby is rich. The prophets speak to how Israel has disappointed God, like children disappoint their parents. Even though God calls the people "in righteousness" (42:6), God's people do not always follow. And yet, like a mother who has gone through the pain and struggle of childbirth, God loves us. That love comes out of the pain and creative effort, the labor in creation.

As a text for preaching on Christmas, this passage provides a counterpoint to the lack of description of Mary giving birth and the idea that "all is calm" on the night of Jesus' birth! Like God crying out in this text, Mary most likely cried out with birth pangs. For both God and Mary, the pain of birth opens up the possibility for something new: a new life, a new child, a new way of being in the world. Preachers can give thanks for the ways that new life comes, through God and through birth.

- When you envision God giving birth, what does that look like?
- How does God give birth to new life throughout the Bible?
- What are the parallels between this text and the birth of Jesus in Luke?

LUKE 2:1–20

Mary Gives Birth

With a text as overinterpreted as the birth of Jesus, it can be hard for a preacher to know where to begin. One approach is to simply retell the story. Although this passage about Mary giving birth to Jesus and the visit from the shepherds probably is familiar to many, the details may be fuzzy (or mixed with the infant stories of Jesus in Matthew). The preacher can remind the congregation of what is actually in the story and what has been added to it. Alternatively, a close reading of the text provides many examples of how God speaks to humans and of different faithful ways that people react to God's message.

The first way that God speaks to people in the text is through tradition. Many commentators have noted that the registration (or census) Luke describes in the first few verses is not historically accurate. There is no external evidence for a census under Herod the Great when Jesus was born.[3] However, tradition dictates that the messiah comes from Bethlehem, the city of David.[4] It is unclear whether Luke was confused or merely taking creative license, but he follows this tradition and uses the oppressive government to get Mary and Joseph to Bethlehem for the birth of Jesus.

The description of the birth of Jesus and the angel's announcement provide contrasting ways that God speaks to people. The verses describing the birth of Jesus are brief and simple (Luke 2:6–7).[5] The time comes for Mary to deliver this child, who has been foretold, and she does. She then wraps him in cloth and lays him in a manger because there is no room for them in the guest room. By contrast, the announcement to the shepherds is dramatic, with an angel telling them the good news and then a multitude of heavenly hosts praising God (2:10–14). Thus, God speaks through the birth of a child and through a multitude of angels.

In addition, God speaks through a sign. The angel tells the shepherds that they will know the child because he is "wrapped in bands of cloth and lying in a manger" (2:12). This description of the child is enough for the shepherds to know that they have found the child when they go to Bethlehem (2:16). There is a surprising lack of details here: how did the shepherds know where to look for the child? Unlike the magi, they do not have a star to follow, but perhaps like them, the shepherds asked others where to look.

When the shepherds arrive and see the child, they tell others what the angels have told them about the child (2:17). Even from the very beginning of Jesus' life, God uses people to tell other people about the miraculous things that God is doing. God could have sent an angel to Mary directly, as before (1:26–38), but instead Mary hears about the shepherds' encounter with the angels and the prophetic words about her son through these strangers.

The ways that the shepherds and Mary react to the news illustrate quite different faithful responses. The shepherds make what they have heard known (2:17), and they return while "glorifying and praising God" (2:20), echoing the angel chorus.[6] Mary, on the other hand, treasures all these words and ponders them in her heart (2:19). Mary has been obedient to what God has asked her to do, and now she has received more amazing news. She provides an example of a quieter way to respond to the miraculous news of Jesus' birth and who he will become.

- What parts of this familiar story are surprising to you on rereading? What did you think would be there that is not?
- Where would you like to have more information? What are the gaps in the story of Jesus' birth?
- Who do you relate to in this story? How do you respond when God speaks?

First Sunday of Christmas

ISAIAH 49:1–7

Called in the Womb

Like Jeremiah, Isaiah says that he was called in the womb (cf. Jer. 1:5):[1] literally, "from the belly of my mother he named me."[2] This text provides a good starting point for a sermon on calling, starting with how God called Isaiah before he was born. Isaiah describes the kind of person that God made him to be while he was still in his mother's womb: God "made my mouth like a sharp sword," and "made me a polished arrow" (Isa. 49:2). For some people, it can be tempting to see the soft, nice parts of themselves as from God and the sharp edges as not of God. But when Isaiah was being formed in his mother's womb, God made him a sharp arrow, ready for use as a prophet.

This text also serves as a reminder that the prophetic calling is difficult. In both Jeremiah and Isaiah, the prophets resist the call. Jeremiah says, "Ah, Lord God! Truly I do not know how to speak, for I am too young" (1:6 NIV alt.). By contrast, Isaiah has tried and failed. He says, "I have labored in vain, I have spent my strength for nothing and vanity" (49:4). Pastors and churches can relate to these sentiments—feeling unqualified for reasons out of their control, or looking back and feeling like the work that they have done is in vain. However, Isaiah does not end there: instead he declares, "Yet surely my cause is with the LORD, and my reward with my God" (49:4).

Isaiah introduces the "suffering servant" featured in this passage and others. It is unclear who this servant is. At one point the servant seems clearly to be Israel when God says, "You are my servant, Israel, in whom I will be glorified" (49:3).[3] But one of the tasks for the servant is to "raise up the tribes of

Jacob and to restore the survivors of Israel" (49:6). It seems unlikely that Israel is called to rescue Israel. Another possibility is that the servant is Isaiah, whom God called as a prophet. Christians have traditionally understood this passage to be about Jesus, called as "a light to the nations" (49:6). And Paul said that it was about his ministry as "a light for the Gentiles" (Acts 13:47).[4] There is ambiguity within the text,[5] allowing space for multiple understandings of the identity of the servant. For the preacher, these multiple meanings create space to talk about how God calls communities as well as individuals.

This passage occurs in the middle of the book of Isaiah, during the Babylonian captivity and after the destruction of the temple.[6] It is a time of despair and questioning for the people of Judah, who must be asking, "Where is God? How could God let this happen?" The central image of the womb is comforting in this text; the prophet is being called back to this safe space where God formed him. Later in the chapter, the image of God as a mother is more direct: "Can a woman forget her nursing child, or show no compassion for the child of her womb? Even these may forget, yet I will not forget you" (Isa. 49:15). This God is faithful and does not forget God's people.

- What are some images you associate with the womb?
- Why does it matter if God calls a prophet while the prophet is in the womb? Why might a prophet claim to have been called while in the womb?
- How is God calling your congregation?

MATTHEW 2:13–15, 19–23

Mary's Family Goes to Nazareth

As in the genealogy of Jesus in Matthew 1:1–17, this text shows the close link that Matthew sees between the history of Israel and Jesus. In the escape to Egypt, Matthew depicts Jesus as a new Moses.[7] Jesus is an infant in mortal peril, yet the one who will later save his people (cf. Exod. 2:1–10). In this parallel story, Herod is cast in the role of Pharaoh, the cruel ruler who plans to kill Jewish babies. But God intercedes directly to save the baby Jesus by having an angel tell his adoptive father, Joseph, to flee to Egypt (Matt. 2:13).

Fortunately for this family, Joseph does what God tells him to do. In fact, throughout the text, Joseph's obedience is the mirror image of God's command.[8] The text does not give any indication of Mary's response, but she must be obedient as well, following Joseph as he does what God tells him to do. In some ways, Mary is in a more difficult position than her husband: Joseph has the divine encounter when he hears from the angel in a dream, but

Mary must trust Joseph's account. The silent Mary in this text is very different from the Mary of Luke, who sings God's praise and names the things that
God has done (cf. Luke 1:46–55). Instead, she is repeatedly lumped in with
Jesus as "the child and his mother," suggesting that women and children are
possessions to be protected in times of danger.

When the family goes to Egypt, Matthew asserts that this fulfills the
prophecy in Hosea 11:1, "Out of Egypt I have called my son" (Matt. 2:15).
Throughout this chapter, Matthew quotes Scripture with almost identical
introductions (called "formula quotations"), thus emphasizing that the events
fulfill prophecy.[9] However, this use of Hosea is strange for several reasons.
First, Hosea 11:1 was never understood in Judaism to be a messianic text.[10]
The context in Hosea 11 is that "Israel" is God's son. Second, in Matthew
2:15, God is sending Jesus and his family to Egypt, not calling them out of
Egypt (though, arguably, Jesus needs to be *in* Egypt for God to call him out
of it later). The main points that both verses have in common is that they are
about Egypt and a son.[11] However, such use of Scripture without necessarily
fitting the biblical context is typical in rabbinic literature of the time,[12] and it
seems clear that Matthew sees a parallel between Jesus saving his people and
the Israelites returning from exile in the prophetic literature.

There are no biographical details about the time the family spends in
Egypt.[13] Instead, the text jumps ahead to Herod's death, when the family can
finally return to Israel (2:19). But Joseph is afraid of Herod's son, Archelaus
(2:22), and with good reason. After Herod's death in 4 BCE, his kingdom
was divided between his three sons: Archelaus, who governed Judea; Philip;
and Antipas.[14] Archelaus was a cruel ruler and ultimately was summoned to
Rome for his excessive harshness.[15] This explains why Joseph takes his family to Galilee (2:23) and underscores how Mary and Joseph protect Jesus in a
dangerous time.

The final formula quotation in this text, "He will be called a Nazorean"
(2:23), does not correspond to any known text from the Hebrew Scriptures.[16]
Scholars have suggested that it is a play on words that creates associations with
both Jesus' hometown of Nazareth and the holiness associated with Nazirite
vows (Num. 6:1–21).[17] For preachers, these formula quotations highlight
some of the potential problems with using a verse in isolation to illustrate
a point. The verse may mean something completely different in its context,
or something that seems vaguely biblical may not actually exist in Scripture!

- How effective is Matthew's use of Hebrew Scriptures to show that Jesus
  is the fulfillment of prophecy?
- What might this story be like if it were told from Mary's perspective?
- How does this story compare with ways in which God speaks to people in
  other parts of Scripture?

Second Sunday of Christmas

ISAIAH 49:8–16

Mothers Do Not Forget

This passage in Isaiah has striking images of God as a nursing mother and a mother who carries a child in her womb. It is a turning point in Isaiah, where God begins to respond to Zion, the personified grieving widow and mother.[1] In a text where it seems as though everything is moving toward celebration, Zion speaks out about her suffering and demands answers from God. Here God's answer is that of a mother who will not forget her children, the people of Israel.

This text begins with a frequent image in Isaiah: the Jewish exiles returning home (Isa. 49:8–9). The servant is a Moses-like figure, leading the people back to their land, but in a much more straightforward way than the original exodus![2] These people will not suffer hunger or thirst or even severe weather (49:10). Instead of forcing the people to take a meandering trip through a harsh desert, God will transform creation for them, turning "mountains into a road" (49:11). God will gather the people who have been scattered in different directions and lead them home (49:12).[3]

This happy prediction leads to one verse of praise (49:13), which is similar to the psalms of praise (cf. Ps. 148:7–10). The prophet does not tell the returning exiles to sing for joy, but rather calls on the heavens and the earth. All of creation will be breaking out in song to celebrate the return of God's people. The second half of this verse explains why the earth and heavens should celebrate: God has comforted God's people and will have compassion on God's suffering ones (Isa. 49:13). This seems like the culmination of Israel's prayers.

But in a dramatic twist, the text does not end in celebration. Instead, Zion speaks, saying, "The Lord has forsaken me, my Lord has forgotten me" (49:14). Zion, frequently personified as feminine in the Hebrew Scriptures, appears as a widow first in Lamentations, lamenting for her children, who are dead or dying (1:1, 16, 18; 2:22).[4] Here, in response to the celebration, Zion cries out in sorrow. She has lost her children, and she is suffering. Zion does not accept the statement that God has comforted God's people: Zion urgently calls on God to explain what has happened and to provide restitution.[5]

God responds to Zion's cry. Instead of dismissing Zion's pain, God relates to Zion as a mother. In an explicitly feminine image, God describes herself as a mother who has breast-fed her child and carried a child in her womb (Isa. 49:15). God has the kind of close bond with Israel that a mother has with a baby that she is feeding with her own body.[6] The assertion that "even these forget" is a way to show the vastness of God's love. It is almost unthinkable for a mother to forget her child, and even if that happens, God remembers. Zion is tattooed on God's palms and always before God (49:16).

For preachers, this text is a reminder to not move too quickly past suffering. It can be tempting, when things improve after a hard time, to want to go immediately to celebration and try to forget the sadness of the past. But Zion reminds God and us to make space for lament, even in times of joy. Like a mother who has miscarried or lost her child, she calls God to account for the pain that she has suffered and asks for answers. Instead of easy answers, God is with Zion in her pain. God knows the suffering of a mother who has lost her child, and God takes Zion's cries seriously. Preachers can use this text to be in solidarity with women who have lost children, and remind them that, like God, the church will not forget them.

- When you think of God as a nursing mother or a pregnant woman, how do you picture her?
- How can churches respond to those who are suffering the loss of a child? What rituals or liturgies can make space for that kind of loss?
- What questions would you like to ask God? Does the answer of God relating to us seem comforting?

MATTHEW 2:16–18

Mothers' Babies Are Killed

This tragic story of the massacre of the innocents comes in the middle of the holy family's flight to Egypt. As in the surrounding passage, this text draws a parallel between Jesus and Moses.[7] Like Pharaoh commanding that all of the

Israelite baby boys be killed (Exod. 1:15–22), Herod orders the deaths of all the children in and around Bethlehem two years or under (Matt. 2:16). But unlike in Exodus, these Jewish children do not have the midwives Shiphrah and Puah to save them (Exod. 1:17).

Scholars have questioned whether these events actually occurred. There is no historical record of Herod ordering the deaths of these infants. The Jewish historian Josephus stated that it was illegal for a king to kill anyone without the authority of the Sanhedrin, the Jewish council in Jerusalem.[8] However, Herod was responsible for numerous atrocities, and this would not have been considered a major event of his reign.[9] Josephus accuses Herod of other illegal executions.[10] Rather than arguing about the historicity of these events, it may be better for preachers to think of this story as a legend—a story involving historical people that has been embellished over time.[11]

As in other places in this chapter, Matthew quotes Scripture to emphasize that the events fulfill prophecy.[12] Here, however, Matthew does not use the formula "in order that," likely to avoid saying that these murders happened to fulfill Scripture.[13] Matthew quotes Jeremiah 31:15, in which the prophet describes the matriarch Rachel weeping for her children after the people of Judah have been taken into exile. But the context for the verse in Jeremiah is hope; God says, "Keep yourself from weeping" because "your children shall come back to their own country" (Jer. 31:16–17 alt.). There is no such hope in this part of Matthew: these children will not return.

All of this occurs because Herod is infuriated when he discovers that he has been tricked by the magi (Matt. 2:16). The word "tricked" here includes the idea of ridicule or being made to look foolish.[14] But distressingly, Herod's anger was caused by the miraculous warning that the magi received (2:12).[15] It is because the magi told Herod about the baby Jesus and the following divine intervention that all these babies are killed. Accordingly, this text raises questions about the nature of God. If God could send a divine messenger to save a child, why only send that messenger to one family?

The grief of the parents of these children in Bethlehem—as well as confusion and anger—is familiar to parents who have lost a child. It can be so painful for parents whose child has died to see other children who are the same age as their child. They may ask questions of God about why one child is cured from a disease when another dies. Just as Matthew draws on the tradition of lamentation from the Hebrew Scriptures, preachers can use this text to be with bereft parents in their pain. Matthew does not provide a tidy ending or platitude: this text ends with wailing and lamentation, a mother who refuses to be consoled.

Usually, this text is preached in the larger context of Mary, Joseph, and Jesus' flight to Egypt. The murder of the babies of Bethlehem is a footnote in a story about the miraculous escape of the holy family to Egypt. But it is worthwhile to approach this text separately. Even in a time of hope, after the birth of Jesus, there is still horror in the world. A merciless king, angry because he has been fooled, responds by killing innocent children. Just as Rachel weeps for her children, these mothers weep for their babies.

- Does it change your understanding of the story to know that there are no other historical accounts of this killing of the infants?
- Mothers have lost their children in times of war, violence, and genocide throughout time. How does this text reflect their pain?
- How does this story make you think differently about the visit of the magi and the holy family's escape to Egypt?

Epiphany

ISAIAH 43:1–7

Bring Daughters

In many of the prophetic books, references to women are few and far between.[1] It can feel like a stretch to say that this text is about women in the Bible when it only has one line about bringing daughters (Isa. 43:6). And yet, there are many women in Israel below the surface of these Scriptures by and for men. In preaching on this text, pastors can remember the women who are not named, point out the feminine aspects of God, and speak prophetically about the ways our language can be more inclusive for those who are not often named.

In the opening lines, the prophet says that God "created you, O Jacob" and "formed you, O Israel" (43:1). But this same God who created and formed Jacob/Israel also created and formed Leah and Rachel. *The Inclusive Bible* translation reinserts these women into the text: "But now, Leah and Rachel and Jacob, hear the word of YHWH—the One who created you, the One who fashioned you, Israel."[2] These women are mothers of Israel, just as Jacob is Israel's father. God repeatedly says, "Do not fear" (43:1, 5), bringing to mind a time when God protected another mother, Hagar, when she was cast out into the desert with her son (Gen. 21:14–19).[3] Like the angel calling out to Hagar, God says not to be afraid.

Another way to make the text more expansive is to change the pronouns for God from "he" to "she." With these feminine pronouns, the description of creation takes on a more maternal character, evoking a mother who knits together a child in her womb, or a feminine spirit creating the cosmos. Like a mother, she names her child (Isa. 43:1; cf. Gen. 29:32) and claims the child as her own.

This prophetic text demonstrates how to use what God has done in the past as a guide for what God will do in the future. With "I am the LORD your God, the Holy One of Israel" (Isa. 43:3), the text reminds Israel of God's introduction to Moses and of how God was with them when they passed through the sea in the exodus (43:2).[4] But this is not the only way that God will save them and protect them. There are other dangers for Israel, represented by rivers, fire, and flame (43:2).[5] God's protection is not limited to how God has saved them in the past; God is with them through all of these threats to their existence.

The description of the nations that God gives in exchange for Israel (43:3–4) may be troubling for Christian congregations. These verses illustrate how, when there is a chosen people, other people are not chosen. This is a place for Christians to remember that we have built on the sacred text of another religion, one that does not include us. And yet, we can hear the prophetic hope that God loves "everyone who is called by my name" (43:7). The tension in these verses is not easily resolved.

When God calls people from all directions, it shows how scattered the Jewish people have become in exile, and that this is not only something that affected men. God calls people from the east, west, north, and south (43:5–6). God calls both "sons from far away" and "daughters from the end of the earth" (43:6). In this context, calling both sons and daughters feels more inclusive than merely sons, but in our congregations today, this may not feel inclusive enough. Nonbinary, trans, and genderqueer church members remind us that language like "sons and daughters" and "brothers and sisters" does not include everyone. As we work to make the women in the Bible more visible, texts like this call us to make space for those who have even less representation in our Scriptures.

- How does it make you feel to add women's names into texts like this one?
- Prophetic texts like this were written for a specific time and place and for the Jewish people. How can we be respectful of that as we use them in our own context?
- What are some examples of language that you would like to be more inclusive in your congregation?

MATTHEW 2:1–12

Mary Meets the Magi

The story of the magi begins in the middle, when the magi are already in Jerusalem (Matt. 2:1). Although the magi are traditionally referred to as "three kings," there is nothing in the passage to suggest that they are male. The tradition that there are three of them is a medieval idea related to the three gifts that they bring. Scholars disagree about who these magi are and where they have come from; there is evidence to suggest that they are itinerant, traveling in large groups with their families.[6] The NRSV calls them "wise men," an inaccurate translation from the Greek *magoi*, or magic/ian.[7] Even the idea that they are wise is in question: early Jewish readers may have seen them as foolish because of their association with magic.[8] In this story, however, the magi are guided not only by astrology, but also by Jewish Scripture.[9]

The magi come to Jerusalem and ask where they can find "the child who has been born king of the Jews" (2:2). This is upsetting to King Herod and all of Jerusalem. King Herod is a paranoid, homicidal king who had ten wives and assassinated many people, including some of his own sons.[10] He was named King of the Jews by Rome, and he has worked hard to get to where he is. It is understandable that he is frightened by the idea of a new king of the Jews: the magi's questions threaten his existence. All of Jerusalem is frightened along with him (2:3). This may seem counterintuitive, considering what a terrible leader Herod is, but the magi's questions indicate that change is coming. It is disruptive and disturbing for the people of Jerusalem to think that God might be about to act in their midst.[11]

Mary is also in the middle of her story. The text says that she is in a house (2:11), a different setting from the nativity scene described in the Gospel of Luke. Though some scholars caution readers to see these accounts as separate, it is interesting to think about this ordinary life coming after the story described in Luke. After all the excitement around the birth of Jesus—angels arriving to deliver news, shepherds worshiping the newborn child—Mary has settled into the daily routine of raising a child. When the magi arrive, they see their visit as the culmination of their journey. For Mary, these are unexpected strangers from another country who have somehow found her and her child and are kneeling to worship him (2:11).

As strange as this must be for Mary, it may also seem like reassurance that she did not exaggerate or imagine the miraculous things that happened around her son's birth. The gifts that the magi bring give her a sense of what his life will hold: the gold that is associated with kings, the frankincense that is used in temple offerings (and associated with the queen of Sheba), and the myrrh for anointing and embalming.[12] With these gifts, the magi foretell that Jesus will be a king, they make offerings to him (as one would to God), and they foreshadow his anointing and death. When Mary accepts these gifts on behalf of Jesus, she must have some sense of the mixed blessings these magi bring.

For preachers, this text can reflect the letdown that occurs after a big event like Christmas. After so much anticipation, going back to ordinary life can be challenging. But the visit of the magi is a reminder that God is still at work on ordinary days, and the gifts of God can arrive at unexpected times and from unexpected people! This text also foreshadows what is to come: the deaths of the babies of Jerusalem and the holy family's flight to Egypt. Even as an infant, Jesus draws good and bad attention, with Mary as a witness.

- How does it change the story to see the magi as groups of families traveling together instead of three kings?
- What do you think Mary's response was when she saw the gifts that the magi brought?
- What are some examples of gifts from God from unexpected sources?

First Sunday in Ordinary Time

PSALM 131

Mother with Weaned Child

In the opening verse of Psalm 131, there is a contrast between how high God is and the lowliness of the psalmist, with imagery that builds up. This rising imagery fits the context of a psalm of ascent, which pilgrims would pray on their way to Jerusalem.[1] When the psalmist says, "My heart is not lifted up" (Ps. 131:1), the Hebrew for "lifted" can be translated to be high, be exalted, be tall, have a proud heart, or to be haughty (cf. 113:5, "Who is like the LORD our God, who is seated on high"). The word for "high" in "My eyes are not raised too high" (131:1) means "rise up," "to be high," or "to be exalted" (cf. 46:10, "I am exalted among the nations, I am exalted in the earth"). Even as the psalmist says that she is not raising her eyes too high, the reader begins to imagine looking up to the heights toward God.

Many scholars think that this psalm was written by a woman because of the use of nursing-mother imagery in it.[2] The psalmist focuses on breastfeeding imagery, describing herself as like a weaned child with her mother (131:2). This is reminiscent of the story of Abraham and Isaac, when weaning was a time for celebration: "Abraham made a great feast on the day that Isaac was weaned" (Gen. 21:8). Weaning usually happened when the child was about three years old, when the child was older and more self-sufficient.[3] For mothers, weaning can be a bittersweet time, with relief that they no longer need to be breastfeeding, but also some sadness that their babies no longer need them in the same way. But it seems odd that the psalmist says a weaned child is calm and quiet: weaned children usually are not calmer than those who

34

are breastfeeding! This may be about self-sufficiency and self-soothing: the psalmist has learned to soothe her own soul.

Alternatively, the Hebrew word that is traditionally translated as "weaned" can also mean "sated" or "satisfied."[4] Instead of a child who is independent from her mother, this may be about a child who is still nursing and sated by her mother's breast. This is a child who is still and calmed. In this context, the final verse calls Israel to "hope in the LORD" (131:3) and thus extends the metaphor. God is the mother, and the psalmist is inviting Israel to enter into God's embrace, like a contented child with her mother. Like a consoling mother, God is here to comfort her people, "from this time on and forevermore."

In addition to the feminist imagery, the psalmist emphasizing her lowly nature may also indicate her gender. Like Teresa of Avila calling herself "unworthy" to protect herself from those who might stop her from writing, the psalmist may be asserting her lowliness to fend off those who would argue that she should not be writing psalms. Those preaching on this text can draw out this tension, of a woman who feels unworthy to speak because she has been told speaking is not what she should be doing. But like Teresa of Avila and other strong women in the church, this psalmist speaks up, sharing her experience of God and of her own body. As a church, we need more women like this to share images of God and expand our understanding of God as a mother who feeds us at her breast.

- How is God like a mother breastfeeding her child?
- What does it mean that the psalmist has been weaned? What do you associate with a child who has grown past the age of breastfeeding?
- How is God like a mother to Israel?

LUKE 2:22–38

Anna Sees Jesus

This text is one of the few stories we have about Jesus' childhood, and it is a microcosm of the ways that God speaks to and through people. The first people in the passage are Mary and Joseph, who are going to the temple for purification according to the law (Luke 2:22). This is the ritual purification of Mary, which occurs thirty-three days after the birth of a son (Lev. 12:4).[5] Accordingly, God speaks to Mary and Joseph through Scripture: they are devout Jews, following biblical instructions for purification and making a sacrifice. The sacrifice they make is "a pair of turtledoves or two young pigeons" (Luke 2:24), specified for poor people who cannot afford a sheep.[6]

The next person named in the passage is Simeon, another righteous and devout man. God speaks to Simeon through the Holy Spirit, which rests on him and guides him to the temple (2:25–27). The temple is enormous; its courtyard is the size of several football fields.[7] But the Holy Spirit guides Simeon directly to the place where he will meet Mary, Joseph, and the baby Jesus. Then God speaks to Simeon through the baby Jesus, the Word made flesh. Simeon holds the baby Jesus in his arms and praises God, saying, "My eyes have seen your salvation" (2:30). God speaks to a man who has been waiting a long time, now seeing Christ in a tiny body.

After prophesying about the salvation he sees in Jesus, Simeon turns to Mary and Joseph, who are amazed (2:33). God speaks through Simeon as he blesses Mary and Joseph. Then Simeon gives Mary a message directly, and it is not an easy one. First, he says, "This child is destined for the falling and the rising of many in Israel, and to be a sign that will be opposed" (2:34). This must be hard for Mary to hear. As a young mother, she wants to protect her newborn son, not to think that anyone would oppose him. Second, Simeon says, "A sword will pierce your own soul too" (2:35). This is also a painful truth: it will be difficult for Mary to see her son separate himself from her and her family, and her heart will break when she sees him killed.

The final person in this narrative is the prophet Anna, an eighty-four-year-old widow (2:36–37). Unlike Simeon, Anna does not need the Holy Spirit to lead her to the temple, where the family is: she is already there. Anna "worshiped there with fasting and prayer night and day" (2:37). Anna knows where she is likely to meet God, and God speaks to her through this place. God uses Anna to speak to others. She praises God and speaks "about the child to all who were looking for the redemption of Jerusalem" (2:38). As a prophet, Anna speaks on behalf of God and tells everyone she meets about what God will do through this small child.

So often in preaching from the New Testament, the focus is on what Jesus says. In this text, he is too young to speak, but God is already speaking. Preachers can point out the different ways that God speaks before and after Jesus, as well as through him. This text demonstrates how God speaks to and through the young and the old, and people of different social classes and genders.

- Who do you relate to most in this text?
- What else would you like to know about Anna?
- How have you seen God speak to and through other people?

Second Sunday in Ordinary Time

ISAIAH 60:1–6

Return to Zion

After all of the suffering and darkness of the exile in Isaiah, this text begins with a bright command: "Arise, shine; for your light has come" (Isa. 60:1). In Hebrew, this prophetic call is to a woman, the personified Zion (Hebrew distinguishes between a male and a female second person, and the "you" here is feminine).[1] Zion, who has lost her children (Lam. 1:1, 16, 18; 2:22) and cried out that God has forsaken her (Isa. 49:14), now shines with the glory of the Lord (60:1). This Zion is embodied: she can rise up (60:1), she has light within her (60:3), she can lift up her eyes and look around (60:4), and her heart will thrill and rejoice (60:5).[2] Zion, the woman who has lost everything, will be radiant (60:5).

The prophet offers signs to show what God is doing: "Nations shall come to your light, and kings to the brightness of your dawn" (60:3); the children of Zion will return from exile (60:4); the abundance of the sea will come to her (60:5); and nations will bring great wealth (60:5–6). This raises the question: how do we read prophecies that are not ultimately fulfilled? Later readers know that the people did not all return, and nations did not bring gold and frankincense to Israel.[3] What is the purpose of a prophecy that does not reflect reality?

One answer is that the prophecy was a comfort to the people of the time. At this point in Isaiah, the exiles are beginning to return. Although the text is directed to Zion, the readers are the Jewish people. Those who have been separated from their home and their community may feel that they no longer belong. The description of the exiles as sons and daughters (60:4) reminds them that they are kin. Moreover, they are beloved young children, being held in their nurses' arms (60:4). The text offers reassurance that their return will be celebrated.

Another possibility is that these gifts from other nations serve to remind Israel who they are. In Psalm 72, the psalmist declares, "May the kings of Sheba and Seba bring gifts," and commands all kings to bow down before the king (72:10–11). The wealth from Sheba would remind the people of the queen of Sheba, who brought gold, precious stones, and spices to King Solomon (1 Kgs. 10:1–13). The prophet evokes this history for these people who have suffered in exile, so that they will remember the richness of their heritage.

For Christians, this text has often been read in parallel with the story of the magi (Matt. 2:1–12). Superficially, there are similarities: kings coming to a bright light, camels, gold, and frankincense. But a close reading of the text makes it clear that this is not a direct foretelling of the visit of the magi to the baby Jesus. Rather than rushing from this to the more familiar story, it is important to read this prophetic text on its own terms, in the context of Isaiah.

It is possible, however, to read the two texts in parallel to see what they reveal about God's epiphany—the divine revelation in the world.[4] In both texts, light is important: the people are in a thick darkness, but God's glory provides clear light (Isa. 60:2; Matt. 2:2). And in both stories, the bodies of women and children are central: the mother Zion and her children, and the mother Mary and her baby (Isa. 60:4, Matt. 2:11). Additionally, people travel to witness the glory of God (Isa. 60:3, Matt. 2:9–10). Reading these texts side by side offers a glimpse of how God appears to people throughout time.

- What emotions do you associate with a mother reunited with her children?
- What is the purpose of prophecy? How do you understand prophecy that does not literally "come true"?
- How does this text connect with the story of the magi?

LUKE 2:41–52

Mary Loses Jesus in the Temple

This text in Luke about Jesus in the temple is the only story from the Gospels about Jesus as a boy. It is clear from the beginning that Mary and Joseph are raising Jesus in an observant Jewish home. Jewish readers would know that, by going to Jerusalem each year, Mary and Joseph are following the requirement in Exodus 34:22–23 that all male Israelites shall go to Jerusalem for Passover, Pentecost, and Tabernacles.[5] This journey would take four or five days from Nazareth.[6] Mary and Joseph do not make this journey alone: they travel with a group of friends and relatives. There are enough people in their group that it takes an entire day on the way back before they realize that Jesus is missing (Luke 2:44).

When Mary and Joseph finally find Jesus in the temple after three days of searching, Mary asks a reasonable question: "Child, why have you treated us like this? Look, your father and I have been searching for you in great anxiety" (2:48). Jesus responds with a question of his own: "Why were you searching for me? Did you not know that I must be in my Father's house?" (2:49). Jesus' response is the first time that he speaks in Luke,[7] and it shows both his immaturity and that he is beginning to understand God's call on his life. As a twelve-year-old boy, he does not understand why his parents would not know where he is. He amazes the teachers in the temple with his questions and understanding (2:46–47), but he is still a boy. Jesus has a glimpse of where God is calling him, but he still has much to learn from his parents. Accordingly, he goes back home with Mary and Joseph and obeys them (2:51).

Although it seems obvious to Jesus where he would be, Mary does not understand what he is saying. She knows that this child is special; the angel told her that when she became pregnant. But she is learning and growing as a mother. In this case, she is probably learning to keep a closer eye on her son! When the text says that Mary "treasured all these things in her heart" (2:51), it is an echo of what happened when the shepherds visited and "Mary treasured all these words and pondered them in her heart" (2:19). For the first several years of Jesus' life, his parents are the ones who are best able to see how he is different from other children, though even they do not have a full picture of who he will become or the ministry he will have as an adult.

This story brings up a question: Is it possible to grow into the person that God calls one to be without hurting others? Jesus hurt his parents by staying behind and by not telling them that he was in the temple, and he probably hurt them again by pointing out that Joseph is not his father (2:49). Children inevitably hurt their parents, sometimes through thoughtlessness and sometimes intentionally. Jesus would go on to bewilder his mother, who probably hopes for a different life for her son. As the stories of Jesus and Mary show, there are no guarantees that following God's will is easy, safe, or without pain. Even the Son of God causes pain to those who are closest to him.

- What do you think it would be like to be Jesus' parents?
- Is it inevitable that children will hurt their parents? How does Jesus hurt his parents in this text?
- When is following God's will painful?

Third Sunday in Ordinary Time

ISAIAH 62:1–5

Zion as Bride

The central image in this text is of Zion as a bride, marrying God. What does it mean to be married to God? The imagery of God in this passage (and throughout Isaiah) as a sometimes-faithful husband may make some readers uncomfortable. Throughout the book of Isaiah, Zion takes on the identity of a woman. Jerusalem is often referred to as Daughter Zion,[1] and in 40:9, she is the "herald of good tidings" about God to other nations.[2] This gendered language can be problematic, as in 1:21, where "the faithful city has become a whore!" Although the marriage in this text is metaphorical, it is effective because it reflects something that can happen in literal marriages.

It is unclear who is speaking in this text.[3] Is it the prophet, speaking for the city, who will not keep silent? Or is it God, waiting for Zion's salvation, who will not rest? The imagery for Zion's vindication is vivid, shining like the dawn and like a burning torch (62:1). Bright lights like these are impossible to ignore. These words also resonate in a modern context. In a time when so many women are speaking up about their experiences of sexual harassment and assault, the words "I will not keep silent" (62:1) take on new life. For a woman who has experienced sexual violence, the first-person pronouns in this text make it possible for her to put herself in this language, saying, "I will not keep silent" and "I will not rest" until the nations see her vindication.

To a nation in exile, these are words of hope. Their holy city will be vindicated, and all the nations and kings will see the glory of the city that was defeated and destroyed. The text goes on to say that the city will have "a new name" (62:2) and be beautiful in the hand of God (62:3). Name changes signal transformation in a variety of ways. For readers, this may suggest name changes in marriage.[4] It may also have special significance for trans people, who choose a new name in which God delights.

At this point in the text, the marriage metaphor comes to the forefront. It may strike some readers as odd for the prophet to say that the land shall be married (62:4). For many women of the time, marriage meant security. Here, instead of being called Desolate, God delights in Zion, and her land shall be married. There is a parallel between the bridegroom and God, suggesting that the marriage is union with God. God is like a repentant husband, as in 54:5–6 ("For your Maker is your husband").[5] This would probably be reassuring for the people of Judah, who felt abandoned by God. It may also be troubling for those who wonder why God abandoned God's people (see 54:7, "For a brief moment I abandoned you") and then decided to return later.

Many young women who have experienced sexual abuse have wrestled with feelings of shame, and churches have contributed to those struggles. When a church tells a young woman that her value is in sexual purity, she may feel broken or less than that after experiencing sexual violence. For women who have had these experiences, this passage may be empowering. The prophetic voice will not be silent or still until a light shines on the truth. The woman is whole and, even though she has been through pain and trauma, God delights in her.

- How does the image of God as a husband make you feel? Is it troubling? Comforting?
- What are examples of times when people receive new names? How do communities celebrate these name changes?
- When do you say, "I will not keep silent"?

JOHN 2:1–11

Mary Attends the Wedding at Cana

According to the Gospel of John, this is Jesus' first miracle. It is a comical story, with some glimmers of the child Jesus, as described in the Gospel of Luke, who abandoned his parents to spend time in the temple and then treated his mother and father badly. The passage starts by saying that this is on the third day, and Jesus has had quite a week. On the first day, he has encountered his cousin, John the Baptist, who declared that Jesus is "the Lamb of God who takes away the sin of the world!" (John 1:29). On the second day, Jesus began to call his disciples; Andrew, Simon Peter, Philip, and Nathanael followed him. But Jesus has not performed any miracles yet. Now, on the third day,

Jesus and his disciples go to a wedding, and his mother is there, too. The wedding takes place in Cana, a town about nine miles north of Nazareth.[6]

This is a text filled with miscommunication, where no one says exactly what they mean. The indirect nature of this story begins with the writing: the Gospel of John does not refer to Mary by name here, but only as "the mother of Jesus." Mary continues this lack of directness when she says to Jesus, "They have no wine." She does not say what she expects Jesus to do about this, but it seems as though she expects him to do something.

Jesus also does not respond in the way one might expect, but instead calls his mother "woman" and asks what concern this is to either of them (2:4). Scholars disagree about whether Jesus' response to Mary—calling her "woman"—is rude. Regardless, Jesus creates distance between himself and his mother by not acknowledging their relationship.[7] He also refuses to do what she wants, instead saying, "My hour has not yet come" (2:4). Mary, in turn, does not respond directly to Jesus, but instead turns to the servants and cryptically tells them to do whatever Jesus tells them (2:5). Despite Jesus' protest, Mary knows that he is ready.

The passage does not say directly when the water turns to wine, but it must be sometime between when the servants fill up the jars and the steward tastes the wine. Instead of asking the servants, who know what has happened, the steward instead turns to the bridegroom and implies that the bridegroom has been holding out on the guests, saving the best wine for last. Even though the interactions may be awkward, the people stay in relationship with each other. After the wedding, Jesus goes to Capernaum with his mother, his brothers, and his disciples. After such a big week, Jesus probably needs some rest!

Why such indirect communication? This may serve as a reminder that the Bible was written in a different time and place. White culture in the United States generally values direct communication, but as Eliseo Pérez-Álvarez, a Latino pastor and theology professor, notes, "Latino culture clicks with this story and Mary's indirectness."[8] To some cultures, this indirectness seems natural. For pastors, this text may also serve as a reminder that God works through awkward, indirect people to create an abundance of wine.[9] God works through the implying mother, the son who thinks he is not ready, the servants who are willing, the snarky steward, and the disciples who see and believe. And this miracle does not just provide what they need, but an abundance thereof.

- How would this story be different if the people communicated directly with each other?
- How is the relationship between Mary and Jesus in this text similar to stories about the two of them? How is it different?
- What are other examples of God working through awkward, indirect people?

Fourth Sunday in Ordinary Time

JEREMIAH 29:1, 4–7

Wives in Exile

This brief text from Jeremiah's letter to those in exile reflects the shattered identity of the community. It is unusual to have a letter in the Hebrew Scriptures;[1] Jeremiah's letter shows that the community is divided into the people taken into exile (597 BCE; 2 Kgs. 24) and those who remain with Jeremiah in Jerusalem. The opening verse (Jer. 29:1) lists the people taken into exile thus far (by around 593 BCE): elders, priests, prophets, and all the people whom Nebuchadnezzar has taken from Jerusalem to Babylon. Jeremiah is one of the few remaining, and he tries to bridge the gap within his divided community with this pastoral letter.[2]

After the exile, the Jewish people had a crisis of faith: Where was God when these deportations happened? The way Jeremiah describes God shows the depth of the crisis. Jeremiah writes on behalf of God, repeating the names for God: "the LORD of hosts, the God of Israel" (29:4). He reminds the people that God is still the God of Israel. And God takes responsibility for sending the people into exile: "the exiles whom I have sent into exile from Jerusalem to Babylon" (29:4). It may seem disturbing to think of a punishing God who would send a people into exile, but for the people of Judah, that is probably more comforting than an absent God or a God who is weaker than the gods of Babylon. At least, this is a God who is in command.

The primary message in this letter shows a theological and practical division between the Jewish people: whether to revolt against those who have taken them into exile. In response to those who want to rise up against their

43

captors, the prophet instead tells them to settle in: they are going to be in exile for a long time. The prophet says to "build houses and live in them; plant gardens and eat what they produce" (29:5). The theology of those who want to fight is rooted in what God has said about the line of David and the temple in Jerusalem as God's eternal home.[3] But Jeremiah has a new word from God for the people: their identity is no longer rooted in Jerusalem or the temple.

The women in the next verse emphasize the length of their stay: it will be long enough for the men to take wives and have sons and daughters, and then for the sons and daughters to be married as well (29:6). A verse from this chapter that is often taken out of context is Jeremiah 29:11: "I know the plans I have for you, says the Lord, plans for your welfare and not for harm, to give you a future with hope." This verse refers to God's specific plans for the people there: they will stay in exile for seventy years, more than a lifetime (29:10). The hope for the future is embodied in the wives and daughters, the ones who will bear children so that they can survive, multiply, and increase.[4]

The final verse fully shows the change in the people's identity. They are no longer a kingdom in control, but a threatened minority. Where they would once pray for the peace of Jerusalem (Ps. 122:6), the prophet now tells them to pray for the peace of Babylon (Jer. 29:7).[5] There is a practical element to this command: if Babylon is harmed, the Jewish people will also be threatened.[6] And it shows that God is calling them in a new direction, based on their changed circumstances.

This text speaks to the realities of those who are part of threatened minority groups, showing how God speaks differently to them than to those in power. For example, it may not be the safest thing for a queer teenager to come out (to declare one's own sexual identity). Rather than telling that person to fight every battle, God may be whispering, "Do what you need to do to survive. This will not last forever." Or for refugees in camps, the most subversive thing may be to celebrate a wedding and bring together family. Jeremiah's letter shows how God cares for those on the margins.

- If you were to write a letter to a divided community that you are a part of, what would you say?
- How does God speak differently to those in power and those who are on the margins?
- What are symbols of a hopeful future for you?

MATTHEW 12:33–37, 46–50

Mary Waits for Jesus

This text is the second place in Matthew where Jesus employs the metaphor of the tree and the fruit (cf. Matt. 7:15–20). The first time he talks about the tree and its fruit is in chapter 7, where it is a general statement. Here he is responding specifically to the Pharisees who have challenged his healing of a man who was blind, mute, and possessed by a demon, saying that his power comes from Beelzebul (12:24).[7] Jesus asserts that his power is for good and therefore comes from God, but these Pharisees cannot speak good things because they are evil (12:34). The careless words that Jesus condemns are their words about his power (12:36).

It is ironic that so soon after repeating the metaphor of the tree and its fruit, Jesus rejects his family of origin. This is the first time that Mary appears in Matthew after the birth narratives,[8] and this text gives a glimpse into Mary's life after Jesus is grown. The person speaking to Jesus tells him that his mother and brothers are standing outside (12:47), suggesting that Mary gave birth to other sons after Jesus. This is consistent with Matthew 1:25, which says that Joseph had no marital relations with her *until* she had borne a son (presumably marital relations began after the birth of Jesus). The tradition of Mary's perpetual virginity did not begin until the second century.[9] However, scholars have debated about the meaning of these verses, interpreting them to be full brothers, half brothers (children of Joseph's prior marriage), or even cousins.[10]

Rather than going out to see his mother and brothers, Jesus declares that his disciples are his mother and brothers (12:49). He then adds that "whoever does the will of my Father in heaven is my brother and sister and mother" (12:50), expanding the circle of his family beyond the disciples to anyone who does the will of God.[11] This includes a mother, brothers, and sisters but not a father, because the only Father is in heaven.[12] Queer readers of this text and others in Matthew have suggested that Jesus opposes the traditional family and encourages an alternative family, or found family.[13] Contrary to the focus of some Christian groups today, Jesus does not seem to see the nuclear family as central to the Christian faith.

For the most part, commentators see this rejection of the family as symbolic; Matthew is interested in the idea of replacing Jesus' biological family by the Christian community.[14] But it is also a narrative: Mary and Jesus' brothers are standing outside, waiting for him, and he refuses to meet with them. There is no indication of what news Mary wishes to tell him, but it seems like it is important and family related, considering that she also brought his brothers. Alternatively, in the parallel version in Mark, his family comes to restrain him because people think he is "out of his mind" (Mark 3:21). In both accounts, Mary must leave without speaking with him. She does not appear again in the book of Matthew (unless the references to the "other Mary" in 27:61 and 28:1 mean her).[15]

Jesus seems to be using his family members as a sermon illustration in a way that clearly conveys his point, but that may be painful for the family members in question. For preachers, it can seem almost inevitable to use stories about one's family to make a point in sermons, but this text may be a caution against doing so. Even though Jesus warns that people need to "account for every careless word" (12:36), his dismissal of his mother and brothers comes across as uncaring, at least, and possibly careless.

- What are some examples of a good tree bearing good fruit and a bad tree bearing bad fruit?
- Do you think the point Jesus made was worth the way he treated his mother and brothers?
- How do you decide whether to use a story from your own family as a sermon illustration?

Fifth Sunday in Ordinary Time

LAMENTATIONS 1:1–6

Jerusalem as Widow

The book of Lamentations begins with a cry of anguish that often begins funeral dirges.[1] The narrator is mourning for the city of Jerusalem, which is empty of people after the exile to Babylon. Jerusalem is personified as a woman, and in the first verse, she is lonely and like a widow (Lam. 1:1). The description of Jerusalem as like a widow shows her vulnerable state and her lack of family support; without the support of a husband, a widow was often poor and marginalized in the ancient Near East.

There is a vast difference between what Jerusalem used to be and what she has become. The narrator describes her as having been "great among the nations" (1:1), but she is no longer. She was also "like a princess," bringing to mind the story of Tamar, whose brother Amnon raped her (2 Sam. 13:1–22). Describing Jerusalem as a woman reflects the vulnerability of women to violence (including sexual violence) in times of conflict. Like Tamar, Jerusalem is a desolate woman, weeping bitterly (Lam. 1:2; 2 Sam. 13:13, 22).

The word "lover" in Lamentations 1:2 does not necessarily mean romantic or sexual partners;[2] it can be translated instead as "those who love her." These lovers who have abandoned Jerusalem are probably nations with whom Judah has entered into political alliances.[3] As a nation, Judah has reached out to others for security, but those other nations have "dealt treacherously with her" and "have become her enemies" (1:2). The prophets denounced these alliances, and now Jerusalem is left alone, weeping.

Judah is also personified as a woman in this text, one who has gone into exile (1:3). Unlike Jerusalem, who was left behind, Judah must "live . . . among the nations, and finds no resting place" (1:3). The language describing Judah also suggests sexual violence: Judah's "pursuers have all overtaken her" (1:3). Although the larger context of this book is the exile, the narrator spends a short amount of time on Judah; the main focus in this text is Jerusalem.

The narrator returns to the cries of mourning, not just by people but also by the roads to Zion and her gates (1:4). This paints a picture of the places that once were bustling but now are empty; there are no people coming to the city on pilgrimage, and no one to celebrate the festivals. Two types of people remain to mourn: the priests and young girls (1:4), suggesting that everyone else has been taken away.

Most of this text focuses on describing the grief and hardship of the city. It is not until verse 5 that there is any mention of blame. The narrator states that this has all happened "because the LORD has made her suffer for the multitude of her transgressions" (1:5). This may be a difficult verse to parse: it describes a disciplinarian God who has punished Jerusalem for her sins. Some feminist commentators have suggested that this depicts Jerusalem as a woman who collaborates in her own abuse.[4] But it also gives Jerusalem some agency. She is not just a woman who had terrible things happen to her; instead, she has had some control over her fate.

This leads to the most tragic image in the text: Jerusalem as a mother who has lost all her children (1:5). Jerusalem's children have been taken away by her enemy, "captives before the foe" (1:5). In addition to the grief of losing her children, she has no one left to support her as a childless widow. The final image of Jerusalem is as Daughter Zion (literally, daughter of my people).[5] Although Jerusalem is depicted as a mother, a lover, and a daughter, she is left without family or friends.

Lamentations does not give a tidy way to respond to grief. Instead, this book practices truth telling.[6] It reflects the raw emotion in the immediate aftermath of violence and loss. For those preaching on this text, it will be important to know the context of the congregation. Are these people who are intimately familiar with grief? If so, this may be a text that allows the congregation to express that grief and heartache.

- When you picture a lonely city, what images come to mind?
- How does the feminine personification of Jerusalem impact your understanding of the loss and grief of exile?
- How can congregations use the raw language of Lamentations to respond to the pain in their own lives?

MARK 6:14–29

Herodias

This flashback about the arrest and beheading of John the Baptizer incorporates elements of stories in the Hebrew Scriptures. The description of the weak king, Herod Antipas, and his powerful wife, Herodias, draws on the story of Jezebel and Ahab (cf. 1 Kgs. 21:1–16), and when Herod tells the girl to ask for "whatever you wish, . . . even half of my kingdom" (Mark 6:22–23), it is a direct quote of the king's offer to Esther (Esth. 7:2). The passage takes on the cadence of a story as it turns into a kind of dark comedy, with the girl *immediately* rushing to the king and the king *immediately* sending a soldier with orders to bring John's head (Mark 6:25, 27). It turns into a grisly bucket brigade,[7] with the guard bringing the head not to Herod, but to the girl, who then gives it to her mother.

Other sources raise questions about whether this is an accurate historical account, beginning with the account in Matthew.[8] In Mark, it is Herodias who has a grudge against John and wants to kill him (6:17), but Matthew states, "Though Herod wanted to put him to death, he feared the crowd, because they regarded him as a prophet" (14:5). Herodias plays a much smaller part in the Matthew version; she is only mentioned as the reason Herod put John into prison; then her daughter is "prompted by her mother" to ask for the head of John the Baptist (14:3, 8). The Jewish historian Josephus raises further questions about whether events happened as in one of these versions of the story. He includes references to John the Baptist and Jesus in his accounts. According to Josephus, Herodias had not been married to Philip, as stated in Mark and Matthew, but to another brother, also named Herod.[9] Josephus blamed both Herodias and Herod for their marriage, but he put all of the blame for John the Baptist's death on Herod, not Herodias.

Why was John the Baptizer in prison? It is not solely because he was a prophet. According to the passage, it is because John told Herod, "It is not lawful for you to have your brother's wife" (Mark 6:18). This is a reference to Leviticus 18:16 and 20:21, which prohibit a man from taking his brother's wife.[10] However, John is not only pointing out the individual sins of Herod and Herodias; he is also challenging the power structure by accusing the rulers of sin. In response to this challenge to his power, Herod has John imprisoned.

At first glance, Herodias comes across as an unsympathetic and vindictive character in this passage. She has a grudge against a prophet because he has pointed out her sin, and she takes the first chance to have him beheaded. But pastors can take this opportunity to be curious about why Herodias acts the way she does. Seen in another light, this is a story of a mother taking steps to protect her family. John has threatened her family by questioning her marriage, and Herodias is like a mother bear, doing whatever it takes to protect her young (cf. Hos. 13:8). It is through her husband's offer to her daughter that Herodias is able to protect her family. Another possibility is that Herodias had no choice in whether to marry Herod. It is possible that, like Bathsheba, Herodias is making the best of a situation outside of her control.

In sermons on this text, preachers usually focus on John and Herod, sometimes also sexualizing the dance by Herodias's daughter. Rather than continuing to objectify and ignore the women, preachers can take this opportunity to place Herodias back at the center of her own story and try to understand her motivations, unpleasant though they may be.

- Is it possible to see Herodias as anything other than a villain in this story? What would the story look like from her perspective?
- Do you think the author intended the story to be humorous?
- What is the warning in this text for prophets and others who speak truth to power?

Sixth Sunday in Ordinary Time

EZEKIEL 16:1–22

Unfaithful Wife

This text in Ezekiel, along with chapter 23, has some of the most disturbing imagery about women in the Bible. Here, Jerusalem is portrayed as an unfaithful wife to God, and God is then cast as an abusive husband. Ezekiel uses the most extreme language possible in this extended metaphor, which is intended to shock his audience into recognizing their sinful ways.[1] Many preachers would prefer to avoid this text. However, the intense language demonstrates how people understood marriage in ancient Judah as well as the limitations of using metaphorical language to describe God.

The first depiction of Jerusalem in this text is as an abandoned baby girl. She is the daughter of an Amorite father and a Hittite mother (Ezek. 16:3)—two groups of people who were in the land of Canaan before the Israelites. Her parents have not done any of the basic things to clean or care for her after her birth, but instead they leave her in an open field to die (16:4–5). God passes by and sees her in her blood (16:6). Although God saves her life and adopts her, God does not clean or care for her either (16:6–7). This young girl, still covered in blood, is abandoned again to grow in a field like a plant.

The description of the female personification of Jerusalem comes entirely from the outside, from literally the male gaze. She never speaks.[2] God, here personified as an older man, passes by again and looks at her (16:8). God sees that she is old enough for sex: her breasts are formed and her pubic hair has grown (16:7–8). She is naked for everyone to see (16:7). Later the prophet describes her as beautiful, but this beauty is a double-edged sword. It does not reflect her, but rather God's splendor (16:14). This beauty attracts the attention of other nations (16:14). The prophet accuses her of trusting in her beauty and playing the whore because of her fame (16:15). So often, a woman's beauty is not considered her own, but something owned by the men in her life or that she owes to others. Like the prophet, others can accuse a beautiful woman of using her physical appearance for gain.

The central metaphor in this text is of Jerusalem as a wife to God. God says, "I pledged myself to you and entered into a covenant with you, says the Lord GOD, and you became mine" (16:8). Importantly, this text highlights the difference between how people in the current day and people in ancient Judah viewed marriage. In ancient Judah, marriage was an important legal and economic transaction, but not a partnership between two equal parties.[3] Instead, the husband had control over the wife, including her sexual and reproductive capacities. A husband could take multiple wives, but for a woman to be unfaithful to her husband was a capital offense.[4]

Often in the Hebrew Scriptures, there is a parallel between the covenantal relationship between God and Israel and the covenantal relationship between a husband and wife. But this text starkly shows the limitation of that metaphor. If God is like a husband and God is in control of everything, then when a foreign nation defeats Israel and destroys the temple, God is necessarily cast in the role of an abusive husband. As has happened to so many women who have suffered abuse at the hands of an intimate partner, the prophet blames Jerusalem for bringing this upon herself.

How should a preacher approach this text? It can be helpful to read it as descriptive instead of prescriptive: this is a description of how it felt to Israel to have suffered military defeat and exile; it is not prescribing God's punishment. It also creates space for the preacher to denounce domestic abuse under any circumstances. Regardless of how this text may have been read in the past, it is unacceptable for parents or spouses to perpetuate violence and abuse against a member of their family. Finally, it gives congregations an opportunity to reflect on their own metaphors and images for God, weighing whether those metaphors are useful in times of crisis.

- How does it make you feel to read this text? Where do you respond in your body?
- What are the primary metaphors that you use for God? What are the potential limitations of those metaphors in times of crisis?
- Should texts like this one be included in the Bible? What are the implications of ignoring images like this or taking these kinds of violent imagery out of our sacred text?

MARK 7:24–37

The Syrophoenician Woman

The story of the unnamed Syrophoenician woman calls us to consider who is an insider and who is an outsider. It takes place during Jesus' traveling ministry: Jesus leaves the area where he has been doing ministry and goes to Tyre, which is part of Phoenicia. He is tired and trying to get away from people (Mark 7:24). But the Syrophoenician woman finds him! She knows that Jesus can heal her daughter, and she begs him to cast the demon out of her (7:26). When Jesus says, "It is not fair to take the children's food and throw it to the dogs" (7:27), he uses a diminutive of "dogs," a slur.

The Syrophoenician woman is undaunted and responds, "Sir, even the dogs under the table eat the children's crumbs" (7:28). By saying this, the woman turns Jesus' words against him: if he is going to call her a dog, she will remind him that even the dogs get fed. Surprisingly, she wins the argument. Jesus says, "For saying that, you may go—the demon has left your daughter" (7:29). Then when she gets home, her daughter is well (7:30), saved because of the words the woman said to Jesus.[5]

This text paints a fairly unsympathetic portrait of Jesus. Commentators have tried various ways to explain his behavior: that this is a test of the Syrophoenician woman, or that this marks an expansion of Jesus' ministry from being solely for the Jews to include the Gentiles. However, Jesus does not require anyone else to pass a test before he heals them, and he has already exorcized demons from a Gentile (5:2–13).[6] Rather than try to explain his behavior away, perhaps this is an example of Jesus' humanity: he is tired and lashes out in a very human way. Then the Syrophoenician woman reminds Jesus of his message of abundance, and he extends this abundance to her and her daughter.

Many preachers approach this passage as an example of Jesus interacting with an outsider, focusing on the Syrophoenician woman as a foreigner and a woman. One translation even uses the heading, "An immigrant's daughter is delivered."[7] But Jesus is in the region of Tyre; so Jesus is the outsider here, in Phoenicia. Syria was a large and prosperous province of the Roman Empire, and Jesus is in this territory. Thus, a better reading is that Jesus is the outsider, not the Syrophoenician woman.

In addition, there is no textual evidence that the Syrophoenician woman is poor; she may be a wealthy, entitled woman, a woman who has everything except a way to heal her daughter. Jesus is the one who is a poor member of a minority group. From this perspective, she seems like a dog of a different kind: the predator at the door, who has already taken so much.[8] Then, when she comes to him, Jesus begs for some bread to give his own children before these voracious dogs take it all. In this reading, the Syrophoenician woman learns from Jesus. As a person of privilege, she may be surprised when Jesus wants to provide for his own people first, but she knows that the crumbs that fall off the table are enough to heal her daughter.

For preachers of more privileged congregations, this passage provides a way to preach about privilege, entitlement, and grace. For example, a white congregation may use this text to examine their reactions to the Black Lives Matter movement. Jesus is essentially saying that the lives of his people do matter, in the face of a society that does not act as if they do.

- Who seems the most sympathetic in the story?
- Does that change when we think of the Syrophoenician woman of privilege? Or when we remember that Jesus was part of an oppressed minority group?
- How can those who have privilege step back when others who have less speak up and ask for justice?

Seventh Sunday in Ordinary Time

EZEKIEL 23:1–21

Oholah and Oholibah

This text has disturbing imagery, as in Ezekiel 16, continuing the metaphor depicting Jerusalem as an unfaithful wife or prostitute, and these chapters are often interpreted together. In this extended metaphor, Jerusalem has a sister, Samaria, who is also engaging in adulterous behavior. In both chapters, it is essential to frame the language in its original context. Modern ideas of marriage and sex work do not map onto these images. For example, Ezekiel uses the word "whoring" here pejoratively, with the intent to be offensive.[1] This strong language is effective and troubling, both for the intended audience and for modern-day congregations.

The prophet introduces the two women as sisters, Oholah and Oholibah, and then explains that Oholah is Samaria and Oholibah is Jerusalem (Ezek. 23:3–4). Oholah literally means "her tent," and Oholibah means "my tent is in her."[2] These tents probably represent the royal shrines in the capitals of the northern kingdom of Israel and southern kingdom of Judah; they may also represent God's presence in these places of worship and, by extension, in these women.[3]

The women's sexual infidelity represents both the alliances that these kingdoms made with other nations and the worship of other gods.[4] Ezekiel repeatedly asserts that the women were engaging in unlawful sexual behavior in Egypt, reflecting his belief that Israel was unfaithful to God beginning in Egypt (23:3; 20:8).[5] First, Oholah lusts after the Assyrians (23:5). Her death and the death of her children (23:10) symbolize the destruction of Samaria by the Neo-Assyrians in 722 BCE.[6] Then Oholibah is unfaithful with the Assyrians,

55

the Babylonians, the Chaldeans, and finally the Egyptians again (23:12–21), representing Judah's alliances with other nations before its defeat and exile.[7]

These are effective metaphors because they work on a literal level as well as figuratively. Ezekiel plays on people's assumptions in ancient Judah that women are uncontrollably lusty, and the audience would know that adultery was a capital offense. These metaphors reinforce negative perceptions of women's sexuality.[8] Even though Judah's offense was worshiping other gods and creating alliances with other nations, Oholah's violent end becomes "a byword among women" (23:10). A woman hearing this prophecy could not help but be reminded of what could happen to her if she went outside the bounds of acceptable sexual behavior.

The extreme punishment that ultimately befalls Oholibah—rape, torture, destruction of property, death, and the death of her children (23:25–26)—seems more like the destruction of a city by foreign invaders than the usual punishment for adultery.[9] For people who had recently been through defeat and exile, these were not imaginary threats; Ezekiel's audience may have seen or experienced these things personally. The extreme nature of Ezekiel's imagery, including fields of bones (37:1–14) and women lusting after men with penises the size of donkeys' (23:20), provides a glimpse of the displacement and suffering of a people in exile.[10]

For preachers in congregations that seem complacent, it may be tempting to follow Ezekiel's example and use shocking language or metaphors. But, as this text demonstrates, the preacher must be careful not to draw on metaphors that can further harm the vulnerable. Before making a parallel to violence, consider whether there are people in the congregation who have experienced that specific kind of suffering and violence. The metaphors we choose to draw on matter because they convey the literal as well as the figurative.

- What makes Ezekiel's metaphor of the two cities as sisters effective? What are the limitations of this metaphor?
- How would you approach describing the kind of violence and loss that the people of Judah experienced in their defeat and exile?
- How does having this kind of graphic sexual language and violence in this text impact how you read the Bible?

LUKE 10:38–42

Mary and Martha

This text seems rather straightforward—there are only three people in it, and it is just five verses long—but commentators do not have any consensus on what it means.[11] It is useful to look at each of the people in turn, beginning with Mary. Mary is Martha's sister, and she sits at Jesus' feet and listens to what he says (Luke 10:39). The language of sitting at Jesus' feet means that Mary is a disciple.[12] It is unusual for a woman to be a disciple in the New Testament; the only woman who is explicitly named as a disciple is Tabitha, a widow in the early church (Acts 9:36).

Preachers need to be careful when approaching this passage, however, because this is a place where Christians can engage in anti-Judaism by arguing that Jesus was ahead of his time in having women as disciples, and that was unlike the Jewish people around him. In the Jewish culture of the time, women had lots of roles, including receiving and giving instruction in synagogues and devoting their lives to studying the Torah.[13] They also were patrons of religious leaders, as Martha is here. It is significant that Mary was a disciple: not because it is new, but because Christians have since tried to argue that women were not disciples in the early church.

The second person in the passage is Jesus. He is confusing, as he often is. The way he pits the sisters against each other contradicts what he says about hospitality elsewhere. Earlier in the same chapter, he instructs his followers to be good guests: "Remain in the same house, eating and drinking whatever they provide" (Luke 10:7). But instead of graciously accepting what Martha offers him, Jesus scolds her for doing too much. And later, when his disciples are arguing about who is the greatest, Jesus says, "The greatest among you must become like the youngest, and the leader like one who serves" (22:26). He goes on to say, "For who is greater, the one who is at the table or the one who serves? Is it not the one at the table? But I am among you as one who serves" (22:27). But in this passage, Jesus says, "Mary has chosen the better part" (10:42), not Martha, who is serving.

The third person in the story is Martha, the one who welcomes Jesus into her home (10:38). Martha is the head of the household. She wants Jesus to be there, but then she is "distracted by her many tasks" (10:40). So Martha goes to Jesus; she wants him to tell her sister, Mary, to help, but instead he scolds her. Perhaps Martha wants Jesus in her home to learn from him, but then she gets stuck with the "women's work" of preparing the food.

Too often, preaching about this text pits the "good" sister against the "bad" sister.[14] However, a closer reading of the text can lead to a reading where Mary and Martha, though arguing in this moment, are equal partners in ministry. Many ancient manuscripts have an "also": that Martha "had a sister named Mary[,] who *also* sat at the Lord's feet and listened to what he was saying."[15] With the "also," both Mary and Martha listened to Jesus and followed him. It is also possible that Mary and Martha were not literally sisters. The language here could mean that they were "sisters in Christ" rather than biological sisters. Read this way, Mary and Martha are more like Priscilla and Aquila:

partners who run a house church together (1 Cor. 16:19).[16] In this reading, they are committed to each other, doing ministry and serving together.

- When you have heard the story of Mary and Martha in sermons, did the preacher pit the two sisters against each other?
- How does this story make you feel about Jesus and the ways he interacts with women?
- Does it change your understanding of the text to think of Martha and Mary as committed partners, leading a church together?

Eighth Sunday in Ordinary Time

HOSEA 1:2–10

Gomer

Hosea is the first prophet to use the metaphor of Israel as an unfaithful wife to God, though it becomes a frequent trope in later prophetic texts (cf. Ezek. 16:1–22).[1] This figure of the adulterous wife is powerful because it evokes both the close connection between God and Israel as well as disgust and revulsion when the wife is unfaithful to her beloved prophet-husband.[2] In this patriarchal culture, where a husband is expected to be in control of his wife, this text presents a marriage in crisis.[3]

Scholars have debated the historicity of this text, falling generally into three categories. First, some scholars have taken this as a literal history of God telling Hosea to take a promiscuous wife. Second, other scholars have read this as metaphorical or symbolic, with Gomer and the three children as fictional characters. Third, scholars have suggested reading this as an explanation of how Hosea ended up with a promiscuous wife: Gomer was chaste when she married Hosea, but she later became unfaithful. There is also a history of understanding Gomer's infidelity as temple prostitution, but there is no textual or archaeological evidence that such a class of prostitutes ever existed.[4] Notably, Gomer is not a professional prostitute, but rather habitually promiscuous.[5]

It is impossible to say what Gomer's perspective is on these events because Gomer does not speak.[6] The only perspective on her comes from the outside, in the description of her as Hosea's unfaithful wife. The use of heterosexual marriage as a metaphor and the lack of Gomer's perspective have theological consequences. As many scholars have pointed out, this aligns masculinity with God and goodness, but femininity with sin and unfaithfulness. It asks the reader to identify and sympathize with a male prophet and God, thus not with a woman.[7]

The image of God as the husband and Israel as wife reflects the historical asymmetry of marriage in ancient Israel. In these marriages, men were in the more privileged position and women were subject to them.[8] Tragically, this metaphor results in casting both Hosea and God as abusive husbands. The punishment for Gomer's infidelity in the following chapter includes isolating her (Hos. 2:6–7) and publicly stripping her naked and exposing her shamelessness (2:3).[9] This text illustrates the limitations of masculine metaphors for God. When God is equated with a man and a husband, with the power to control and physically abuse a metaphorical wife, that creates an image of God with embedded male violence; readers should be wary of uncritically accepting such an image.[10]

However, buried in this overly masculine text is a feminine image of God. Gomer gives birth to three children with symbolic names (1:4–8). The daughter's name, Lo-ruhamah, means "not pitied" or "no mercy." *Ruhamah* is associated with the word for womb in Hebrew; it refers to God's maternal compassion, which comes from the divine womb.[11] *Lo* means "not." Thus, at first, her name is a sign that God will no longer have compassion for Israel (1:6). But the final verse of this text restores the relationship between God and Israel, saying that these are God's people (1:10). Perhaps this name is a reminder that, even when it feels like God no longer has compassion for God's people, even God comes around to say that the people are "Children of the living God" (1:10).

For those preaching on this text, it is important to place the marriage, whether literal or symbolic, in its social and historical context. This text provides an opportunity to show the potential violence in seeing the marriage as a power-over relationship instead of a mutual agreement between two equals. It also gives the congregation incentive to reflect on their metaphors for God and the power structures inherent in the images they use to describe a God who is ultimately indescribable.

- The metaphor of marriage between people and God is a strong one. What other metaphors could capture this sense of broken relationship?
- What are the limitations of using the metaphors of man and husband for God?
- What do you imagine this text would sound like if it were told from Gomer's perspective?

LUKE 20:27–38

Marriage after Resurrection

In this text, the Sadducees invoke the law of levirate marriage (Deut. 25:5–10) to have Jesus take a position on an ongoing debate they have with the Pharisees.[12] This is the only time that the Sadducees appear in Luke, and he introduces them as "those who say there is no resurrection" (Luke 20:27; cf. Acts 23:8), presumably because the Gentile Christian readers would not know about them.[13] The Sadducees were the elite party, based in Jerusalem, and connected with the high priesthood.[14] The name Sadducee comes from "Zadok," the high priest in the days of David and Solomon, whose descendants were high priests for generations.[15] The Sadducees were conservative, only recognizing the authority of the books of Moses.[16] They left no writings and disappeared after the destruction of the temple.[17]

The case that the Sadducees describe to Jesus involves a woman whose husband dies, and she successively marries his six brothers in turn, in each case after her current husband dies (20:28–31). Under the law of levirate marriage, if a man dies with no son, his brother shall marry his widow, and their firstborn son will carry on the name of the man who died (Deut. 25:5–6). For those who do not believe in resurrection, this was a way for the man to be remembered after death as well as a solution for his inheritance. An example of levirate marriage occurs in Genesis 38, when Tamar tricks her father-in-law into impregnating her because he will not follow the law and give her in marriage to his third son after the first two sons die. It is also the reason why Boaz offers Ruth to a closer relative before marrying her (Ruth 4:1–6) and why, when Ruth has a son, the women of the neighborhood say, "A son has been born to Naomi" (Ruth 4:17; under the law of levirate marriage, this child is carrying on Naomi's son's name).

The Sadducees are trying to make a point about the ridiculousness of resurrection, and their point is rooted in culture. It is acceptable for a man to have several wives, but it is what Leviticus calls a "detestable" practice for a woman to have seven husbands.[18] The text moves quickly past this imaginary widow to the argument, but it is a place where preachers can instead center on this woman's experience. Although this is an extreme example, it is based in the reality that women who lost their husbands, in addition to feeling grief, would also be left in a vulnerable position socially and financially. This widow is passed like property (really, she is property) from one brother to the next.

Jesus responds by saying that, after the resurrection, people "neither marry nor are given in marriage" (20:35). Like the angels, they do not die (20:36), and thus they have no need to marry or have children.[19] This description of life after the resurrection calls into question the social structure that levirate marriage supports. Two purposes of levirate marriage are (1) to continue the man's name and inheritance and (2) to protect his widow. This is part of the protection of patriarchy, which assumes that a woman needs the protection of a man (her father, her husband, or her son). If there is no marriage in the age to come, then Jesus is describing a time when women will not need this kind of protection.[20] Jesus is setting aside patriarchy!

Next, Jesus argues that there is resurrection of the dead by saying that God is "God not of the dead, but of the living" (20:38). Because God is the God of Abraham, Isaac, and Jacob (Exod. 3:6), they must be alive in some sense.[21] This argument is another place where women are left out or overlooked in the text. As *The Inclusive Bible* reminds us, God is not just the God of Abraham, Isaac, and Jacob, but also "the God of Sarah and Abraham, and the God of Rebecca and Isaac, and the God of Leah and Rachel and Jacob" (20:37).[22] We could expand this further to include Hagar, Zilpah, and Bilhah (Gen. 16:3; 30:4, 9). Preachers can right the wrongs of leaving women out by bringing them back in when we read the Scripture.

- What are the upsides to a law like levirate marriage? What are the drawbacks?
- How would you respond to the question the Sadducees ask Jesus?
- When you envision an ideal afterlife, what does it include?

Transfiguration Sunday

HOSEA 11:1–11

God as Parent

This first-person account from God in Hosea reflects the complex nature of God in the prophets. It also has a three-part narrative journey: (1) the past and Israel's journey from Egypt, (2) Israel's present exile, and (3) Israel's future return.[1] God is present for each of these parts of the journey, and the metaphors for God in the different parts illustrate the ways that the people of Israel understand God.

In the part about the past, God speaks as a parent, with Israel (also called Ephraim) as God's son. As a parent, God is intimately involved in raising Israel, first calling Israel (the Hebrew can also be translated as "naming"), teaching the child how to walk, carrying him, and then healing him (Hos. 11:1–3). This is one of the few places in the Bible where God is truly without gender: the author does not explicitly call God "mother" or "father." Some scholars have suggested that these are activities that mothers primarily perform, so this is an example of God as a mother.[2] But for preachers, this is an opportunity to think beyond traditional gender roles. God may be a nurturing father, mother, or nonbinary parent.

By contrast, in the part about the present, God is potentially destructive. In response to Israel's rebelliousness, God considers making Israel like Admah and Zeboiim, two cities on the plain that were destroyed with Sodom and Gomorrah (11:8; Deut. 29:23).[3] This is a reminder that God can and has destroyed cities in anger; it suggests that God may do the same to Israel. Although it is not explicit, this may be a continuation of the parent metaphor: under the law, parents could bring a rebellious child before the elders and have him condemned him to death (Deut. 21:18–21).[4] It also shows the anguish that God feels during this internal dialogue, leading to God's decision to spare Israel.[5]

A feminist argument has been that this is an example of motherly compassion, with God as a mother who will not have her son put to death.[6] Proponents of this argument have pointed to "mortal" in Hosea 11:9, saying that it is literally "man." Accordingly, God is saying, "I am God and not a man." However, as Gale A. Yee points out, the contrast here is between the created and the creator, not male and female.[7]

Finally, in the part about the future, where the people of Israel return, the metaphor shifts. Now God is like a lion (11:10), which is usually a threatening image. Indeed, the children come trembling when they hear the lion's roar (11:10). But then the children, here described as like doves, follow the lion back to their land. For people in the ancient Near East, the image of birds following a lion would be familiar: birds would follow a large predator in the hope of finding food. Accordingly, this metaphor connects with the beginning of the text: God is again a source of food for the people. This final metaphor brings together the two earlier sides of God: God can be both a nurturing and feeding parental figure and a terrifying and destructive force. Ultimately for the people of Israel, it is good to have God on their side, leading them home.

This text reflects the ways that the people of Israel are trying to bring together the aspects of God they know in their present circumstances. They believe in a God who brought them out of Egypt and protected them in the wilderness, but now they are experiencing violence: "the sword rages in their cities" (11:6). To make sense of this, they see themselves as rebellious children, bringing this punishment upon themselves. But they believe it will not last forever, that the God who has protected them in the past will provide for them again.

- When you think about God as a parent, what parental attributes do you think God has?
- How does it make you feel to think about God without gender? Does this passage suggest a particular gender for God to you?
- How do you reconcile the different aspects of God, the nurturing and frightening parts of the Creator?

MARK 5:25–34

The Woman with Hemorrhages

This story of the woman with hemorrhages appears in all the Synoptic Gospels (cf. Matt. 9:20–22; Luke 8:43–48). It is a physical story, unambiguously about bodies. This unnamed woman has suffered from hemorrhages in her body for twelve years (Mark 5:25). When she hears about Jesus, her response is tactile: she says to herself, "If I but touch his clothes, I will be made well" (5:28). When she reaches out and touches his cloak, she feels in her body that she is healed of her disease (5:29). Jesus feels this as well; he is immediately aware that power has gone forth from him and that it has happened because someone touched his clothes (5:30). Even in this jostling crowd, Jesus can tell the difference between those who are pressing against him and this woman who knew his touch would heal her.

The healing stories in the Gospels demonstrate how much God cares about people's bodies. Jesus cares about the sick and suffering around him: he does not just care about their souls, but about their bodies as well. When he feels the healing power go forth from him, he wants to know whom he has healed. Even when his disciples laughed and said that there was no way to know who had touched him in the crowd, he persists in looking for this woman (5:31–32). And when she comes to him in fear and trembling, he calls her daughter and confirms that she is healed of her disease: her faith has made her well (5:33–34).

Sermons on the hemorrhaging woman are a place where anti-Judaism can creep into preaching. This happens when preachers focus on purity codes.[8] A typical sermon in this vein sounds like this: "Under Jewish law, this woman was unclean and ostracized, but Jesus didn't care about the Jewish law, and he let her touch him anyway." This approach is problematic for several reasons. First, there is nothing in the text about Jewish purity laws.[9] In fact, immediately afterward, Jesus goes with a leader of the synagogue to raise his daughter from the dead, and the synagogue leader says nothing about Jesus being "impure" after touching the woman who was bleeding.[10] Second, impurity was a fact of life within Jewish culture at the time. People became impure for all sorts of reasons, and this did not mean that they were ostracized or isolated. The woman's problem here is that she has spent all her money trying to get well, but she is suffering and getting worse (5:25–26).[11]

With the recent rise of anti-Semitism and violence against Jewish people, Christian preachers need to be especially aware of anti-Judaism in our understanding of the Bible. This is not a new phenomenon; Christians have participated in anti-Semitism throughout our history. Christians have perpetuated stereotypes about Jewish people, failed to help Jewish people who were facing genocide, and participated in killing Jewish people. Even if we are not the ones doing the violence, there is anti-Semitism in our history and in the ways in which we read our sacred text. We need to be aware of that, listen to Jewish people when they tell us that we have made mistakes, and do our best to root this out of our tradition going forward.

- When does the healing take place in this story? What does that moment teach us about how Jesus heals?
- Have you heard this story preached in a way that followed some of these anti-Jewish tropes? How would you approach it differently?
- What more would you like to know about this woman with hemorrhages? What do you imagine her life was like after Jesus healed her?

Lent, Easter, and Pentecost

Ash Wednesday

GENESIS 3:1–24

Eve and Adam

When preaching this text, the preacher's first task is to defamiliarize the story. So much doctrine has been inserted into the narrative of the garden of Eden that listeners probably think they know what it says and means. However, this is a much stranger story than the children's version! Here the serpent is not a devil or a demon, just the craftiest animal (Gen. 3:1). There is also no mention of original sin. In this text, the reader is left to wonder: what does it mean to be "like God"? What are God's motives in providing the two trees and forbidding the humans from eating the fruit of one? The preacher can help the congregation pay attention to what is actually in the text by retelling the story.

In the dialogue between the serpent and the woman, the serpent is cunning and manipulates the woman into questioning God's motives (3:1–3). The serpent tells the truth: they will not die when they eat the fruit, but instead they will know good and evil (3:5).[1] Although the woman has often been portrayed as a temptress in this story, she is actually the protagonist.[2] She is the one who moves the story forward. Unlike her passive husband, the woman is curious and thoughtful, and she decides to learn more. Curiosity and knowledge can complicate simple narratives, but that is not a reason to avoid them. This is a story of growth and change, with real-life consequences. The woman sees for herself that the tree is good for food, so she eats it and shares the fruit with her husband. This may reflect women's role in feeding her family.[3] After this, the woman takes on the role of creating new life out of her own body and part of the man's, continuing God's creative process (3:16, 20).

69

This text provides a different image of God than in earlier chapters. This is a God who walks in the garden at the time of the evening breeze (3:8), suggesting a God who is embodied and enjoys the feeling of the cool breeze in the evening. God also calls out to the man, asking, "Where are you?" (3:9). Does God not know where they are? Is this a God who is all-knowing? Finally, this is a God who acts as a judge, understanding that the humans have violated the command not to eat from the tree, and thus responding with curses and judgment (3:10–19).

Although the judgment from God is written as a curse, it also provides an explanation for how people have gone from an idyllic garden to the hard life that the writer knows. It also explains why the serpent goes on its belly instead of feet: because it tricked the woman (3:14)! Much has been made of the curse against the woman. Interestingly, the labor that the woman has in childbirth (3:16) is a parallel to the hard labor that the man has in working in the fields (3:17). Both will labor and struggle in this new order. In addition, the woman will still long for sexual intimacy, even with the risks of pregnancy and childbirth.[4] Historically, some have interpreted this passage as making women subservient to men. If that is the case, that subservience is part of the punishment rather than God's original ordering of the world. Everything has changed, and all of creation yearns to return to an earlier, easier time.

For preachers, this kind of idealizing of the past may sound familiar. When things are difficult in the present, it can be tempting to look back on a time when life seemed simpler. It can be easy to make the transition to ask, "Whose fault is this?" Unfortunately, people at the margins often receive the blame, such as immigrants and refugees, queer people, and people of color. In this story, we see how the woman is punished for her curiosity. Preachers can use this text to challenge their congregations about idealizing the past and blaming marginalized groups.

- What seems new in this familiar story?
- When God says, "Your desire shall be for your husband, and he shall rule over you" in Genesis 3:16, that is a punishment. Why do some people make it a goal?
- When do we idealize the past because the present is difficult? Who gets the blame?

MATTHEW 25:1–13

The Ten Bridesmaids

This story of the ten bridesmaids, which appears only in Matthew, is one of Matthew's descriptions of the kingdom of heaven. Neither Jesus nor Matthew ever say directly what the kingdom of heaven is, probably because it is beyond our comprehension. Instead, Jesus tells stories like this one to say what the kingdom of heaven is like.[5] This parable includes ten women and demonstrates that the choices they make will impact what happens to them. It also continues Matthew's concern for women at the final judgment (cf. Matt. 24:19, 41).[6]

This is a strange story, with some unexpected details. The setting is the return of a groom to his father's house.[7] The bridesmaids (literally, "virgins," also translated as "maidens") may be wedding guests, but probably they are servants waiting for the groom to return.[8] Even taking into account different cultural marriage customs, some things seem odd. First, where is the bride? Second, why is the bridegroom appearing so late? Third, would there really be shops open this late at night to sell oil to the foolish bridesmaids?[9]

Rather than reading this as a literal story or an explanation of marriage customs in Jesus' time, most scholars have seen this story as an allegory, with the characters representing aspects of Jesus' return.[10] In this reading, the bridegroom is Jesus and the bridesmaids are the church members: some of the people in the church are ready for Jesus' return, and others are not. This message would be especially important for Matthew's original audience, church members in 70 CE who eagerly awaited the second coming of Christ. Placing this text in the context of the early church provides a shift in focus. Instead of being a story about who is in or out, the emphasis is on encouraging people in the church to keep the faith.

A lamp is a small clay vessel containing oil and a wick and, in this text, Matthew is drawing a parallel between oil and faithful living.[11] By lighting the way for the bridegroom, the bridesmaids are fulfilling the command to "let your light shine before others, so that they may see your good works and give glory to your Father in heaven" (5:16). Accordingly, the bridesmaids are doing the good work that Jesus calls them to do, which will make them ready for the second coming.

There are still some troubling aspects to this text. It seems contrary to other parts of the Gospel that the wise bridesmaids will not share their oil. But they are facing the dilemma that, if they share, no one will have enough oil.[12] Notably, the bridesmaids without oil are not impoverished. They have enough funds to go to the dealer and buy some (25:9–10), suggesting that they are financially independent.[13] They are not poor, simply unprepared to fulfill their duty.

Another troubling aspect is the response of the bridegroom—especially as the embodiment of Christ—when he says, "Truly I tell you, I do not know you" (25:12). Preachers will need to decide how to address this. One approach is to say that the bridesmaids are focused on the wrong thing: their primary job is to welcome the bridegroom, but they are distracted by getting oil.[14]

Another possibility is that this text is about the ongoing relationship between people and God: as in any relationship, both parties are responsible for maintaining the relationship, or they will not know each other.

The end of the text says to "keep awake," but the better translation is "be prepared."[15] The problem is not that the foolish bridesmaids fall asleep—the wise bridesmaids do too! The issue is that the foolish ones are not prepared ahead of time. In the end, the readers are left with the understanding that Christ's return may be delayed.[16] Rather than preparing for one final return, people in the church should live a life of preparation, knowing that Christ may come later than people hope.

- How does this story reflect the kingdom of heaven? What questions do you have about the kingdom of heaven after reading it?
- Is it easier to read this as a text about who is in the kingdom of heaven or left out of it? Why or why not?
- What are some ways that people in the church can live a life of preparation for the coming of Christ?

First Sunday of Lent

PSALM 17:1–9

Under God's Wings

The psalmist begins this psalm with a cry to God, and she is convinced that her cause is just. She offers to let God try her heart, test her, and visit her by night (Ps. 17:3). Some translators have put this in the conditional: "*if* you test me." Others translate it in the past: "you *have examined* me." The psalmist continues, "If you test me, you will find no wickedness in me" (17:3). This is a strong claim, reminiscent of Job, who was blameless, according to the text. Yet this psalmist is not claiming to be completely blameless, but rather that she is in the right. She feels this in her body—in her lips that are free of deceit, in her feet that have not slipped (17:5), and in her heart.

The description of God is also embodied: the psalmist asks God, "Give ear to my prayer" (17:1) and "Let your eyes see the right" (17:2). She follows the words of God's lips (17:4) and says that God saves those who seek refuge at God's right hand (17:7), a place of presence and power.[1] The psalmist asks God to guard her as the "apple of your eye" (17:8), literally, the pupil of the eye. In Hebrew, the word for pupil can also mean "middle of the night" or the "deepest blackness." It is in these dark places that the psalmist encounters God and finds safety.

Then the psalmist asks God, "Hide me in the shadow of your wings" (17:8), a decidedly inhuman description! This is one of many places in the Bible describing God with wings (cf. Pss. 36:7; 57:1). After the other embodied descriptions of God, this image of God with wings is a reminder that God is not human. It puts God in a category with other supernatural beings in the

Bible, such as the seraphs and cherubs that prophets describe. These angel wings also provide protection: the ark of the temple was placed under cherubs' wings in the holy of holies (2 Chr. 5:7–8).

In addition to being embodied, this image of God with wings is feminine, like a mother bird who stretches out her wings to protect her young.[2] Jesus draws on this image when he says, "How often have I desired to gather your children together as a hen gathers her brood under her wings!" (Matt. 23:37). The psalmist wants to be under the protection of God's wings, in the shadow—another dark, safe place. Later in the psalm, the psalmist says, "As for me, I shall behold your face in righteousness; when I awake I shall be satisfied, beholding your likeness" (17:15). She meets God in the dark places and recognizes herself; when she sees God face-to-face, she is satisfied.

When preaching on this text, the preacher can invite the congregation into the embodied experience of the psalmist, asking those listening to think about how they encounter God in their bodies. The psalm also provides an opening to think about how we envision God with a body. This text goes much farther than the often-depicted image of God as a bearded man on a cloud! The psalmist describes God as having some human characteristics as well as additional features like wings. The image of God as a mother hen reminds us that God is neither male nor female but incorporates characteristics of all genders. Being present in our own bodies can help us feel the presence of God and embrace the mystery of a God who is both embodied and beyond bodies.

- What makes you want to cry out to God for justice?
- When you imagine an embodied God, what does that God look like?
- How is God like a mother hen gathering her children?

MARK 12:38–44

The Widow's Offering

The story of the widow's mite is familiar for many. It is a passage that pastors like to call on during the church "stewardship month" or "giving drive." The message in those sermons often sounds like this: Be like the widow and give generously! A deeper look at the passage, however, reveals much more subversive and interesting messages.

Scribes in the ancient Near East were trained in reading and writing, usually with competence in some area such as law or economics.[3] Essentially, the scribes in this text are like Jewish lawyers. This is a place where it can be easy for preachers to slip into anti-Judaism, perpetuating the idea that Jesus is saying that all scribes are bad and the widow is good. In the context of the chapter as a whole, that clearly is not the case: just a few verses before this text, Jesus has a conversation with a righteous scribe (Mark 12:28–34). Instead of reading this as Jesus denouncing all scribes, it makes more sense to read it as Jesus warning his followers to beware of the particular scribes who "like to walk around in long robes, and to be greeted with respect in the marketplaces" (12:38).

Jesus says that these scribes "devour widows' houses and for the sake of appearance say long prayers" (12:40). Jesus is not condemning the scribes for wearing fancy robes and wanting the best seats; he is outraged that the scribes are oppressing those whom they should be protecting.[4] The word for "devour" in Greek is the same word used in the New Testament for when a dragon devours. Jesus is using strong language to invoke the Hebrew prophets, who repeatedly called on the people of Israel to care for the widow and the orphan (cf. Zech. 7:10; Mal. 3:5).[5] These scribes, who are experts in the law, are sinning against God by devouring widows' houses.

We know little about the widow in this text, only that she is poor and that she puts two small copper coins into the treasury (Mark 12:42). Not all widows were poor in this time, but this one is. Perhaps she is poor because a scribe has devoured her house? This is a powerful image, of a widow whose home has been taken away by the people who are supposed to protect her.[6] She has only these two coins left, but she knows what is right. Instead of turning her back on her religious tradition, she walks out in front of that unscrupulous scribe and gives her last two coins. The widow has her dignity, and she will not let the scribe have the last word.

Jesus uses this widow as an object lesson for his followers. He does not engage her or try to help her. This may be because Jesus is also poor: he also may not have had any money to give. It is also possible that the widow serves as an example to Jesus. When Jesus says, "She out of her poverty has put in everything she had, all she had to live on" (12:44), the literal translation is "She has given her whole life." As Jesus will do a few chapters later, this unnamed widow gives her whole life.

For preachers, it will not be a stretch to find modern comparisons to the widow and the scribes in this text. Many today face losing their homes to lenders, and governments do not protect those who are living on the edge. Preachers can follow the example of Jesus in showing respect for people who have little, learning from how they maintain their dignity in a world that tends to ignore and ridicule them.

- What is the lesson of the widow who gives her last two coins to the treasury?
- How do you understand Jesus' response to her?
- What are some modern parallels to this story?

Second Sunday of Lent

ISAIAH 66:10–14

God as Comforting Mother

This text depicts strong feminine imagery of the returning exiles nursing from Jerusalem's breast and of God as a mother providing for the people's needs. The larger context extends these feminine images to include God as a midwife, helping Jerusalem give birth without pain. The lectionary text includes only a small amount of the end of Isaiah, which turns from comfort to God's judgment, but reading it in this larger context helps to expand our understanding of God and what we consider maternal.

The verses leading up to this text describe Zion in labor and giving birth (Isa. 66:7–8). Amazingly, "before she was in labor she gave birth; before her pain came upon her she delivered a son" (66:7). This is incredible for two reasons. First, Zion is giving birth to a nation in one day (66:8)—faster than any nation has ever been born.[1] Second, the lack of pain suggests a return to Eden. That story explains that women giving birth in pain is part of the punishment for Eve eating the fruit that God commanded her not to eat (Gen. 3:16), but here there is no pain.

God knows that these are incredible statements and responds by casting herself in the role of the midwife, saying, "Shall I open the womb and not deliver? . . . Shall I, the one who delivers, shut the womb?" (Isa. 66:9). As in many stories throughout the Bible, God is the one who is responsible for wombs being open (for pregnancies).[2] Here, the Creator God is intimately involved in the birth process, delivering the child.

Then the prophet calls for the people to rejoice with Jerusalem, noting that they have been mourning over her (66:10). The prophet describes the relationship between Jerusalem and the people as mother and child, with the returning exiles nursing at Jerusalem's "consoling breast" and saying they may "drink deeply with delight from her glorious bosom" (66:11). The comfort that the prophet has declared since Isaiah 40:1 now comes from Jerusalem's breast, which provides everything that the people need.[3]

The feminine imagery then expands from Jerusalem as mother to God as mother. The milk from Jerusalem's breast becomes the river of prosperity that God extends to the people, which includes "the wealth of the nations like an overflowing stream" (66:12). The people do not just nurse: they are also carried and dandled (66:12), their every need fulfilled. God comforts the people "as a mother comforts her child," repeating the word "comfort" three times in 66:13.[4]

But, in what seems like a sharp turn, the language turns to judgment.[5] This text cuts off just as the judgment is beginning, only mentioning God's indignation (66:14). The chapter and book end with vivid descriptions of God's anger, describing God's fire, sword, and all those slain by God (66:16). Some commentators have explained this as a shift in God's role as a parent in Isaiah, going from disciplinarian to nurturer.[6] In the end, however, God is in both roles. This raises questions about how we describe mothers: do only the verses describing nurturing and comfort reflect God as a mother? Or can motherhood include the disciplinarian side of God?

For preachers, this is a complex text. The prophet calls for rejoicing, but it comes at the end of a long period of sadness. God is a comforting mother and a vengeful disciplinarian. Even the mention of Jerusalem may be difficult for some congregations. Given the amount of violence and struggle over Jerusalem, it can be hard for those who love her to rejoice. Depending on whether the congregation needs to rejoice or mourn, this text offers the preacher space for both.

- What associations do you have with midwives? How do you envision God as a midwife delivering a nation?
- What images does breastfeeding conjure for you? Does it seem like a comforting metaphor?
- When is it important for congregations to look at the larger context rather than focusing on one joyful event?

JOHN 8:1–11

The Woman Accused of Adultery

This story of the woman accused of adultery is not included in most reliable early manuscripts of John.[7] It appears in later versions, sometimes in other locations: other places in John, or in Luke. The description of "the scribes and the Pharisees" only occurs this one time in John but is common in Luke.[8] The placement here breaks up the larger narrative; some scholars suggest that it should be read on its own without the context of the rest of the chapter.[9] It may have been part of the oral tradition about Jesus that people shared before the Gospels were written. Regardless, the story is popular and familiar to many, particularly Jesus' command, "Let anyone among you who is without sin be the first to throw a stone at her" (John 8:7). Perhaps this passage has remained in the Gospels despite its questionable origin because this is the kind of Jesus that people want to believe in: a Jesus who stands with the accused.

The unnamed woman in this text has been accused of adultery. The Jewish leaders bring her alone to Jesus, without the other party to the adultery. The scribes and the Pharisees point to the law of Moses to accuse her. However, unlike their claim that this law commands them to "stone such women," the Scriptures they reference state that both offending parties must be put to death (cf. Lev. 20:10; Deut. 22:22). They say this to test him (John 8:6), and Jesus has no good options: if he says that they should not stone her, that goes against Torah, but stoning for adultery was illegal under Roman law.[10] Instead of picking one of these choices, Jesus bends down and starts writing on the ground. What he writes is unknown, but by doing this, Jesus is de-escalating the situation: he is not responding in the same way that the leaders are questioning him. Jesus does not stare them down; he simply says that whoever is without sin should cast the first stone, and then bends down again to write on the ground. This gives the leaders an opportunity to leave, and they do.

This is a text that is easy to read in an anti-Jewish way: contrasting the punitive law of Moses proffered by the scribes and the Pharisees with a forgiving Jesus. This thread of anti-Judaism provides a compelling reason to read this passage in the context of the chapter. Later, Jesus says to the Jews, "You are from your father the devil, and you choose to do your father's desires. He was a murderer from the beginning and does not stand in the truth, because there is no truth in him" (8:44). This language reinforces the anti-Jewish subtext of this story text.

Some scholars have tried to downplay the harshness of the passage, arguing that it is in response to the intensity of the conflict between Christians and Jews at the time the Gospel was written.[11] But this anti-Jewish sentiment is present in the original chapter of John. For pastors who decide to preach on this text, it is important to beware of creeping anti-Judaism. Instead of ignoring these difficult texts, we can name them and face the violence that Christians have done to Jewish people based on anti-Jewish sentiment in our sacred text.

- Does knowing that this story is not in the most reliable manuscripts change your perspective on it?
- What else could Jesus have done to de-escalate the conflict between the woman and her accusers?
- How have you heard this story preached or taught? Did that sermon have anti-Jewish elements?

Third Sunday of Lent

JUDGES 16:6–21

Delilah

Although Samson is most often associated with Delilah, there are actually five women in the Samson story. Delilah is the only one who is named. A potential way to approach a sermon on Samson is to tell the story of the other four women, putting his interactions with Delilah in context. As the story begins, the first woman is Samson's mother, who is barren and thus has borne no children (Judg. 13:2). An angel of the Lord appears to her and tells her that she will conceive and bear a son (13:3). The angel also specifies that Samson will be "a nazirite to God from birth" and is not to drink alcohol, eat anything unclean, or have a razor on his head (13:4–5). Samson's mother accepts what the angel says and helps her husband to understand (13:23).[1]

The second woman in the story is Samson's wife. After Samson has grown into a man, he sees a Philistine woman who pleases him, so he demands that his parents get her for him as his wife (14:1–3). His parents try to convince him to marry an Israelite woman, but he insists on his choice (14:3). On the way to talk to her, he tears a lion apart and later eats honey that bees made in the lion carcass (14:5–9). At the wedding feast, Samson tells a riddle to the Philistines based on the lion, and the Philistines go to his wife. They threaten to burn her and her father's house if she does not get Samson to explain the riddle (14:15). She cries for seven days until Samson explains the riddle to her (14:17). When the Philistines answer Samson's riddle, he suggests that his wife has been unfaithful and abandons her (14:18–19). Samson's wife is then given to his best man (14:20).

The third and fourth women in the story do not get much description. The third is the wife's sister. After a while, Samson goes back to his wife, but her father will not let Samson go into her room (15:1). The father says that he thought Samson had rejected his wife and instead offers up her sister (15:2). Ancient readers would have seen this as a reasonable solution,[2] but Samson refuses; he catches three hundred foxes, lights their tails on fire, and sends them through the Philistines' fields of grain (15:4–5). The fourth, unnamed woman is a prostitute that Samson sees in Gaza (16:1). The people of Gaza know Samson is there, so they wait all night at the city gate, planning to kill him in the morning (16:2). But Samson doesn't stay the night, only until midnight. Then he takes the city gate and carries it to the top of a hill forty miles away (16:3).

Finally, there is Delilah. She is from Sorek, which suggests that she may be a Philistine.[3] Samson falls in love with her (16:4), but there is no indication that she loves him.[4] The Philistine rulers offer Delilah an enormous amount of money to find out what gives Samson his strength: eleven hundred pieces of silver (by contrast, a priest would make ten pieces of silver in a year).[5] Delilah never hides what she is trying to do: she has already tried to give Samson to the Philistines three times. In this story, Samson is usually presented as the hero, while Delilah is the conniving woman who betrays him. But in the context of the story as a whole, Samson's behavior toward women is appalling, and he has broken all of his nazirite vows (and his marital vows!).[6] Preachers can use Samson's interactions with all of these women to examine whether Delilah is consistent in her words and actions and not the villain of the story.

- How does putting the story of Samson and Delilah in the context of the other women in Samson's life change your perspective on their interactions?
- What else would you like to know about Delilah?
- Could you tell this story with Delilah as the hero who makes the right choice for her people?

JOHN 4:7–15

The Woman at the Well

The Jews and the Samaritans both descended from ancient Israel and practice similar religions, but they "do not share things in common" (John 4:9).[7] The stories that each group tell about themselves deepen our understanding of the interaction between Jesus and the unnamed woman. The Jews speak of the Samaritans as foreigners, descendants of foreign colonists from Cuthah and other places in Mesopotamia (2 Kgs. 17:24). The Jews see the Samaritans as unclean mischief-makers and exclude them from the temple in Jerusalem by formal edict.[8]

The story that the Samaritans tell about themselves is quite different. The Samaritans believe that they have descended from the remnant of the ten tribes, in the northern kingdom of Israel, some who were not deported when the northern kingdom fell in 722 BCE.[9] The Samaritans consider themselves the bearers of the true faith of ancient Israel. They are strict and Torah observant, and they practice their faith at a shrine on Mount Gerazim, which competed with the temple in Jerusalem. There was tension when some Jews returned from exile in Babylon because the Samaritans opposed the rebuilding of the temple.[10] About 160 years before Jesus met the woman at the well, Jewish troops destroyed the shrine on Mount Gerazim.[11]

Jesus and the Samaritan woman bring all of this history with them when they meet at the well, and it informs her question when she asks, "How is it that you, a Jew, ask a drink of me, a woman of Samaria?" (John 4:9). Preachers on this text often bring the perspective that Jesus is willing to meet with the outsider woman. But Jesus is in Samaria! He has traveled to a place where *he* is a foreigner and an outsider. The Samaritan woman is in her hometown, engaging with a man from the group that destroyed her people's holy place.

After this passage, Jesus states that the woman has "had five husbands, and the one you have now is not your husband" (4:18). To modern readers, this may seem like judgment about the woman's sexual history, but it would have had a different meaning for people in the early church. The story of a man meeting a woman at a well is familiar: in well-known stories, this is how a man meets his wife (cf. Gen. 24:1–27; 29:1–10; Exod. 2:15–21).[12] But Jesus' response indicates that this is not that kind of story. Jesus does not seem concerned by the woman's sexual history; instead, his words show that he knows who she is and sees her.[13] His description of her husbands is a statement of fact, not judgment. This is how she knows he is a prophet (John 4:19, 39).

The Samaritan woman has experienced so much loss. It is not clear whether some or all of her husbands have died or divorced her. Perhaps this is why she is willing to engage with Jesus: she has already lost so much, so what else does she have to lose? When what Jesus says to her does not make sense, she questions him (4:11) and reminds him of their shared history (4:12). And when she hears what he has to offer, she knows that is what she wants.

This text provides an example of two vulnerable people who each have something to give each other. Jesus is vulnerable when he asks for water: he is human and needs water to survive. But he has something to offer the woman as well: a spring of living water and a connection with the God that they both worship. Preachers can name this need and remind the congregation that God meets us with the same offer: a spring of water gushing up to eternal life.

Like the woman, we can engage with God and ask questions when things do not make sense. And like this woman, we can ask for God's living water.

- How does knowing the history of the Jews and the Samaritans deepen your understanding of this story?
- Why do you think Jesus mentions the woman's sexual history?
- What is the living water that Jesus has to offer?

Fourth Sunday of Lent

JOB 28:1–20

Wisdom

This lyrical poem in the middle of the book of Job begins with a description of valuable metals that can be found in the earth, including silver, gold, iron, and copper (Job 28:1–2). Later, it describes jewels, including sapphires, onyx, and pearls (28:6, 16, 18). Although the reader will find that there is something greater than these natural wonders, that does not take away from the loving description of their value and beauty. This listing of precious metals and jewels brings to mind what the queen of Sheba gave to Solomon from her wealth when she visited and witnessed to his wisdom (for more on the queen of Sheba, see the commentary on 1 Kgs. 10:1–13).

The text describes a person who seeks out these precious things in the earth (Job 28:3), leaving the identity of the person ambiguous. The description of "miners" in the NRSV translation is interpretive; in Hebrew it is "he" or "one."[1] Some interpreters have suggested that it is a description of God, putting an end to darkness, as in the creation narrative.[2] Or it may be some combination of God and people, with mining mirroring God's creative work in the world.[3] The language illustrates the great lengths to which people go to find things of value, and the lurking danger of the earth, which produces food on the surface but is "turned up as by fire" below (28:5).

Then the text turns from human searching to animals. The narrator gives the example of a falcon and birds of prey (28:7); these birds are a symbol of being able to see far and wide, with their extraordinary eyesight and ability to fly over vast territories,[4] but this also suggests that animals are searching as well as humans. The poem goes on to say that proud wild animals and lions have "not passed over it" (28:8). When the poem finally states that what they are seeking is "wisdom" (28:12), this search expands to the entire cosmos. Personified voices of the deep and the sea say that it is not in them (28:14). All of creation is seeking wisdom!

What is wisdom in this poem? Like the deep and the sea, this wisdom seems to be personified. In some translations, Wisdom is capitalized; in others, the translators use feminine pronouns for wisdom to reflect the feminine nouns for wisdom in Hebrew (as in 28:20–21 CEB): "But wisdom, where does she come from? Where is the place of understanding? She's hidden from the eyes of all the living, concealed from birds of the sky." God is the one who knows the way to this feminine wisdom (28:23). Wisdom is mysteriously both with God and separate from God.

At the time Job was written, mining may have seemed like new, impressive technology: today mining has a different connotation. Instead of evoking wonder, mining for precious metals and jewels brings to mind the legacy of colonialism and environmental destruction. How can we read Job 28 now, as we recognize climate change and degradation? Sarah Stokes Musser argues, "Despite what might seem to be similarities between human and divine control over the natural order, the presence of wisdom makes all the difference."[5] As this poem points out, humans can mine for gold and jewels, but that is not the way to find wisdom.

- What images do mining for precious metals and jewels conjure for you?
- Why do you think the narrator repeats the questions asking where wisdom is to be found?
- How do you imagine personified wisdom? Do you envision wisdom as feminine?

JOHN 11:17–35

Mary and Martha's Brother Raised

This story is sometimes called the death and resurrection of Lazarus (as in the NASB heading), but later Lazarus died, and the account is actually more about Lazarus's sisters Mary and Martha (for more on Mary and Martha, see the commentary on Luke 10:38–42). Of the forty-four verses about these events, only seven have their setting at Lazarus's tomb (John 11:38–44).[6] Much more of the chapter is about the interactions between Jesus and Mary and Martha. Although the story seems to end triumphantly, with Lazarus raised from the dead, the author describes the grief, anger, and hope of Martha, Mary, and Jesus in detail.

The story begins with Mary and Martha sending a message to Jesus, saying that their brother Lazarus is ill (11:3), but Jesus waits two more days to leave after receiving the message (11:6). By the time Jesus arrives, Lazarus has been in the tomb four days (11:17). This is significant because of the Jewish belief that the soul lingers near the body for three days until the soul "sees that the color of its face has changed" and leaves the body for good.[7] The author is establishing that Lazarus is truly dead.

Mary and Martha are mourning for their brother, and other Jews have come to console them (11:19). This may be a ritualized mourning observance, like the Jewish practice of sitting "shiva" for a week at home, when people come to console the mourners.[8] The town of Bethany is close to Jerusalem, which probably indicates that the Jews have come from Jerusalem to comfort the sisters. The reference to Jerusalem also reminds the readers how close Jesus is to Jerusalem, where his life is at risk (10:31, 39; 11:8).[9]

When Martha learns that Jesus is coming, she immediately goes out to meet him (11:20). Martha confronts Jesus (11:21). Martha has expected Jesus to do something, and the complaint in her statement fits well in the Jewish tradition, such as the psalms of complaint.[10] She follows this up with a statement of faith: she knows God will do whatever Jesus asks of him (11:22). Jesus responds to Martha by telling her that her "brother will rise again" (11:23), but understandably, Martha thinks that he means in the end times (11:24). Then Jesus tells her, "I am the resurrection and the life," which leads Martha to a formal confession of faith, that Jesus is "the Messiah, the Son of God, the one coming into the world" (11:25–27).[11] This is exactly the statement that John's Gospel would like every reader to make,[12] and here it comes from the mouth of a woman. It is similar to Peter's earlier confession (6:69), though he does not use the term "Messiah."[13] By naming Jesus as the Messiah, Martha is saying that Jesus carries their eschatological hopes.[14]

Jesus does not go to Mary, but instead sends Martha with a message for her to come to him (11:28). It is unclear why Jesus does this, but one possibility is that he wishes to speak to Mary privately, as he did with Martha. If that is what Jesus desires, it is not to be. The Jews who are with Mary follow her, thinking she is going to the tomb (11:31). Mary repeats Martha's words, with the same dashed hope, sorrow, and complaint that Jesus did not do anything (11:32).

The fact that Jesus weeps (11:35) has caused consternation among commentators. It seems unlikely to some that he is feeling sorrow at the death of his friend, because he earlier told the disciples that he was glad this happened for their sake (11:15). The Greek in verse 35 suggests that Jesus is angry and indignant, not that he feels compassion. This suggests that the death of his friend has reminded him of his own imminent death. He may be feeling anger at the Jews mourning at the tomb because some of these Jews will go to the Pharisees and tell them what Jesus has done (11:46), which will lead the chief priests and the Pharisees to plan to put him to death (11:53). All these possibilities reflect the humanity of Jesus as well as his divine knowledge of what is to come.

- Both Mary and Martha speak up about their sorrow that Jesus did not heal their brother. How can churches incorporate language of sorrow and complaint like this?
- When Jesus is talking with Martha about resurrection, is it clear what he intends to do? How would you interpret his words?
- Why does Jesus weep?

Fifth Sunday of Lent

PROVERBS 1:20–33

Wisdom Calls

The book of Proverbs is primarily a text by a male narrator to a son or sons, despite the command "Do not reject your mother's teaching" (Prov. 1:8). Some translations have made the language more inclusive by changing "son" to "child" and "sons" to "children,"[1] but it is fundamentally a guide for privileged young men. Given that context, it may be surprising that one of the primary characters is a feminine personified Wisdom! This text introduces Wisdom, who appears throughout the book. She goes against some of the stereotypes we may have of what makes an ideal woman in the Bible: Wisdom is loud, crying out and raising her voice (1:21–22). She is also in the busiest parts of the city: the squares, the busiest corners, and the entrance to the city gates (1:21–22).[2] And Wisdom is available for everyone: really, she is unavoidable.

When Wisdom begins to speak, it becomes clear that this is not her first time giving her message. She starts out with "How long?" to indicate that she has been calling out to the people for a long time (1:22). Wisdom uses the language of the prophets here, saying that she has called and stretched out her hand, but no one has heeded her words (1:24; cf. Jer. 7:13).[3] When she addresses the people as simple ones, scoffers, and fools (Prov. 1:22), her words are not mere insults. Wisdom distinguishes between those who are merely naive and those who persist in their ignorance.[4] Those who have heard Wisdom but continue to hate knowledge are setting themselves up for catastrophe.

Wisdom goes on to describe the calamities that will come through the chaos of natural disasters: panic that "strikes you like a storm" and calamity "like a whirlwind" (1:27). For readers today, these descriptions evoke the natural disasters that come with climate change, a fruitful parallel for those preaching on this text. Like Wisdom, scientists are letting us know that if we persist in ignorance, there will come a time when it is too late to act. Like the scoffers in this text, we will call out for help after ignoring Wisdom (1:28).

The final verse in this text sums up the message of Proverbs: those who listen to Wisdom "will be secure" (1:33). There is a tension here, because there is ample evidence that this is not true. Biblical stories and lived experience demonstrate that wise and good people experience catastrophes just like those who make bad decisions. In fact, when disasters strike, the vulnerable are most at risk. This is why it is important that Wisdom is speaking with a prophetic voice. The message of the prophets in the Hebrew Scriptures is to protect the vulnerable. Wisdom is speaking here to the most privileged in society—the ones who have responsibility for the vulnerable. Their poor choices and failure to listen to Wisdom will lead to disaster not just for themselves, but also for those in their care.

Wisdom is a strange character for feminist preachers: a woman personifying wisdom, written by a man for men. She is often compared with the "strange woman," who appears later in Proverbs and leads young men astray. Some scholars have argued that the women in Proverbs are merely types, and they exacerbate the problem of seeing women as either all good or all bad. Preachers can avoid this kind of good/bad dichotomy by paying attention to the details of these feminine characters and pointing out how they differ from lazy stereotypes.

- How do you picture Wisdom after reading this text? What is surprising about her?
- How can churches address the most privileged in society and help them to accept responsibility for their actions?
- If you were to personify Wisdom, what would she look like? How would she be similar to or different from the Wisdom personified in this text?

LUKE 8:1–15

Women Accompany Jesus

In the beginning of this text, Luke explicitly states that there are women in the group following Jesus. Luke names three women in particular—Mary Magdalene, Joanna, and Susanna—and states that there are "many others" (Luke 8:2–3). At least some of these women have been cured of evil spirits and infirmities, like Mary Magdalene, who had seven demons go out of her: having seven demons would have been much worse than having one (for a more in-depth discussion of Mary Magdalene and her reception history, see the commentary on John 20:11–18).[5] Luke identifies Joanna as the wife of Chuza, who manages Herod's estate.[6] This suggests that Joanna is elite and raises the question of whether she has left her husband to follow Jesus.[7] Susanna is otherwise unknown.[8]

Luke says that these women provide for Jesus and his disciples "out of their resources" (8:3), suggesting that they are wealthy. The Greek verb translated as "provided" indicates service as well as financial support. This word comes up again in the story of Martha and Mary (10:38–42), and Jesus uses it to describe his own ministry (22:27).[9] In the early church, this service was not limited to domestic chores but also included serving at the table for Eucharist and proclaiming the word.[10] Although these women are not explicitly called disciples, as is Tabitha (Acts 9:36),[11] they are a central part of the community of faith surrounding Jesus.

In this context of the women's support, Jesus tells the parable of the sower. Jesus describes a sower who sows his seed, with some falling on rocks, some being eaten up, some choked by thorns, and some falling on good soil (8:4–8). The seed that falls on good soil yields a hundredfold, which seems to be quite miraculous, considering that the average yield probably is around tenfold.[12] Although there is no explicit connection between this parable and the support that the women provide, it is not much of a stretch to suggest that these women are like those who till the soil, making it possible for Jesus to sow these seeds.

The disciples then ask Jesus to explain what the parable means (8:9). It is unclear to whom Jesus is speaking in this part of the text; he could be speaking to only the disciples, the inner circle that travels with him (including the women), or the entire crowd. However, unlike in the parallel text in Mark, Jesus and his disciples do not withdraw from the crowd (Mark 4:10).[13] Accordingly, this explanation probably is for everyone present, including the women.

In response to the disciples' question, Jesus explains the meaning of the parable: the seed is the word of God (Luke 8:11). He goes on to describe the different kinds of soil as people who hear the word of God: some will have the word taken away from them, some do not have roots but fall away at testing, some are choked by the thorns of riches, and some hold it and bear fruit. Probably the disciples think that they are in the final category but, in fact, when the time of testing comes, they scatter! It is the women who stay with Jesus to his crucifixion and burial, and then seek him after the resurrection (23:49, 55; 24:1–10). In the end, it is the women who embody the good soil, holding the word of God in their hearts and bearing fruit "with patient endurance" (8:15).

- How does it change your understanding of the parable of the sower to read it in the context of the women providing for Jesus and the disciples?
- What questions do you have about the women who follow Jesus?
- What are the qualities of good soil? How does this metaphor of the soil help you to understand the good news?

Sixth Sunday of Lent

PROVERBS 8:1–4, 22–31

Wisdom's Gifts

The opening lines of Proverbs 8 mirror the description of Wisdom in 1:20–21, where Wisdom is in the street, the square, the busiest corner, and the entrance to the city gates. But here the narrator goes even further: Wisdom is also on the heights and beside the way: Wisdom is present everywhere (Prov. 8:2). She calls out to everyone who lives (8:4); no one can say they have not heard the voice of Wisdom. As the poem goes on, Wisdom describes the creation of the cosmos and her place in it, including the three realms of sky, waters, and land, which for people in the ancient Near East encompassed all of reality.[1] Wisdom has expanded from being present everywhere in the city to being present in all of creation.

Wisdom's description of the creation of the world evokes the creation stories in Genesis 1–2 and places her within them. The relationship between God and Wisdom is ambiguous. Is Wisdom something that God has acquired? Or did God create Wisdom? The identity of Wisdom in verse 30 is famously difficult to translate; the primary interpretations are (1) architect's plan, (2) master worker, or (3) little child.[2] Each of these translations reveals different facets of Wisdom and the nature of God.

The interpretation of Wisdom as an architect's plan envisions Wisdom as a kind of blueprint for creation.[3] God acquires Wisdom in the beginning, and Wisdom is present throughout all of time. In this metaphor, Wisdom is available for all to see in creation: the created order reflects Wisdom and her imprint everywhere.[4] Thus God uses Wisdom as a guide for creation, and

Wisdom is a separate entity from God. Wisdom understands how the world works, and people should listen to her and keep her ways (8:32).

Seeing Wisdom as a master worker or artisan paints a picture of Wisdom as working beside God in creation.[5] Reading this in parallel with the first creation story (Gen. 1:1–2:4), one can imagine God speaking and Wisdom creating. This image also brings to mind crafts that women have traditionally done, like sewing, weaving, or knitting. Wisdom is a master worker with God, making beautiful things on earth, above, and below.

The best understanding of Wisdom is probably as a "little child."[6] Bringing forth usually refers to the birth of a child (8:24). In this metaphor, God is a mother giving birth to a daughter, Wisdom. This is the image that most closely links God and Wisdom: they are as close as a mother and a daughter. The daughter Wisdom delights in God's creation, smiling, frolicking, and having fun.[7] This picture of Wisdom is pure joy, and it connects God with humans: Wisdom is God's delight, and Wisdom delights in humans (8:31).[8]

For preachers, this text provides a wealth of images to describe Wisdom, many of which have parallels to people in a congregation. The text celebrates those who have lived a long life and have grown in wisdom. It honors those who are skilled at crafts and create beautiful things with their hands. It invites us to see the wisdom in the ordering of the universe. And it recognizes the wisdom in a little girl's laughter and delight. Instead of choosing one of those metaphors, the text invites preachers to layer the images and help the congregation to see the wisdom around and within them.

- When you picture Wisdom, what images come to mind?
- How does it change your understanding of Wisdom to see her as an architect's plan, a master worker, or a little girl?
- Who in your congregation embodies wisdom?

MATTHEW 27:11–23

Pilate's Wife

Throughout this text, Matthew heightens the tension. At each step, it seems possible that Jesus will not be crucified: people are making decisions about whether to continue toward crucifixion or to let him go. One of these moments is the interruption by Pilate's wife. She appears only through a message, not in person, but she makes an appeal to her husband to have nothing to do with Jesus (Matt. 27:19). Although we all know how the story ends, this text gives preachers a chance to mirror this rising tension and explore each of the moments that could have led to a different outcome.

The first moment is when the story seems as though it could go a different way as Jesus and Pilate encounter each other. Pilate is the prefect of Judea in 26–36 CE, thus the Roman official that Jewish leaders need to work through to get Jesus executed (capital cases are reserved to the Romans; see John 18:31).[9] For Pilate, if Jesus is claiming to be "The King of the Jews," that is a treasonous threat to the Roman Empire.[10] Jesus' response in the NRSV translation, "You say so," is enigmatic; the translation in the NIV, "You have said so," seems more affirmative (27:11). But when given the opportunity to defend himself against the accusations by the chief priests and elders, Jesus does not respond (27:12).

Next, Matthew raises the possibility that Pilate will release Jesus as part of the festival custom (27:15). The only evidence for this custom is in the Gospels, and it is historically unlikely that Roman officials would release a political prisoner during the nationalistic festival of Passover, when the Jewish people are gathered and at their most patriotic.[11] But in terms of this story, it gives hope that Jesus will be the one to be released.

Matthew contrasts Jesus with another prisoner, here named Jesus Barabbas (27:16). The name Barabbas ironically means "son of his father," drawing a contrast between him and Jesus as the true Son of the Father.[12] It is likely that Matthew added the name "Jesus" to heighten this contrast.[13] In the parallel passage in Mark, Barabbas is a political prisoner with the rebels, and he has committed murder during "the insurrection" (Mark 15:7). Here, Matthew merely describes him as "a notorious prisoner" (27:16).

As Pilate is posing the question to the crowd about which prisoner to release, he is interrupted by a message from his wife (27:19). This unnamed woman, who only appears in Matthew, appeals to her husband on behalf of a man she has never met, but who has disturbed her dreams. This divine revelation through a dream connects Pilate's wife with people in the Hebrew Scriptures who received messages from God in dreams (cf. Gen. 37:5–10), as well as with the magi and Joseph in Matthew 2. Like the magi, she is a Gentile with whom God communicates about Jesus through a dream. She continues the theme of Matthew by calling Jesus a "righteous man" and tells her husband to have nothing to do with him (27:19 RSV).[14]

After receiving this message from his wife, Pilate turns back to the crowd and the question he had begun to pose: Should he release Jesus or Barabbas? According to this account, Pilate has misgivings about going ahead with the execution of an innocent man, which he later demonstrates by washing his hands (27:24). However, if he thinks that the crowd shares his uncertainty, he is mistaken. The crowd, persuaded by the chief priests and the elders, shouts repeatedly, "Crucify him!" It is in this moment that Jesus' fate is sealed: Pilate will hand Jesus over to be crucified (27:26). Each step has led to this conclusion.

- In this text does it seem possible that the story will have a different ending?
- According to Matthew, Pilate knows that the Jewish leaders have handed Jesus over "out of jealousy" (27:18). Does that seem like the correct explanation?
- What else would you like to know about Pilate's wife? What would this story be like if it were told from her perspective?

Maundy Thursday

PROVERBS 9:1–6

Wisdom's Feast

In this culmination of the description of the feminine personified Wisdom, the ways Wisdom acts are reminiscent of other wise women throughout the Bible. First, Wisdom builds a house (Prov. 9:1). Homes and domestic life are often associated with women in the Hebrew Scriptures (e.g., Gen. 18:9), and Wisdom builds this feminine space with her own hands. Scholars have debated about the meaning of the seven pillars:[1] they may be the mythic pillars of the earth or like pillars in ancient temples.[2] Wisdom, who was present at the creation of the cosmos and worked with God as a master craftswoman (Prov. 8:27–30), now applies the same wisdom to her own house, a microcosm of all creation.[3]

Next, Wisdom prepares a feast (9:2). Like the wise Queen Esther (Esth. 5:4) or Abigail sending a feast ahead of her (1 Sam. 25:18–19), Wisdom knows that providing food and wine will help her convince those she invites. The meat and the wine she offers are good to consume, representing the hearty wisdom that she makes available to everyone. Wisdom herself sets the table (Prov. 9:2), putting everything in its place so that it will be welcoming to her guests. After building the entire house, she attends to every detail within the domestic space.

Then Wisdom invites her guests (9:3). Wisdom not only calls out to the people herself, but she also sends her servant girls with invitations (9:3). This is the first place to mention that Wisdom has female servants, and it creates an image of a household of women, with Wisdom at its center. Another wise woman, the queen of Sheba, said when she visited Solomon: "Happy are these your servants, who continually attend you and hear your wisdom!" (1 Kgs.

10:8). If this is true of Solomon's servants, how much more so the servants of Wisdom! It is easy to envision the women going out with joy to share the wisdom that they have learned.

This chapter makes the binary clear between Wisdom and the Strange Woman (here called Folly).[4] The first six verses are about Wisdom and the last six are about Folly, with many parallels between them. Wisdom and Folly both go out into the high places and make the same call: "You who are simple, turn in here!" (cf. Prov. 9:4, 16). Both women have built their houses and offer feasts to the simple ones. This binary and flattening of women to good versus bad is a reminder that Proverbs is a book by men for men, the lessons of an older man to his son.[5] For a young, straight man, these women would probably be attractive. Fortunately, we live in a time when the message of the Bible is not only for young, straight men. Although the device of framing Wisdom and Folly as two opposing women is problematic, the choice between wisdom and folly is one that everyone gets to make. The narrator here does not paint folly as unappealing. On the contrary, Folly's water is sweet, and her bread is pleasant (9:17). The young man and the reader have the option of choosing folly, which will satisfy them in certain ways.

This text also makes clear that, when a person chooses wisdom, that choice involves giving something up. Wisdom tells the simple ones that they must "lay aside immaturity" (9:6). And this is not a choice made once and for all: those who choose wisdom will start on the path to walk in "the way of insight" (9:6). Those who are preaching on this text can use the example of the appeals of Wisdom and Folly, then round out the lesson with other examples of ways that both wisdom and folly can be appealing. With other illustrations, the feminine personifications of wisdom and folly become just one way to describe wisdom and folly, rather than a description of the two options for women.

- When you envision Wisdom's house, what do you imagine it looks like?
- Who are Wisdom's servant girls? Who spreads the message of wisdom in the world?
- Instead of creating a binary between good and bad women, what are some other images you can think of to embody Wisdom and Folly?

MARK 14:1–9

The Woman Anoints Jesus

In this text about the unnamed woman who anoints Jesus, Jesus announces that "wherever the good news is proclaimed in the whole world," part of that good news will be about a woman! Jesus' view of the good news is expansive:

it is not just about his own life, teachings, and ministry, but also about the service that others do around him and for him. Instead of scolding this woman, Jesus proclaims that she is part of the gospel message.

The context for this story is the upcoming Passover and the chief priests and scribes' plot to kill Jesus (Mark 14:1). By naming Passover, Mark associates the reign of God with this festival and its theme of liberation.[6] The Jewish leaders' desire to arrest Jesus by stealth to avoid a riot (14:1–2) underlines the vulnerability of the Jewish people in the Roman Empire and the ways that these religious festivals would stir up nationalistic sentiment. The woman's public anointing provides ironic contrast: the chief priests and scribes seek to secretly betray Jesus while the unnamed woman publicly prepares his body for burial.[7]

The anointing carries two meanings. Pouring the ointment over his head suggests royal anointing, as when Samuel poured oil over Saul's head to anoint him as king (1 Sam. 10:1).[8] Alternatively, it could be preparing a body for burial.[9] The ointment is nard, a fragrant perfume that also appears in Song of Songs (Song 1:12; 4:13, 14).[10] The woman never speaks, but by pouring the ointment, she is engaging in a prophetic act. Jesus has been predicting his own death (Mark 8:31; 9:31; 10:33–34),[11] but his disciples have not understood him. However, this woman knows what is to come.

Those around Jesus in this story do not understand what the woman is doing and instead feel that they have the authority to scold her (Mark 14:4–5). These others are not named here, but in the parallel accounts they are either the disciples (Matt. 26:8), a Pharisee (Luke 7:39), or Judas (John 12:4–5). These others draw on a pious excuse to condemn the woman: the perfume was worth almost a full year's wages, and the money could have gone to the poor (Mark 14:5).[12]

But Jesus, in turn, scolds them (14:6). He says that what she has done is a good deed or an act of charity in itself, preparing his body for burial, the equivalent of giving to the poor.[13] Jesus also exposes the hypocrisy of these others: they can show kindness to the poor themselves, whenever they wish (14:7). This woman has most likely spent her own money to buy this costly ointment,[14] and she is more aware of the timing and the type of charity that is appropriate than these others, who are not engaging in charity at all.

Then Jesus declares that this unnamed woman will be remembered (14:9). This is a preaching moment: Jesus is preaching to his followers as well as anyone who later reads or hears this text. Mark reminds the followers that the good news of Jesus will be shared throughout the world.[15] Jesus also demonstrates that the good news is expansive. The gospel is not just about Jesus' life, death, and teachings; it is also about how others play a role in his mission.[16] This woman's prophetic act is part of the gospel that will be proclaimed in the whole world.

Those who preach on this text can follow Jesus and make sure that this woman's story is told wherever the gospel is proclaimed! This story also gives preachers a chance to address the false piety of questioning someone else's good act by pointing to something else that they should be doing. Here is a type of "whatabout-ism" (e.g., "Why are you talking about the environment? What about orphans?!"). There are many ways for followers of Jesus to do acts of service, and it does not help to tear each other down when someone is not doing the work in exactly the way another expects.

- This scene is dramatic and does not have many details. How do you envision it playing out?
- When have you encountered "whatabout-ism"?
- If you imagine yourself as one of the people in this text, who are you? How do you respond?

Good Friday

DEUTERONOMY 32:10–20

God as Mother Eagle

The text from the song near the end of Deuteronomy includes several vivid metaphors for God, including God as a mother eagle, a rock, a woman giving birth, a protector, and a provider. It also demonstrates the limitations of these metaphors for God. Although the book of Deuteronomy is traditionally attributed to Moses, the language is most like classical Israelite prophecy.[1] In particular, many of the images for God are similar to language in Isaiah.

The first description of God in the text is of God as a sustainer, the one who has sustained Jacob/Israel in the desert (Deut. 32:10). This is a nurturing image of God: God protects Israel from the "howling wilderness waste," shields him and cares for him, keeping him as close as the center of God's eye (32:10). But what about when Israel is no longer sustained and protected? Does that mean that God has abandoned Israel?

The next image the author uses to describe God is as an eagle that "hovers over its young" (32:11). This takes the protective description of God from the previous verse and makes it explicitly parental: God is a mother eagle, using her body to protect her young. In this description, God also helps her young fly, as the eagle "spreads its wings, takes them up, and bears them aloft on its pinions" (32:11). This verse brings to mind Isaiah 40:31, that "those who wait for the LORD . . . shall mount up with wings like eagles." And yet, describing God as a bird of prey like an eagle may be troubling for some readers.

After God sets Jacob "atop the heights of the land" (Deut. 32:13), God becomes a provider—another nurturing image. The poetry describes a vast

100

array of food that God provides, produce of the field, honey from the crags, curds and milk, meat, wheat, and the finest wine (32:13–14). Unfortunately, this turns from a lovely feast to what reads now like body shaming. Israel (also called Jeshurun) grows fat and bloated (32:15). If God has provided all this food, why is God upset when Israel eats it?

One of the most troubling implicit metaphors in this text is of God as a spouse. When it says that God is "jealous" (32:16), that is a term from marital relationships.[2] God becomes upset when Israel is unfaithful and turns to other gods, like a jealous spouse. The writer invokes the image of God as a Rock to demonstrate God's unchanging faithfulness (32:15), but God also seems like a sullen spouse who turns away, saying, "I will hide my face from them" (32:20).

The final metaphor in this text is strongly feminine: God as a mother giving birth. The writer says that Israel is "unmindful of the Rock that bore you; you forgot the God who gave you birth" (32:18). This literally means "writhed in travail" and refers to labor pains.[3] It is similar to the description of God in Isaiah 42:14, where God says, "I will cry out like a woman in labor, I will gasp and pant." This birthing imagery for God is powerful, but it is immediately followed by God spurning God's sons and daughters (Deut. 32:19). For those who have felt abandoned by parents, this metaphor for God may be painful.

Each of these images provides an insight into the nature of God and how God interacts with people. They also illustrate the difficult relationship between Israel and God. When people see God as nurturing, supportive, and their sole provider, they may feel as though God is abandoning them when things do not go well. This text is a source of strong feminine images of God, and it provides an opportunity for preachers to challenge congregations about the metaphors that they use to describe God. Because God is beyond what we can comprehend and name, every metaphor for God will eventually fail.

- What are the images you use most often to describe God? How do these images help you understand the nature of God?
- What are the limitations for the metaphors we commonly use for God?
- How does it impact your understanding of God to think of God as a mother eagle or as a woman experiencing labor pains?

JOHN 19:23–30

The Women Watch

This text typically is associated with Holy Week and Good Friday (and that is where it falls in this lectionary), but its themes go beyond that specific event. The people and events give preachers and congregations an opening to talk about various aspects of death and dying, both for the person who is dying and those around them. It raises issues of what happens to the person's belongings at death, how others can bear witness to death and suffering, and the example Jesus sets of how to die well. The text does not give easy answers but instead walks us through some of these stages of death.

In the opening of this text, the soldiers have already crucified Jesus and now are waiting for him to die (John 19:23). They divide up his clothes, a common practice at a Roman execution.[4] For John, this is a fulfillment of Scripture (Ps. 22:18).[5] However, it also raises the question of what happens to a person's belongings after death. Jesus has only the clothes on his back, but most people have more possessions. Through the lens of Jesus' death, people in the congregation can think about what kind of legacy they are leaving with their belongings and how they would like the things they own to be distributed after their death.

The text then goes on to describe the women who stand at the foot of the cross (19:25). The language is ambiguous: this could either be three or four women, depending on whether Jesus' mother's sister is Mary the wife of Clopas or those are two different women. Most scholars think there are four women since it is unlikely that two sisters would both be named Mary.[6] All four Gospels state that the women watch, but with different women named. The only woman who is consistently named is Mary Magdalene; this is the first reference to her in the Gospel of John (for more on Mary Magdalene, see the commentary on John 20:11–18).[7] The diversity of these lists suggests a rich tradition of faithful women who attended Jesus' death.[8] While in the other Gospels the women stand at a distance, here they are close enough to converse with Jesus.[9] They do not run away in the face of death, but gather to bear witness.[10]

When facing their own death, many people wonder what will happen to their loved ones. This is true for Jesus when he sees his mother (19:26). Mary may be in a vulnerable position, losing her son. Jesus sees her grief and makes arrangements for her physical and emotional care by designating the Beloved Disciple as her adopted son (19:26–27). This kind of chosen family is familiar for many queer people, who may not have the love or support of their families of origin.[11] Jesus shows support for these kinds of chosen families, to provide the care that biological relatives may be unwilling or unable to give.

After he has made these arrangements for people he loves, Jesus knows that all is finished (19:28). He says that he is thirsty, perhaps for God's living water. In the end, he bows his head and gives up his spirit (19:30), suggesting the Holy Spirit, a gift of life that comes through Jesus' death.[12] Not everyone has an opportunity to make final decisions in the moments before death: some deaths come quickly and unexpectedly. Throughout his story, Jesus shows how living his life well has prepared him for a good death. For some, the idea of death is too scary to face. But Jesus gives this example of how knowing that one's death is coming can be a gift, an opportunity to put things in place.

- When you picture the women watching Jesus on the cross, what do you imagine?
- Why did Jesus give the Beloved Disciple to Mary as an adopted son?
- What are the ways that Jesus is an example to us in life and death?

Holy Saturday

HOSEA 13:2–16

God as Angry Mother Bear

The first three chapters of Hosea have a sustained metaphor: Israel is like an unfaithful wife to God. In this text, the metaphors layer on each other. The prophet has many ways to describe the people, the nation, and God. The Hebrew is difficult to interpret, with potentially opposite translations. Although this may be hard to follow, the barrage of imagery captures the prophet's difficulty in describing what is happening around him and his understanding of God.

The first set of images describes the people of Israel. Because they have been unfaithful to God and worshiped other gods (Hos. 13:2), they will dissipate. The prophet compares them to four things that people would have observed: the morning mist, the dew that goes away, chaff swirling from a threshing floor, or smoke from a high opening (houses at the time did not have chimneys, so smoke would escape through other apertures).[1] The people of Israel who once seemed so solid are now like these ephemeral things that are scattered and disappear.

The next series of images describe God. Because the people have forgotten that God had protected them since the time of Egypt and fed them in the wilderness (13:4–6), God will become like a giant animal of prey. God here is like a lion, a leopard, or a bear (13:7–8). This combination of animals combines in the hearer's mind and creates a terrifying predator in wait for its prey: the people. It also includes one of the most terrifying feminine images of God in the Bible, the mother bear robbed of her cubs (13:8). This maternal image is not nurturing but instead destructive, tearing the people open in her grief.

The metaphor that follows is also of childbirth, but one that has gone terribly wrong. Ephraim, whom the prophet has described as God's son (11:1–4), is now back in the womb (13:12–13). The pangs of childbirth have come, but Ephraim "does not present himself at the mouth of the womb" to be born (13:13). Israel's sins are like an untimely birth: if the child does not come on time, the result will be pain and possibly death.[2]

At this point, the Hebrew becomes difficult to translate. Each line that begins in the NRSV translation with "shall I" could also be translated as "I shall," and "ransom" could be translated as "compassion."[3] God may be saying, "I will be your plagues" and "I will be your destruction" (13:14). Thus it is unclear whether God is one who saves the people from death or sends them to their death. This ambiguity captures the ambivalence of the prophet, who sees God as both the savior and one who is responsible for the violence that is befalling Israel. The prophet returns to the wilderness, but this time instead of feeding and protecting the people, God destroys them. The wind comes as a blast from the east, the fountain dries up, and the spring is parched (13:15). All of Israel's treasures are stripped, and there is no comfort or protection from their God.

In the final image, the prophet returns to the metaphor of the unfaithful wife, in a feminine personification of Israel. The prophet blames her for what will happen to her: because she has been rebellious, she will be killed, her children will be dashed to pieces, and pregnant women will be ripped open (13:16). This is intentionally shocking language: the prophet hopes to get the people's attention.[4] It also reflects the reality of war: those who are most vulnerable (in this case, children and pregnant women) are often the ones who suffer violence.[5]

This may be a difficult passage for preachers, but it also provides an example of a time when single words or metaphors fail to capture the full intensity of a catastrophe. In a time of crisis, the preacher can invite the congregation to add their own images of how they feel: it is like *this*, and like *this*, and like *this*. The prophet illustrates the very human desire to blame everyone: the nation, oneself, and God. Rather than trying to present this in one illustration, Hosea offers a multitude of images and metaphors.

- What images in this text speak to you? Which ones do you find most disturbing?
- What metaphors would you use to describe God when God is angry?
- What is a time in your life or the life of your congregation when you had a hard time coming up with words or images to describe what was happening?

LUKE 23:50–56

The Women See the Tomb

The story of Joseph and the women going to the tomb encapsulates aspects of privilege, as well as how a person with privilege can use that advantage to help people who are more marginalized. Joseph is immediately named in the text, which calls him a "good and righteous man" and names his hometown of Arimathea (Luke 23:50–51). He is a member of the council (the judicial authority, also called the Sanhedrin), and this is the first time Luke states that the council's decision to execute Jesus was not unanimous.[6] Thus Joseph has enough authority that he can disagree with the majority. Joseph is not a disciple, but rather a good Jew who is "waiting expectantly for the kingdom of God" (23:51).

By contrast to the description of Joseph, the women are not named. Luke merely says that they are the "women who had come with him from Galilee" (23:55). These are the women who have provided for Jesus and his disciples (8:2–3) and watched Jesus' crucifixion (23:49). Luke does not name them here until after they are witnesses to the resurrection (24:10), when he says they are "Mary Magdalene, Joanna, Mary the mother of James, and the other women." Like Joseph, these women are faithful Jews, waiting until after the Sabbath to prepare Jesus' body for an honorable burial.[7]

Joseph uses his privileged position to do something the women cannot: ask Pilate for the body of Jesus. The Romans did not usually allow family members or supporters to take an executed person's body for a decent burial.[8] However, Joseph is neither a family member nor supporter, and he has access to Pilate in a way that Jesus' followers do not. Joseph is also following the law stating that criminals are to be buried on the same day they are executed (Deut. 21:22–23), another indication that he is a faithful Jew.[9] Joseph takes Jesus' body down himself and wraps him in a linen cloth (Luke 23:53). The fact that he has a new tomb in which to place Jesus suggests that he is wealthy.[10]

The relationship between Joseph and the women is unclear. The women follow him and see how Jesus' body is laid (23:55) before the stone is rolled in front of the tomb (24:2). Perhaps Joseph has invited the women to come with him to place Jesus in the tomb. In any event, after he puts Jesus in the tomb, Joseph makes space for the women to see where Jesus is buried, to grieve for him, and to prepare his body according to their customs. Joseph does not use his power to take over or tell the women what to do, but rather makes space for the women after using his privilege to help them.

Luke establishes these women as eyewitnesses to Jesus' life, ministry, death, and resurrection. They have seen him during his life, watched his death on the cross (23:49), and now see where he is buried. Soon they will return and be the first ones to learn about the resurrection (24:1–10). These women are the ones who bear witness at each stage; they can verify that this is the right tomb and that Jesus was placed in it.[11] Their eyewitness is the link between these critical events and provides the "chain of evidence" for the Christian claims about Jesus.[12] Even though their witness will seem like "an idle tale" to the apostles (24:11), these women will be vindicated.

- Why do the women go to the tomb with Joseph?
- What else would you like to know about these women and their experience at the tomb?
- What are some examples of people using their privilege to make space for people who are marginalized?

Resurrection Sunday

SONG OF SOLOMON 1:1–8

Beloved

"Let him kiss me with the kisses of his mouth! For your love is better than wine" (Song 1:2). The love poetry of Song of Songs can be shocking in its directness, and it is strikingly different from the other poetry in the Bible. This is a book dominated by women's voices: more than fifty of the verses are ascribed to a female speaker; the male speaker has only thirty-six.[1] There are three voices in this book: the unnamed young woman, the unnamed young man, and the collective voices of the "daughters of Jerusalem," who serve as a chorus in responding to the lovers.[2] Song of Songs is also the only place in the Bible where a woman speaks directly about what she wants and needs, not through a narrator.[3]

In addition, the relationships in this text and book are described in terms of women: the young woman talks about her mother's sons (1:6) rather than saying they are her brothers (or her father's sons), and later she says that she is in her mother's house (3:4). After so many stories about fathers and sons (and fathers' houses), this focus on women's relationships and homes may feel like a relief to the reader! The text continues to follow the woman's perspective as well as her sexual fantasies and desires. This overwhelmingly female perspective has made some commentators suggest that a woman wrote Song of Songs.

This text is a poem about pleasure. The descriptions are tactile and evocative: kisses that are sweeter than wine, the lover's name that is like perfume poured out (1:3). The young woman takes pleasure in herself: she announces that she is "black and beautiful" (1:5). She describes the feeling of the sun on her skin as she works with her hands in the vineyards (1:6) and compares her skin to the dark fabric of the tents of Kedar and the curtains of Solomon (1:5). The images evoke taste, touch, smell, and sound, engaging all the senses. For preachers, this text invites slow reading and reflection on the tactile imagery. It reminds us that blackness is beautiful—a counter to other places where darkness is associated with evil and light with good.

Song of Songs has made readers uncomfortable—Jewish and Christian communities have not known what to do with this book. For centuries, the church tried to say that these verses were an allegory for Christ's love for the church, that instead of a book about two young lovers, it describes the all-encompassing love that God has for God's people. That interpretation seems like a stretch for a book that never mentions God.[4] Instead of seeing it as separate from the rest of the Bible, preachers and congregations can reflect on what it means to have this sensual poetry as part of our sacred text.

This text ends with the young woman asking her lover where he pastures his flocks. She wants to know where he is so that she can go and be with him: she longs to be with him. He tells her where to go, to follow the tracks of the flock to where he will be (1:8). As noted above, there have been questions about why Song of Songs is included in the Bible, but this longing transcends the longing between two specific people. These verses offer an invitation to touch, to smell, to hear, to taste, and to see the beauty of those we love. It is a reminder that our bodies call to us, and God is the Creator of these bodies.

- Have you heard this text in a sermon before? How did the preacher approach Song of Songs?
- What imagery stands out to you in this text?
- How is the love between people sacred?

MARK 16:1–8

The Women Go to the Tomb

As soon as they can, when the Sabbath has ended, Mary Magdalene, Mary the mother of James and Joses, and Salome buy spices and go to anoint Jesus in the tomb. These are the women who have looked on from a distance as Jesus was crucified (in Mark 15:40). After the disciples have fled, these women have remained, and as a result, "Mary Magdalene and Mary the mother of Joses saw where the body was laid" (15:47). These women know where to find the body of Jesus, and they know that there is a large stone in front of the tomb.

The stone is what concerns them on their way to the tomb: who will roll it away from the entrance? (16:3). But when they arrive, that is not an issue.

Instead, the stone is already rolled away, and when they enter the tomb, there is a young man dressed in white (16:4–5). Who is this mysterious man? Probably an angel: it was common for Jewish texts of the time to refer to an angel as "a man" (cf. Dan. 8:15–16; 9:21).[5] The parallel text in the Gospel of Matthew specifies that the man is "an angel of the Lord" (28:2). Alternatively, the man's white clothes suggest that he may be a vindicated martyr.[6] Whoever this man is, he has a divine message for the women.

The man tells them not to be alarmed; he knows that they have come to seek Jesus, but Jesus has been raised and is not there. He proves this by showing the women the place where others laid Jesus (16:6). The man then tells the women to go back to the disciples, especially Peter, and tell them that Jesus has been raised and is going ahead of them to Galilee (16:7). He reminds them that Jesus told them that this would happen: "But after I am raised up, I will go before you to Galilee" (14:28).[7] But the women do not go back to the disciples to tell them what has happened. Instead, they say nothing to anyone because they are afraid (16:8).

Who are these women who come to the tomb? Mary Magdalene is the most well known: the Gospel of Luke describes her as "Mary, called Magdalene, from whom seven demons had gone out" (8:2). The other Mary's sons, James and Joses, also appear in parallel passages (Matt. 13:55; Mark 6:3) as the brothers of Jesus,[8] but it is unclear whether this is Jesus' mother, Mary, in Mark 16:1. Salome appears only here. The Gospel of Mark says that these women have followed Jesus and "provided for him when he was in Galilee," along with many other women (15:40–41).

When the man tells these women to go back to the disciples and tell them what has happened, he is calling them to preach. In this account, they refuse the call. But in other Gospels, they do what the man tells them to do and tell the disciples (cf. Matt. 28:8), who do not believe them (Luke 24:11). Preachers can point out the original ending of this story, that it ends with fear and silence, unlike the other Gospels. But these women are called to preach, and they will have more opportunities to do so. Eventually, they will tell their story.

- What else would you like to know about these women who come to the tomb?
- How does it change the story of the resurrection to end on a note of fear and silence?
- What do you think made the women eventually break their silence?

Resurrection Evening

SONG OF SOLOMON 2:8–13

Lover

Preachers approaching this text may consider comparing it favorably with romance novels. Romance is a genre with a specific structure: certain people are attracted to each other, but something keeps them apart until they finally are able to be together. The books have a central love story and a satisfying and optimistic ending. There are authors who are really good at writing within this structure, writers who can describe chemistry between people and come up with convincing reasons why they cannot be together; thus it is so satisfying when they finally are together. But romance novels are often belittled, in part because they are in a genre that is overwhelmingly written by and for women. The vast majority of people who read romance novels are women, and women write most romance novels. Things that are by, for, and about women are often seen as lesser than those for men; intimate relationships are seen as less serious than other, more masculine topics. And these are books that are about women's desires, which can be threatening, so people mock them.

It is not hard to see the parallels between romance novels and Song of Songs. This is a book that centers around a love story, and most of it is in the woman's voice. Like romance novels, this book of the Bible seems threatening, and people mock it, maybe for similar reasons. Its text is entirely from the woman's perspective: even when we hear what the lover says, it is because she quotes him.[1] The woman hears her beloved before she sees him (Song 2:8). She watches through the window as he bounds toward her (2:8). The lovers

111

gaze at each other through the window, on the inside and the outside, longing to be together.

When her beloved calls to her to come away, the poetry is evocative of spring and young love.[2] In Israel, winter is the rainy season, and everything blooms in the spring.[3] In the time of year when everything is blooming, the outdoors calls like the beloved calling to his lover. It is the time when "the winter is past, the rain is over and gone" (2:11). Looking outside, "the flowers appear on the earth" and "the time of singing has come" (2:12). Everything is in blossom and fragrant, and there is new fruit to eat later in the season (2:13). The approach to desire and sexuality in this text is so different from how Paul talks about sexuality in the New Testament. And yet, as uncomfortable as Song of Songs has made people feel, it has remained in the Bible. This text has something to say to us about God and our relationship with the divine—not as an extended allegory of God's love for the church, but in the ways in which God creates beings to love each other.

In this glorious description of spring, flowers, and new love, there are animals. The young woman compares her beloved to a gazelle (2:9), and the young man tells her, "The voice of the turtledove is heard in our land" (2:12). Both these animals were significant in ancient Israel. The gazelle is a clean animal (for eating); the word for gazelle also means "beauty," "glory," and "honor." A turtledove is a bird often sacrificed as an offering to God (Lev. 1:14; 12:6). These animals are pleasing to God, according to the tradition. In this love story, the animals are clean for eating and sacrifice, and the plants are fresh and sweet. There is no shame when the beloved says, "Arise, my love," and tells her to come to him. This love is a gift from God, the longing that the two feel is a gift from God, and the animals are a gift from God.[4]

- How can Song of Songs counter messages in our culture that sexuality and sensuality are shameful?
- What metaphors would you use to describe the feeling of new love?
- What if this were the only part of the Bible we had? How would we think about God if this were our only sacred text?

JOHN 20:11–18

Mary Magdalene Sees Jesus

There is a lot of misinformation about Mary Magdalene! Preaching on this text gives the preacher the opportunity to address the misinformation about her and to celebrate how God has called women to preach. The idea that Mary Magdalene was a prostitute or a fallen woman began in the sixth century

CE, when Pope Gregory the Great conflated Mary Magdalene with several other biblical women.[5] These included Mary of Bethany, who anointed Jesus' head, and the unnamed sinner woman who anointed Jesus' feet. It is unclear why Pope Gregory did this (perhaps he thought it would be easier to remember if these stories all featured the same woman), but in doing so, he damaged Mary Magdalene's reputation. This changed her from a follower and supporter of Jesus to a sinner and a prostitute.

However, Mary Magdalene was a popular saint associated with "worldliness" and became the patron of hairdressers, scent makers, seamstresses, and cosmeticians.[6] Preachers should take care when talking about Mary Magdalene and her reception history, because it can be easy to disparage sex workers in this conversation. In addition, preachers should be wary of categorizing things associated with women (like cosmetics and hairdressers) as less important than more "masculine" pursuits. At the same time, it is important to point out how these gendered stereotypes have been used against Mary Magdalene for centuries.

Instead, we can construct a positive narrative of who Mary Magdalene was, based on what we know of her from Scripture. The first place where Mary Magdalene appears in the Gospels is in Luke. When Jesus was going out to teach, he was accompanied by "some women who had been cured of evil spirits and infirmities: Mary, called Magdalene, from whom seven demons had gone out, . . . and many others, who provided for them out of their resources" (Luke 8:2–3). Thus there were women who traveled with Jesus and supported his ministry out of their own resources. In each of the Gospels, when these women are listed, Mary Magdalene is named first.[7] This text also tells us that Jesus had healed Mary Magdalene: seven demons had gone out of her. There are various theories about the origin of the name Magdalene. Magdalene means "tower of strength," and some scholars suggest that this name was given to her as a descriptor.[8] It is more likely that it refers to where she came from, the town of Magdala, a city on the shore of the Sea of Galilee.[9]

All four Gospels place Mary Magdalene at the foot of the cross when Jesus was crucified.[10] She followed him to the end and beyond: in every Gospel, she goes to the tomb (sometimes with other women), which is where she is at the beginning of this passage. Even though Mary Magdalene has followed Jesus for so long, she does not recognize him when she sees him (John 20:14). Maybe she is consumed by grief and confusion. Or she might want to pursue her task. This whole week has been so terrible, but now she has a task: find the body and bring it back (20:15). But then Jesus says her name, and she recognizes him (20:16).

This text reveals some interesting things about Jesus in his interactions with Mary Magdalene. First, Jesus chooses to speak to Mary Magdalene, not the other two disciples at the tomb, who leave wondering and confused. Second, Jesus both does and does not want to be seen: if Jesus wanted Mary Magdalene to recognize him, he could have immediately said her name or made himself known to her. Third, Jesus is in the middle of something mysterious. He says to Mary, "Do not hold on to me, because I have not yet ascended to the Father" (20:17). Why is Jesus ascending to his Father? How does he do that? These are questions that we cannot answer. Finally, Jesus commissions Mary to tell the others (20:17). Thus Jesus chooses Mary to be the first preacher, the one to share the good news of his resurrection and return.

- Why do you think church leaders and others have painted Mary Magdalene as a sex worker despite the lack of biblical evidence?
- Why does Jesus choose Mary Magdalene to be the first to hear the good news?
- Does this make Mary Magdalene the first preacher? What qualifies a message as preaching?

Second Sunday of Easter

ESTHER 1:10–22

Vashti

Esther is one of the few books of the Bible named after a woman, and this text focuses on another woman: this king's first queen, Vashti. Some preachers may be tempted to put Vashti and Esther at odds with each other, portraying Vashti as the bad queen and Esther as the good queen, but Vashti demonstrates strength and character in this short passage about her.

The book of Esther takes place in the Persian period and reflects life in the Jewish Diaspora.[1] However, Jews do not appear in this first chapter, which starts with a series of feasts that King Ahasuerus gives for his officials and ministers (Esth. 1:3–8). While King Ahasuerus is feasting, Vashti also gives a banquet for the women (1:9). When the king calls for her, Vashti refuses to come. The text does not explain why, merely stating that she refuses (1:12). The Hebrew text says, "The heart of the king was good in wine," making it clear that the king is drunk, so he may not have been thinking clearly.[2] He has already shown his palace and his generosity, and now he wants to show off his wife. King Ahasuerus sees Vashti as an object—a beautiful thing that he owns and wants to show off to the peoples and the officials. There have been arguments among rabbinic scholars about whether the king was asking Vashti to wear *only* her crown.[3] Regardless of how she was dressed, the king wanted her to come to reflect his power, but Vashti says no to the king.

Vashti's refusal to do as the king commands is terrifying for the king and for the men in his court. Instead of going to confront Vashti directly, the king asks his advisers what to do under the law (1:13). His advisers overreact and make

115

what has been an instance of personal disobedience into a matter of state.[4] These men fear that their wives will follow Vashti's example and disobey them, so they suggest using all the resources of the state to respond to the threat that Vashti poses! The king's adviser Memucan suggests that the king replace Vashti, so that "all women will give honor to their husbands" (1:20).

King Ahasuerus wants to be seen as strong, but he is weak and controlled by the people who surround him. He completely overreacts and declares that he will never see Vashti again and that "every man should be master in his own house," and he announces this decree to all the people in all the lands he rules (1:22). Ironically, this gives Vashti exactly what she wants: not to see the king![5] It also means that more people hear about Vashti's actions than would have without the decree.

The book of Esther famously does not mention God, which may be why many churches do not spend much time on it. However, Vashti uses the agency that God has given her to tell the king that she will not come. In a culture that sees her merely as an object, Vashti knows who she is and what she will not do. This sets up the rest of the book, which will eventually lead to the Jewish Esther becoming queen, but preachers do not need to move further into the book to see God at work in this text. Vashti makes a decision about what will happen with her body, and this has terrible consequences for her. She loses her status and disappears from the narrative. However, this text also shows the weakness of the male-dominated power structure. Whether or not it was true, the men in power thought that she could take them all down.

- Why does Vashti refuse to see the king?
- What would have been a more appropriate reaction to her refusal?
- Can you think of other examples of a man overreacting when a woman will not do what he wants?

MATTHEW 28:1–10

Mary Magdalene and Mary

This account of the women going to the tomb in Matthew answers many of the questions in Mark. There is no question here of who rolled away the stone, the identity of the man in white clothing, or whether the women share the news of the resurrection. But there are still aspects of this text that are mysterious. For example, none of the Gospels explain what happened during the resurrection.[6] Instead, the story picks up as the women approach the tomb. Accordingly, this text shows how the Bible comes with a human perspective. Here the perspective is from the two women who approach the tomb.

Matthew states that two women go to the tomb: Mary Magdalene and the other Mary (Matt. 28:1). Mary Magdalene is the only woman who appears in all the Gospels as one of the women at the tomb. The identity of the other Mary is unclear. She is most likely Mary the mother of James and Joses, sometimes called Joseph (27:56; cf. Mark 16:1; Luke 24:10),[7] but some scholars have suggested that she might be Jesus' mother, Mary. Unlike the disciples, who have deserted Jesus and fled (Matt. 26:56), these women stay with Jesus to witness his crucifixion (27:56) and his burial (27:61).[8]

By contrast with the account in Mark, these women do not bring spices to anoint the body. This is because the woman in Bethany has already anointed Jesus' body for burial (26:12). Such anointing would not be possible in this account because of the guards stationed outside the tomb (27:65).[9] Instead, these women come "to see the tomb" (28:1). They plan to keep the vigil that they have maintained during Jesus' death and burial, expressing their undying devotion to what seems to be a lost cause.[10] But instead, through a series of dramatic events, God communicates with the women. First, there is an earthquake (28:2)—a sign of the end time.[11] Then an angel dressed in white clothing appears, descends from heaven, and rolls back the stone (28:2–3). The appearance of the angel takes away the threat of the guards: they are "like dead men" and more frightened than the women (28:4).[12] The last time an angel has appeared to bring a message in Matthew is to tell Joseph to return from Egypt (2:19–20). Now the angel informs the women that Jesus has been raised from the dead and invites them into the tomb to see where he lay (28:5–6). Finally, the angel calls the women to preach. He tells them to go quickly to the disciples and share the good news with them (28:7).

Though in Mark, the women leave in terror and do not say anything to anyone (16:8), here the women leave "with fear and great joy" to go and tell the disciples (Matt. 28:8). On the way, they encounter Jesus (28:9). Jesus repeats what the angel has said nearly verbatim, telling the women to share the news with the disciples (whom he calls "my brothers," perhaps forgiving them for abandoning him) and says that he will see them in Galilee (28:10). The women worship him and take hold of his feet (28:9), demonstrating that Jesus is resurrected in body and not a ghost or a phantom.[13] Thus Matthew answers the question of who first encounters Jesus after the resurrection: these two women, whom Jesus calls to preach to the disciples.

For preachers, this text offers a wide spectrum of the ways that God communicates to people: through their grief, powerful events like an earthquake, an angel, a direct encounter with the risen Christ, and the preaching of others. People also encounter God through the narrative in this text, which shares the good news of Jesus' resurrection. This text gives preachers an opening to celebrate with the women, join in the call to share the good news, and invite people in the congregation to share the ways that they have felt God speaking to them.

- What are some of the ways in which God communicates with people, both in this text and otherwise?
- When you imagine the resurrection, what does it look like?
- Why do you think Jesus appears to these women and tells them to share the news of his resurrection with the disciples?

Third Sunday of Easter

ESTHER 2:1–18

Women Taken / Esther Is Queen

The book of Esther begins with the most powerful class of people in the Persian Empire: King Ahasuerus and his officials and Queen Vashti. Very quickly, however, it turns to the least powerful people in the kingdom: the oppressed and enslaved. The context of this story is the Persian Empire, after the Babylonian period. The Babylonians had defeated the city of Jerusalem, destroyed the temple, and deported many of the people. This exile created a time of theological crisis for Israel: Where is the all-powerful God? Esther is a novella set in the context of this continued exile, roughly half a century after the Persians defeated the Babylonians (539 BCE); it is likely a work of fiction, yet with some true historical elements. Esther is an orphan, marginalized, and powerless. This mirrors the Jewish people's position as marginalized and powerless exiles.

It is rare for churches to hear sermons about Esther; when pastors approach this text, they often do it badly. This text is not just an introduction to Esther (or Hadassah) and Mordecai: it is also about the women who were taken from their homes and "gathered" into the king's harem. Some commentaries and sermon series call this a "Miss Persia" competition or compare it to a reality show like *The Bachelor*. Perhaps some preachers turn this into a joke because it makes them uncomfortable. Specifically, several Christian commentaries have made the unfortunate choice of blaming Esther for her participation in her enslavement.

In Hebrew, it says that Mordecai was among the people taken into exile. Historically, that does not make sense; it would make Mordecai over

119

a hundred years old. Translators and commentators have tried varied ways to fix this, such as dismissing it as a clerical or editorial error. The NRSV translation changes it to say that Kish (Mordecai's great-grandfather) was the one taken into exile.[1] But taken literally, this ambiguity says a lot about how people experience trauma: trauma impacts families for generations (and even on a genetic level). Something that may have happened to Mordecai's ancestor feels like it happened to him because, in a way, it did.

When the women are taken away, this layers a new trauma on the generational trauma. The king orders his servants to "gather all the beautiful young virgins to the harem in the citadel of Susa" (Esth. 2:3). This citadel may be a fortress on high ground, protecting the city, or a palace. It would be a place that the Jewish people in exile could see. They would look up to the citadel dominating the city and wonder what was happening to the women who had disappeared.

Although the Persians were famously tolerant toward the Jews,[2] this text reveals the fear and uncertainty of a system of complete power and control over a group of people. It doesn't matter how benign the system usually is. When the king has full control, the people must do what he says. This is the part of slavery that is inherent but not always discussed: when a person owns another person, the owner can do whatever they want with the enslaved person. When the enslaved person is a woman, that means owners can use their bodies for work, sex, and children. On a large scale, this can be too much to comprehend, so we look at individual stories, like Esther. For a more recent historical parallel, the preacher can tell the story of Sally Hemings, whom Thomas Jefferson enslaved and who bore his children.[3]

This story in Esther probably is not historically true,[4] but it points to a deeper truth: the stories of these women who were enslaved and survived. For Esther, disobedience would be suicidal.[5] For pastors, preaching on this text is an opportunity to bear witness to women who do what they need to do to survive. Preachers can lift up the names of women who have been enslaved, like Esther/Hadassah and Sally Hemings, and honor those whose names we do not know. This text provides a chance to face the ways that people used their bodies, without making uncomfortable jokes or minimizing their experiences, and to recognize their pain, their struggle, and their strength. This is holy work.

- Does it change your understanding of this story to see it within the context of sexual abuse and oppression?
- How does this story mirror the stories of women in slavery in U.S. history?
- How can churches make space for the stories of people who have experienced this kind of trauma?

LUKE 24:13–24

The Women Are Not Believed

The story of the two disciples on the road to Emmaus can be read in a variety of ways, depending on the perspective of the reader. There are several gaps in the description, which makes it an interesting text for sacred imagination. The first gap is in the identity of the two disciples on their way to Emmaus. Halfway through the text, Cleopas is named (Luke 24:18), but he is otherwise unknown (though some traditions equate Clopas and Cleopas).[6] There are no details about the other disciple, leading commentators to speculate that the disciple may be a woman or a stand-in for Luke's reader.[7] Whoever they are, these are not part of the male inner circle in Jerusalem; they are part of the extended group of Jesus' followers.[8] As they walk together, they talk, trying to figure out the meaning of what has happened.[9] Then a third person joins them; this is Jesus, though they do not recognize him (24:15–16). It is unclear why "their eyes were kept from recognizing him," but the passive voice suggests that God is preventing them from seeing the man they are discussing.[10] This may be symbolic: even those who see him do not recognize him later. It also creates narrative tension: the readers know something that the disciples do not.

When Jesus asks the disciples what they are talking about, his question is literally, "What are these words that you have been pitching back and forth to each other?"[11] Jesus' question gives the disciples (and Luke) an opportunity to retell the story. Through the disciples' retelling, the reader can see that they have already decided that some parts are significant: (1) Jesus was a prophet (24:19); (2) they hold the chief priests and leaders most accountable for Jesus' death (24:20), not the Romans or all of the Jews;[12] (3) they "had hoped" that Jesus would redeem Israel (24:21); and (4) this is the third day since these things took place (24:22).

Then the disciples describe the women's experience of going to the tomb. There are so many ways to interpret what they say! This is the first time that the appearance of the angels is described as "a vision of angels" (24:23). Combined with the earlier statement that the women's "words seemed to [the apostles] an idle tale" (24:11), this report seems less credible than the more detailed account of what the women saw.[13] One thing that the preacher should avoid is saying that the disciples did not believe the women because Jews do not accept the testimony of women (an anti-Jewish reading of the text).[14] It is possible that the story is too good to believe or that the disciples are merely puzzled or confused.[15] Whatever the reason, these disciples have heard the women's testimony about the resurrection, but they still do not understand what has happened.

Because there are so many ways of reading this text, it is a place where preachers can invite the congregation into the story. One approach would be to read it aloud multiple times, asking people to imagine themselves in the text. Where do they see themselves? With whom do they most identify? What does it sound like when each person talks? What is it like for these disciples to both see Jesus and not see him? Instead of trying to find definitive answers to the questions that this story raises, the preacher can guide those listening into the mystery and many of its possibilities.

- When the two disciples were talking to each other before encountering Jesus, what do you think they were saying? How would you tell the story of Jesus' death?
- Why would the disciples be kept from recognizing Jesus?
- Why do you think the disciples were astounded at the news the women told them?

Fourth Sunday of Easter

ESTHER 5:1–8

Esther's Banquet

This is the moment when Esther puts her plan to save her people into action. It is also the time when the tensions between Esther's Jewish identity and her identity as queen are highest. The text begins "on the third day" (Esth. 5:1), that is, the third day of fasting. In preparation for her meeting with the king, Esther has asked all the Jews in Susa to hold a fast on her behalf, and she also has fasted with her maids (4:16). In the book of Esther, Jews fast and Persians feast.[1] By fasting, Esther aligns herself with her Jewish people.[2] But the text also says that Esther put on her royal robes (5:1), literally clothing herself in royalty.[3] Her clothing shows her status as queen. Esther is pulled between two identities here, a feeling that is familiar to anyone from a minority group who has gained access to privilege.

As Esther stands in the court of the king, the stakes are high. When Mordecai came to convince her to save her people, she informed him that if anyone goes to the king inside the inner court without being called, they will be put to death unless the king holds out his scepter (4:11). She has not been called for thirty days (4:11), so she has no way to gauge whether the king will receive her. This is the moment where Esther lives out her famous response, "If I perish, I perish" (4:16). Esther is the outsider, waiting for the king on his throne in the palace to see her (5:1). Fortunately for Esther and the Jews, Esther gains the favor of the king, who holds out his scepter to her (5:2).

When the king says to Esther that he will answer her request "even to the half of my kingdom" (5:3), this is a formulaic response, which they both know he does not mean literally.[4] However, it is a reminder of the power of the king and his ability to give extravagant gifts. Instead of coming right out and making her request, Esther invites the king and Haman to a banquet (5:4). In doing so, Esther brings both of them into her territory: the king, who has the power to grant her request; and Haman, her enemy.[5] As queen, she has learned to work within this system of power and to keep her enemy close.

Esther continues her strategy when the men come to her banquet. She gives the king wine, which she knows puts him in the mood to make offers (cf. 1:10–11). When the king repeats his offer to grant Esther's request, she again invites the king and Haman to another banquet (5:8). Scholars have been baffled concerning why Esther takes this approach. Is she putting off her request because she is afraid? Or is this another part of her strategy? As a literary device, it serves to increase the suspense: by this point, everyone wants to know what Esther's request will be!

Considering how carefully Esther has planned so far, it is likely that this is a further part of her plan. Perhaps she is following a social convention of courting the king's favor before making her request.[6] By having the king repeat that her request "shall be fulfilled" (5:6), she is guaranteeing that he will say yes to her request when she finally makes it. And she seems to be lulling Haman into false security; he later goes out and brags to his wife that the queen invited no one but the king and himself to the banquet she prepared (5:12). Esther has set a trap for her enemy and ensured the safety of her people.

- How does this text reflect the tensions between Esther's competing identities?
- Do you find Esther's indirect approach frustrating? Or is it a model for change?
- What are other examples of people who have taken risks to protect their communities?

LUKE 7:11–17

The Widow's Son Raised

This text about Jesus raising the widow's son echoes two stories in the Hebrew Scriptures where a prophet raises a woman's son.[7] The first is the story of Elijah reviving the son of the widow at Zarephath (1 Kgs. 17:17–24). In that passage, Elijah has escaped from the wrath of King Ahab, and he follows God's command to go to Zarephath (17:1, 8–9). A widow there feeds Elijah from a jar of meal and a jug of oil that God miraculously refills (17:12–16). When the widow's son becomes ill and has no breath in him, Elijah carries the boy into the upper chamber, stretches himself over the boy three times, and cries out to God to let his life come into him again (17:17–21). God hears Elijah's plea, and the child is revived (17:22). Elijah gives the child to his mother, and the mother says to Elijah, "Now I know that you are a man of God" (17:23–24).

The second story is of Elisha raising the Shunammite woman's son (2 Kgs. 4:18–37). This woman is not a widow, but a wealthy woman who, with her husband, provides for the prophet Elisha (4:8–10). One day, when her son is in the field with his father, he complains about his head and later dies (4:18–20). Elisha goes to the house and sees the child lying dead on the bed (4:32). Elisha prays to the Lord, then lies upon the child, putting his mouth on the child's mouth, his eyes on his eyes, and his hands on his hands, and the child becomes warm (4:33–34). Elisha then gives the boy back to his mother (4:36).

In this text, Luke draws parallels between the stories of the prophets and Jesus, but there are some significant differences between this story and the stories of the prophets. In the stories of Elijah and Elisha, the prophets have established relationships with the mother. Here, there is no indication that Jesus knows the mother or the son. It seems unlikely that he does so, since he encounters them outside the gate of the town as he and his followers arrive (Luke 7:11–12). In addition, both Elijah and Elisha pray for God's intervention to revive the child, while Jesus takes on the role of God as the one who can bring someone back to life.[8] Finally, the prophets physically stretch themselves over the children to bring them back, but Jesus is able to do that with a simple command to rise (7:14).[9] Like the prophets, Jesus gives the son back to his mother (7:15). Jesus is aware of both these stories; he has even referenced them in his first sermon, specifically describing the widow at Zarephath (4:26).[10]

Luke says that Jesus is moved by his compassion for the unnamed widow (7:13). In fact, this is the only time that Luke says Jesus has compassion.[11] It is unclear whether Jesus' compassion is because of the widow's grief or because of her potentially vulnerable economic and social position as a widow, though not all widows at the time were poor, and the text does not mention her economic condition.[12] The crowds watching Jesus, however, would have been very familiar with the Hebrew Scriptures' commands that people are to care for widows and orphans (e.g., Exod. 22:22; Isa. 1:17). Jesus is following in this tradition, as well as taking on the role of God as parent to orphans and protector of widows (Ps. 68:5).

Like the widow at Zarephath, the crowd recognizes Jesus as a prophet; they are seized with fear as they recognize that God is working through Jesus (Luke 7:16). It is unsurprising that the word spreads throughout the surrounding country, considering that Jesus has a large crowd with him and meets another large crowd leaving the city (7:11–12). A lot of people see this miracle! But these people also know what kind of man of God this Jesus is:

one who has compassion for widows and uses the power of God to continue God's message of protecting the vulnerable, like this unnamed widow.

- Why do you think Jesus stops to help this widow and raise her son?
- How is this text similar to and different from the accounts of Elijah and Elisha restoring sons to life?
- What else would you like to know about this widow and her son?

Fifth Sunday of Easter

ESTHER 7:1–10; 9:20–22

Esther

This dramatic conclusion to Esther's story is the only part of the book of Esther in the Revised Common Lectionary. The verses included in the RCL tie up the story neatly: Esther tells the king about Haman's plot to kill the Jews, reveals that she is Jewish, and saves her people. Haman gets what he deserves. The Jews celebrate, and Mordecai creates the holiday Purim. However, the text selection omits several important things.

In the first gap (Esth. 7:7–8), the king leaves the feast while Haman stays to beg Esther for his life. When the king returns, he sees Haman on the couch where Esther is reclining and thinks that Haman is sexually assaulting the queen. The king is angry when he thinks that Haman is violating his wife; that is when Haman is taken away. Why does the lectionary leave this out? Because it makes for a neater narrative? Or because sexual assault is uncomfortable to talk about in church? In addition, some scholars have commented that Esther's lack of response to save Haman is "unattractive."[1] In a book that prioritizes the physical beauty of women, Esther is judged by standards of attractiveness even when she is risking her life to save her people.

In the second gap, the Jews strike down all their enemies with the sword, killing 800 people in Susa, the ten sons of Haman, and 75,000 in the king's provinces (9:5–17). This is what the people are celebrating (9:22). The RCL omits the violent aspects of this story, but preachers should not.[2] Even though this is probably not historically accurate, it speaks to a deeper truth. The murder of Jewish people is historically true, in ancient and modern times. It makes

127

sense that the wish of a captive people would be to feel that God is on their side in conquering those who wish to kill them.

The book of Esther famously does not mention God; maybe that is one of the reasons why so little of it is included in the Revised Common Lectionary. It is unfortunate that one of the few books in the Bible that has a woman at its center gets so little attention in the RCL, but that also demonstrates how anyone who chooses texts from the Bible for preaching will necessarily omit portions. In a sacred text that is almost entirely about men and their experiences of God, what does it mean to omit passages from the few books that are primarily about women?

Commentators have not known what to do with Esther's statement in 7:4, "If we had been sold merely as slaves, men and women, I would have held my peace; but no enemy can compensate for this damage to the king" (7:4). It may seem odd that Esther would have kept silent about her people being sold into slavery. But within the context of the book, the young women were already enslaved by the king, and the Jews are under foreign rule. Esther knows this and focuses instead on how the destruction of her people—and her own death—would harm the king, damaging his property. In this context, she knows that her people will continue to be oppressed, but it is possible to save their lives by appealing to the king's interest.

For preachers, this text is a good example of the kinds of stories that are left out of the narrative and why. In some cases, parts of the Bible make people uncomfortable, and it is easier to skip over them than to try to reconcile violence with characters that otherwise seem like heroes. Alternatively, some people seem less important than others. But preachers can challenge their listeners to engage with difficult texts and highlight the stories of people who might otherwise be forgotten.

- Why do you think the RCL chooses the verses it does from these chapters?
- How does it change the preached story to include the verses where Jews kill their enemies?
- How can preachers use this text to talk about sexual violence and the ways that stories about sexual violence are silenced or ignored?

LUKE 13:10–17

The Crippled Woman

In many ways, this text reads like a "what not to do" when preaching about women and people with disabilities. Both in how Jesus acts and in ways that this text has been interpreted, there are a lot of potential pitfalls for the preacher. At the same time, the possible problems in the text give preachers openings to talk about how we read these healing stories in our context and better ways to engage with people who have disabilities.

For a text that is ostensibly about Jesus healing a woman, this text moves quickly past the healing itself into the argument.[3] Rather than spending time on the unnamed woman and her healing, the text instead becomes an argument between Jesus and the synagogue leader about the Sabbath (Luke 13:14–16). For many people with disabilities, this is a familiar feeling: being seen as a lesson instead of a person. Preachers need to approach texts like this one with care. Healing stories like this have been used in harmful ways against people with disabilities—leading nondisabled people to put their hands on people with disabilities, as Jesus does (13:13), or praying for their healing. This can have a dehumanizing effect, making the disabled person feel like a project, broken, or less than whole.

So, how can preachers approach this text? One way is to center on the woman herself and not make the mistake of using her as a lesson or moving too quickly to the argument. There is not a lot of information about her in the text, but there is some. Jesus encounters the woman in the synagogue (13:11), so she is part of this worshiping community. Jesus confirms that she is Jewish when he calls her "a daughter of Abraham" (13:16). It does not seem as though the woman has come to see Jesus; instead, he calls her over to him (13:12). She has been in this condition for eighteen years, and when Jesus frees her from the spirit that has bound her, she praises God (13:11–13).

Jesus describes this woman as bound by Satan (13:16), which is a quite different understanding of chronic illnesses and disabilities than we have today. Like centering the woman, this is an opportunity for the sermon to center the lived experiences of people with disabilities. If you are a person with a disability, you may want to share your own responses to healing stories like this one. Or this may be a place to hear stories from people in the community who are disabled, to let them talk honestly about their experiences.

Another issue with the text is how it presents women. As many commentators have pointed out, this story is parallel to the story in Luke 14:1–6, where Jesus heals a man with dropsy. In both, Jesus performs a miraculous healing on the Sabbath, which leads to an argument about whether it is lawful to heal on the Sabbath. This is a pattern in Luke: to pair a story about a woman with a story about a man.[4] As a result, Luke has more stories about women than any other Gospel, but it also increases the stories about men by the same amount! This approach illustrates the problem of addressing structural and historic inequalities by attempting to make everything equal. Rather than trying for an equal division between male and female (and leaving out nonbinary people altogether), the better approach is to let women have their own stories.

A final pitfall in the story is misunderstanding Jesus' argument about the Sabbath. This is not a story about Jesus versus the Jews, nor is he arguing to abolish the Sabbath. Jesus is engaging within the Jewish context here, by teaching in the synagogue (13:10), and he is arguing with the synagogue leader about what is appropriate on the Sabbath.[5] Jesus uses a principle common to the rabbis by arguing from the lesser to the greater: They would untie their animals to bring them to water on the Sabbath; should they not do more for the woman than they would do for an animal?[6] Accordingly, Jesus is arguing from within his tradition rather than against it.

- What questions do you have about the woman whom Jesus healed in this story? What more would you like to know about her?
- How can churches center the perspectives of people with disabilities instead of using them as a lesson?
- How does it change your perspective to think about Jesus arguing from within his Jewish tradition instead of against it?

Sixth Sunday of Easter

JOB 1:1; 2:1–10

Job's Wife

The book of Job begins like a folktale: "There once was a man in the land of Uz whose name was Job" (Job 1:1). The initial description of Job says how upright he is and lists all the things he has, including seven sons and three daughters, as well as extensive livestock and servants (1:2). In this description, as in most of the book, the narrator does not mention Job's wife. The sons and daughter are "born to him" (1:2). This omission continues in the interaction between God and the Accuser, who first talk about how blameless Job is (1:8) and then agree to test his integrity by taking away what he has (1:11–12).

By the second chapter, Job and his wife have lost so much: oxen, sheep, camels, and their children (1:13–19). Up until this point, the losses have been joint: perhaps they thought that God was inflicting both of them. But then the Accuser makes it clear that this is a test for Job alone by convincing God to allow Job to have sores all over his body (2:7). At this point, it is clear to everyone that Job is the focus of this suffering. He sits alone in the ashes, scraping himself with a piece of pottery (2:8).

Job's wife only has one line, but scholars have debated the meaning of what she says for millennia. The Hebrew for "cursed" here is actually "blessed," a euphemism that Job uses in the previous chapter, when he would offer burnt offerings in case his children have "cursed God in their hearts" (1:5).[1] Why does Job's wife tell him to curse God? Some theologians, including Augustine and Calvin, have suggested that she is an aid to the Accuser in this moment.[2] Others have argued that she cannot bear to see her husband in pain; accordingly, she tells him to curse God—a capital offense (Lev. 24:10–16), which would lead to his death.[3]

Biblical scholar Carol Newsom asserts that the word "integrity" is ambiguous here: it points to a conflict between Job's social integrity and his personal integrity. If Job holds on to his social integrity and blesses God as he did before, he will lose his personal integrity by failing to acknowledge the ways that God has harmed him. But if Job holds on to his personal integrity and is honest about what God has done, that would lead him to curse God, violating his social integrity.[4]

Job lashes out at his wife's words, saying, "You speak as any foolish woman would speak" (Job 2:10). He insults not only his wife, but women in general in his angry response, and far too many preachers have taken Job at his word. But, as Newsom points out, after this, Job does not speak again until chapter 3, in which he sounds much more like his wife. Job does not curse God, but he curses the day he was born (3:3).[5] The tension between personal and social integrity that Newsom names develops into questions that the other characters argue throughout the rest of the book, without satisfactory answers.

After this confrontation, Job's wife disappears from the book of Job. Even in the end, when Job has ten more children (42:13), she is not included in the description of his family.[6] It may be that this woman who questions God and her husband is too threatening. But she has not been forgotten! Job's wife has been the subject of paintings, literature, and plays, showing the impact of even a small, assertive female character in the Bible.

- In a book almost entirely comprised of men and masculine figures, imagine changing the genders of the characters. How would this passage read differently if it depicted a feminine God and a female Accuser discussing a blameless woman?
- Later, what would it be like if Job were a woman who was comforted by her female friends? Would you expect the conversations to progress in the same way or differently?
- What do you think Job's wife meant when she told him to curse God and die?

LUKE 13:31–35

God as Mother Hen

This short text raises many issues about the relationships that Jesus has, with others and with his tradition—as well as expanding our understanding of Jesus' identity. First, Jesus interacts with a group of Pharisees, who warn him that Herod Antipas wants to kill him (Luke 13:31). It is unclear from the text whether these Pharisees are offering a sincere warning. It would not be out of character for Herod to want to kill Jesus, but later Herod wants to see Jesus and hopes he will perform a sign (23:8). At that point, Herod does not kill Jesus but returns him to Pilate (23:11).[7] Accordingly, it seems more likely that these Pharisees are trying to scare Jesus or get rid of him instead of honestly warning him.

Jesus responds with a message for Herod, connecting the group of Pharisees with him (13:32). In reply, Jesus calls Herod a "fox," a potentially dangerous insult.[8] Jesus is not comparing the ruler to a stately lion, but to a cunning and destructive fox.[9] Whatever the source of the threat, Jesus does not take it seriously but instead says that he will continue to do his work. Rather than destroying things, Jesus is "casting out demons and performing cures" (13:32). In simply describing his work, Jesus sets himself up as someone who heals and makes whole.

Jesus also uses an animal metaphor for himself, but it is one that may be surprising. Unlike the dangerous predator he uses to describe Herod, Jesus sees himself as a mother hen, desiring to gather her brood under her wings (13:34). In this description, Jesus invokes the description of God as a mother bird in Psalm 17:8, with God's maternal care for God's people. It is a gender-bending image, showing Jesus' nurturing and tender side. Jesus has not come to fight with the rulers like an animal of prey, but rather wishes to protect God's people.

The larger context of this image is Jesus' lament about Jerusalem, which connects him with the prophets in the Hebrew Scriptures (e.g., Lam. 1:1–7). Jesus explicitly describes himself as a prophet when he says that he must be on his way "because it is impossible for a prophet to be killed outside of Jerusalem" (Luke 13:33). Like the prophets, the words of Jesus here can be read on multiple levels. When he says, "Your house is left to you" (13:35), he evokes both the Babylonian destruction of Jerusalem, with the exile, and the future destruction of the temple.[10] In addition, when Jesus says, "On the third day I finish my work" (13:32), that may be a straightforward description of what he plans to do or a reference to his own death and then resurrection on the third day. In his lament over Jerusalem, Jesus mourns for the city and foretells his own death there (though not yet).

In his final statement, Jesus also demonstrates his connection to his Jewish culture and identity. He tells them that they will not see him until they say, "Blessed is the one who comes in the name of the Lord" (13:35). This is from Psalm 118:26, which is one of the psalms recited on festivals, including Passover.[11] The disciples will say it when Jesus enters Jerusalem (Luke 19:38).[12] Thus, Jesus is connecting himself with his tradition while also anticipating what will happen when he finally goes to Jerusalem.

For those preaching on this text, the multiple identities and relationships offer an opportunity to talk about how Jesus fits within the prophetic tradition as both an insider and an outsider. He is clearly part of his community and religious tradition, while also being outside of it. Jesus is nonbinary in his use of metaphor when he describes himself as like a mother hen. For anyone who has felt both part of a community and outside of it, Jesus' words may feel familiar.

- With what animal would you expect Jesus to compare himself?
- In this text, Jesus knows that his death is coming, but he is not afraid of the threat on his life. Why do you think that is?
- How is Jesus like and unlike the prophets in the Hebrew Scriptures?

Ascension (Thursday)

PSALM 123

Maid and Mistress

Psalm 123 is one of the Psalms of Ascent (Pss. 120–134) for pilgrimages to Jerusalem that Deuteronomy 16:16 requires Jewish men to take three times a year. Although these pilgrimages were required only for men, the men would have taken other members of their household with them.[1] The various voices in this psalm as well as the feminine imagery reflect the diversity of people who might have sung this psalm on the way to Jerusalem. This short psalm reveals a lot about the Israelites' relationship with God and with each other!

The psalm begins with a single voice, one person lifting their eyes (Ps. 123:1). This establishes a spatial relationship between the psalmist and God: the psalmist is below while God is "enthroned in the heavens" (123:1). In the next verse, the single voice becomes many as "the eyes of servants look to the hand of their master" (123:2). It is easy to imagine one person beginning the song, with others joining on the second verse. When reading this psalm in the liturgy, it is a good practice to assign the different parts to diverse voices.

The following stanzas may seem merely like a doubling of the previous lines, but there are some key differences. First, the image of God in these lines is feminine: God is described as a mistress (123:2). In this context, the mistress would be the highest-ranking female of a household, in charge of household management.[2] Second, the text has gone from multiple (and presumably male) servants to one "maid," as translated by the NRSV. In the class structure of the time, the "maid" would be one of the lowest ranked and most vulnerable members of the household. Continuing the high/low description

135

in verse 1, this puts the Israelites in the position of the lowest person in the household, with God in the highest.

But the translation of "maid" is misleading. The Hebrew word more accurately means enslaved woman or girl, frequently associated with sexual and reproductive duties.[3] This word also occurs in the story of Sarai and Hagar, where Sarai gives her "maid" to Abram to bear children for them (Gen. 16:1–6). In the story of Leah and Rachel, their father Laban gives Zilpah and Bilhah to his daughters when they are married (29:24, 29), and Rachel and Leah then give these women to their husband, Jacob, to bear children for them (30:3–5, 9–10).

Understanding this aspect of the word "maid" complicates the reading. What does it mean for God to be a mistress if one of the things a mistress may do with her hand is to give an enslaved woman to a man for sex and reproduction? Feminist preachers of this text may feel pulled in different directions.[4] On one hand, this is one of the few feminine images of God in the Psalms, and it broadens our perspective on God's supposed gender (as well as the ways the Israelites envisioned God). On the other hand, it reinforces unjust power systems, including the ownership and sexual exploitation of women. This may be a metaphor for God that no longer serves us.

In the third verse, the psalmist repeatedly asks for mercy from God. Unlike some other psalms, the psalmist does not say that God has granted that mercy or go on to recite the great things that God has done. Given the variety of voices within the psalm, this may be a place for the enslaved women to cry out to God. They certainly have "had more than enough of contempt" (Ps. 123:3). A close reading of Psalm 123 gives preachers an opening to remember the enslaved women in the Bible, along with all those who cry out, "Our soul has had more than its fill of the scorn of those who are at ease, of the contempt of the proud" (123:4).

- When you imagine the people going to Jerusalem on a pilgrimage, what do you picture? Who is part of the household?
- Is the image of God as a mistress (or a master) a useful metaphor for you?
- How can churches make space to acknowledge the pain of the enslaved women in the Bible?

LUKE 15:1–10

The Woman Finds Her Coin

This text begins with the tax collectors and sinners coming to hear Jesus (Luke 15:1). In this context, sinners are those who fracture community welfare; tax

collectors, often Jews working for the Roman Empire, were considered trai-
tors and corrupt.[5] The Pharisees are upset to see Jesus welcoming and eating
with the sinners and tax collectors, possibly because, as the previous chapter
reports, Jesus goes to eat at the house of a leader of the Pharisees (14:1). Jesus
uses this space to tell three stories about counting and who is included in the
kingdom of God.[6]

In the first story, Jesus describes a man with a hundred sheep. His hear-
ers would know that this man is wealthy because that is a substantial flock.[7]
Although readers now may have positive associations with shepherds in the
Bible, in Jesus' time, they had acquired a reputation as shiftless, thieving
trespassers.[8] Jesus subverts this stereotype by describing the man as one who
would know when one sheep out of one hundred was lost (he would need to
count) and would go on a search for the lost sheep (15:4). This man is also
part of the larger community, inviting his friends and neighbors to rejoice
with him when he has found the sheep (15:6).

Jesus immediately follows this story with one about a woman who has lost
a coin. This second story takes place in the woman's house, the sphere associated with women (15:8). Unlike the man, the woman is not wealthy. Jesus
uses the word "drachma" for silver coin, a laborer's day's wages. Accordingly,
the woman's entire savings is ten days' wages.[9] The woman's house provides
a glimpse of a typical house at the time, with a dirt floor, a small door, and
no windows.[10] She searches intently, lighting a lamp and sweeping the house
until she finds the coin (15:8). Once she has found the coin, she calls to her
(female) friends and neighbors to celebrate with her (15:9).[11]

The image of the shepherd with the sheep on his shoulders is a familiar one
for Christ; it appears in catacomb art as early as the third century.[12] However,
these stories have exactly the same structure: the person loses something, they
search for it, they find it, and they call friends and neighbors to celebrate with
them.[13] If the man who searches for his lost sheep is an image of God, then
so is the woman who searches for her lost coin.[14] But it apparently has been
easier for people in the church to see God reflected in the wealthy man who
finds his lost sheep (as well as the man in the third story, the forgiving father
of the prodigal son) than to see God in the impoverished woman.[15]

Luke frames these stories as being about repentance: there is joy in heaven
and in the presence of the angels over one sinner who repents (15:7, 10). This
seems strange because sheep and coins cannot repent! It makes more sense to
read these stories as about the nature of God. By using the man, woman, and
father as models, Jesus describes a God who carefully tracks and notices what
or who is lost. This is a God who will go out and find the one who is missing,
like Jesus eating with the sinners and tax collectors. And this is a God who
celebrates with the community after finding the lost.

- Is the image of the man carrying a sheep on his shoulders more familiar as a metaphor for God than the woman searching for her coin? If so, why do you think that is?
- What does the image of God as a less wealthy woman teach us about the nature of God?
- Who do you identify with the most in this text? Who do you identify with the least?

Seventh Sunday of Easter

PROVERBS 7:6–23

Strange Woman

This text is a dramatic cautionary tale from the parent to the son about the dangers of an adulterous woman. Sometimes called the Strange Woman or Woman Folly, this woman represents many different "strange women" who threaten the young man.[1] Although some scholars have argued that this depiction is really about sin and folly, not gender, it has gendered language and a distinctly feminine threat! Because this text (and type) has been used against women, it is in the preacher's best interest not to gloss over the gendered aspects of the language.

This woman has often been interpreted as the opposite of the female personification of Wisdom throughout Proverbs. However, a close reading of the text demonstrates that there are many similarities between the two characters.[2] Both the Strange Woman and Wisdom speak loudly (Prov. 7:11; 1:20). Rather than stay in the home, they are in public places in the city (7:12; 1:21). But they focus on different things. Wisdom calls out for people to seek knowledge; the Strange Woman is focused only on her own sexual gratification. The Strange Woman is explicitly sexual (7:16–18), and that sexuality is threatening. When comparing these women, it is important to remember that men have created them as examples for other men. Ultimately, this is not about women or how they should be in the world, but a reminder from male leaders who believe that women's sexuality can create threatening desire in young men.

Some scholars have speculated that the Strange Woman is a foreigner, but there is no evidence of that in this text. On the contrary, she says that she

139

"had to offer sacrifices" (7:14), indicating that she is an Israelite and has paid her vows to God. This woman seems to be very wealthy; when she seduces the young man, she describes her elaborate linen and spices (7:16–17), and she later says that her husband "took a bag of money" when he left (7:20). But many women in the ancient Near East were more vulnerable, especially foreign women in Israel. Reading her as Other can serve as a reminder that women who are seen as outsiders can be vulnerable when people believe their community is in peril.[3]

Ultimately, this text is a sexual ethic directed at young men, telling them to master their desires and fantasies and control their impulses.[4] The final verses show the dire consequences of choosing poorly: it can lead to death (7:23). The narrator uses graphic language of various animals being led to slaughter to demonstrate the danger that the young man is in (7:22–23). He is not the only one at risk; his actions are threatening on a larger level. In this patriarchal system, adultery violates a man's exclusive right to his wife's sexuality and offspring. By violating that, the young man threatens the stability of the entire system.[5]

Sexual ethics are not only an issue for people in biblical times: they have also been divisive issues in many churches recently. Reading a text like this one gives preachers an opening to talk about their congregation's sexual ethics and how people in the church want to convey that message to young people. Do they want to use scare tactics, like the parent in this text? In an era of sexually transmitted infections like HIV/AIDS, it is possible that sexual activity can lead to death, as the text describes, and people in the church will want to prevent this kind of risk. Texts like this one give a point of comparison for churches to engage in conversation about their priorities and values.

- What other examples of seductive women come to mind when you read this text? Do these examples reduce women to binaries and stereotypes?
- How can you use this example of a sexual ethic from a different time and place to reflect on the sexual ethics within your congregation?
- What kind of sexual ethics does your congregation wish to impart to young people?

LUKE 18:1–8

The Widow and the Judge

In this parable about being persistent in prayer, Jesus begins with an unexpected figure: a judge who does not fear God or man and is only looking out for his own self-interest (Luke 18:2). By beginning with "a judge in a certain city," Jesus intends this judge to be a stock character.[6] But a judge should be one who adjudicates disputes, maintains harmonious relations, and takes special care of widows, orphans, and immigrants (Deut. 24:17–18; 27:19).[7] This judge is the opposite.

Then Jesus introduces the second character in the story, the widow who comes to the judge for justice (Luke 18:3). There is little information about the widow: we do not know the facts of her case or her financial situation. However, considering the stock-character nature of the judge, she probably is intended to evoke the stereotype of the poor widow.[8] This is supported by the fact that she is going to the judge for justice; it is likely that she is calling on the judge to make a third party give her something owed to her, either money or property.[9]

This widow is persistent! She keeps coming to the judge and asking him to grant her justice against her opponent (18:3). At this time judges usually would sit in public places to hear cases, so the widow is making her request in front of the whole town.[10] Although the judge refuses for a while, he eventually needs to pay attention to the widow (18:4). When he says that the widow "keeps bothering me," the literal translation is "so that she may not wear me out by continually coming" (18:5).[11] His concern may be metaphorical—this widow is making him look bad—but it could also be literal.[12] The humor of the widow beating the unethical judge until he hears her case gets lost in the English translation. Either way, the threat works: the judge decides to grant her justice (18:8).

Luke frames the parable as being about constant prayer (18:1). One way to read it is a lesser to greater argument: If even this terrible judge will grant the widow's request, how much more so would a just judge like God grant requests for justice? Another way of reading it is to include the context of the widow—a vulnerable and marginalized person—being persistent in seeking out justice. Read this way, Jesus is encouraging people to persistently seek out justice for those on the margins, including advocating for themselves.[13] This is an active approach to prayer, a vision of God's desire for the world. The humor in the story is also a way to oppose people who use their power unethically, countering them by laughing at them and challenging their authority.[14]

This seems like a triumphant place to end, with the widow getting justice, but the text instead concludes with waiting and a question. Jesus assures his listeners that God's justice will come quickly (18:8), but the disciples (and readers) know that is not always the case. It can be hard to keep the faith when we see injustice in the world. Even Jesus seems to question this, wondering whether there will be faithful people on his return. Thus, rather than a triumphant ending, this text ends in a questioning, wistful place.

- How does this story about the widow and the judge seem like prayer? How does it not?
- When you picture the widow going to the judge for justice, how do you imagine the scene?
- Does this text make it easier or harder to continue to engage issues and people when you see injustice in the world?

Pentecost Sunday

JOEL 2:23–32

Daughters Shall Prophesy

With so many prophetic texts about destruction and despair, it can be a relief to hear Joel the prophet calling for the people of Zion to rejoice and be glad (Joel 2:23). But this is not a call to joy that forgets the pain of the past. Woven throughout this text are reminders of the destruction that the people of Israel and Judah have endured, plus some ambivalence toward the God they are now called to praise. The prophet paints a picture of a hopeful future that is occurring and is yet to come, but he still cannot completely break free from the oppressive structures of his culture.

Little is known about the prophet Joel or the context in which this book was written. A major theme throughout the book is the swarm of locusts that have eaten and destroyed (2:25). This may refer to a literal swarm of locusts that have ravaged the crops and caused agricultural and economic collapse.[1] Alternatively, it may refer to the destruction of Israel and Judah's defeat and exile. Some commentators have suggested that the four kinds of locusts symbolize four different invasions.[2] In the first-person description of the locusts, the voice of God says that they are "my great army, which I sent against you" (2:25), reflecting the understanding that God is the one responsible for natural disasters like locusts and for invading armies.

In the context of this destruction, the prophet describes the rejuvenation of the land through plentiful rain, which will bring threshing floors full of grain and overflowing vats of wine and oil (2:23–24). The prophet writes these visions of restoration in the prophetic perfect: it is a future action that the prophet presents as one that God has already completed.[3] God also removes their shame, meaning the condition the people are in when they fail God.[4] Because the people are returning to their covenant with God, God is upholding God's part of the covenant by providing for the people.[5] God also assures them twice that they will not be put to shame again (2:26–27), assuring the people that they will not suffer from invasions by armies or locusts as they have repeatedly endured.

Then the language changes to a prediction of the future, when God's day of judgment will come. God will send God's spirit (also translated as wind or breath) over all the people, calling them to prophetic declarations. The prophet says that one of the signs of this coming day is that "your sons and your daughters shall prophesy" (2:28). In the Religious Society of Friends, this verse has been central to the argument, since the seventeenth century, that God calls women to speak. The prophet envisions a world in which God's power comes on people regardless of gender or age.

However, the following verse shows that this is not a perfectly equal world. The prophet states that God will pour out God's spirit on "the male and female slaves" (2:29). Although the prophet's intent probably is to show that God's spirit will come on people regardless of social standing, the prophetic imagination does not extend to a world in which there are no enslaved people. For preachers, this is a reminder that even when we try to envision an ideal future time, our imaginations are limited by the structures of our own time.

Many Christian commentaries on this text quickly move to the story of Pentecost in Acts 2, where Peter quotes it (2:17–21). The expansiveness of the language—"Everyone who calls on the name of the LORD shall be saved" (Joel 2:32)—makes it ripe for people throughout the church to read themselves into the text. But a close reading reminds us that Joel is for a particular time and people: it specifically refers to Mount Zion and Jerusalem, and in context "everyone" means all Judeans.[6] Preachers should hold this tension in interpreting a text that is both specific and continues to speak to people throughout time.

- Does this text make you want to rejoice? Or lament what has happened? Or both?
- When you imagine the spirit of God being poured out over all people, what does that look like?
- How can Christians acknowledge the specific Jewish context of this text while also celebrating the way it appears in the New Testament?

ACTS 1:14; 2:1–8, 14–18

Women Pray and Prophesy

The story of Pentecost is foundational for the church as a description of how the Holy Spirit has filled the followers of Jesus and sent them into the world to share the good news. It also demonstrates the diversity of people whom God calls to preach and to speak. This group includes people of different genders and ages; when the Holy Spirit fills them, they are led to speak in different languages. Amid this celebration, however, Christian preachers should be careful with the quote from the prophet Joel and consider how we see our faith as fulfillment of the Hebrew Scriptures.

Luke states that those who constantly devote themselves to prayer include "certain women, including Mary the mother of Jesus" (Acts 1:14). These women are the ones who have followed Jesus from Galilee (Luke 8:1–3), witnessed his death and burial (Luke 23:49, 54–56), and reported his resurrection (24:1–10, 22–23).[7] By including them, Luke makes it clear that women will continue to play a significant role in the church.[8] This mention of Mary is the first time that Luke has called her by her name since the story of Jesus' birth.[9] Just as she was filled with the Holy Spirit to speak when she was pregnant with Jesus (Luke 1:46–55), she is one of the people who are moved by the Holy Spirit to speak in tongues at Pentecost.[10]

When the "sound like the rush of a violent wind" comes from heaven (Acts 2:2), this evokes the wind of God (also translated "breath" or "spirit") that hovered over the deep at creation (Gen. 1:2). This divine wind is a feminine image of God, an image that appears in creation and in this rebirth. Her appearance here shows the continuity of God's work in creation. The tongues of fire are also a continuation of the divine presence (Exod. 19:18; Isa. 66:15–16).[11] As the tongues of fire rest on them, the followers are filled with the Holy Spirit, a parallel to God filling the first person with breath (Gen. 2:7).

The gift that the Holy Spirit gives here is the ability to speak in other languages (Acts 2:4). The followers then go out to speak, and Jews from every nation can understand them because they are speaking in the native language of each (2:6). This is unnecessary because all of the people listening would have understood Greek.[12] But rather than use the one language of the empire, God affirms the diversity of those gathered.[13] This is a church made up of mainly visitors and immigrants—people who speak in different languages and come from different cultures.[14] The Holy Spirit is leading people of different genders to speak in different languages, showing that the truth of God can be shared and heard in many different ways.[15]

When Peter addresses the crowd, he makes it clear that he sees this out-pouring of the Spirit on people of different genders, class, and age as a fulfill-ment of the prophecy in Joel 2:28–32 (Acts 2:17–18).[16] The original context of the part of Joel he quotes is that a swarm of locusts have eaten and destroyed the land (2:25), which may be symbolic of the destruction of Israel and Judah's defeat and exile. The prophet mourns this destruction but then offers a prom-ise from God that all of these things will be restored (for more on this text, see the commentary on Joel 2:23–32).[17] Peter makes small but significant changes to the text, changing "afterward" to "in the last days" and adding "they shall prophesy."[18] By doing so, he is emphasizing the end-time nature of the Scrip-ture rather than reading it in context.

Peter is not the only one to suggest that what is happening in his commu-nity is the fulfillment of Scripture; the passage from Joel has been referenced throughout Christian history. This presents a challenge for Christian preach-ers, because Joel 2 has its own specific context and is part of the Jewish tradi-tion. Thus, even in the celebration of Pentecost and the giving of the Holy Spirit, preachers must approach with humility, knowing that we are using something that is not entirely ours.

- Why does Luke state that the women, including Mary, are present?
- Why does the Holy Spirit lead the disciples to speak in different tongues instead of having everyone understand one language?
- How can Christians use Jewish texts that speak to us without completely appropriating Jewish tradition and culture?

The Season after Pentecost

Trinity Sunday

GENESIS 1:1–2:4

Creator

In this first creation story, there are multiple feminine images of God. The first is the "wind from God" (Gen. 1:2), which can also be translated as "breath" or "spirit"; it is a feminine noun in Hebrew. This life-giving, feminine aspect of God sweeps over the face of the waters and is connected to God's creativity (Ps. 104:4).[1] Although the original writer would not have meant this to be the Christian Holy Spirit, the Hebrew text includes a feminine image of God at work in the world from the beginning.

Another feminine image of God in the creation story is God as creator. Christians often refer to God as a divine parent, and in this text, God appears as mother, giving birth to the cosmos. Like a mother growing a child within her, God forms new life.[2] In addition, God does not simply create a static world where everything stays the same. Instead, God empowers the waters and the earth to bring forth the plants and animals, which will continue to create and give birth. This first occurs with the earth putting forth vegetation, with "plants yielding seed, and fruit trees of every kind on earth that bear fruit with the seed in it" (Gen. 1:11–12). These plants go on creating, bearing seed and fruit. Later, God lets the waters bring forth living creatures and blesses them, saying, "Be fruitful and multiply and fill the waters in the seas, and let birds multiply on the earth" (1:20–22). Finally, after letting the earth bring forth living creatures of every kind, God creates humans and gives the humans the same blessing as the air and sea animals: "Be fruitful and multiply" (1:28). This is a creator God, who wants the plants, animals, and people to go on creating.

A third feminine image of God appears in the way God creates humans: "In the image of God, God created them; male and female God created them" (1:27 alt.). This description specifies that there is something about being male and female that reflects the image of God.[3] It suggests that God is male, female, nonbinary, and everything in between. God is not reflected solely in the image of man, but in both male and female.

However, the creation of humans is not the end of the story. There is still one more day. On the seventh day, "God rested from all the work that God had done" (2:2 alt.). This is the Jewish Sabbath, and it sets forth a weekly rhythm of creativity and rest. Like a mother who has done the hard work of giving birth, God rests. And this rest is holy: "God blessed the seventh day and hallowed it" (2:3). As part of creation, God reminds us that rest is necessary and holy.

Unfortunately, many have taken this account of birth and creation as a license to destroy the world that God has created. They have understood the language of subduing the earth and having dominion as a command from God to kill animals and overdevelop the land. But God blesses the animals in the same way as humans: God gave the animals "every green plant for food" (1:30). If we take this blessing seriously, then it is a sin against God for humans to destroy the habitats of the animals that God has created and blessed.

Reading this description of God as creating the heavens and the earth is like listening to a poem or a call to worship, especially in the refrain "God saw that it was good." It was most likely written by a priest whose goal was to "describe creation with such harmony and beauty that it would inspire the people of Israel to praise and worship their creator."[4] In preaching on this text, the preacher can further inspire the congregation to praise God for creation, to continue creating, and to protect the vulnerable in God's creation.

- Does it expand your understanding of God to think of God as a mother giving birth to all of creation?
- What does it mean to be created in the image of God? How do humans reflect God's image?
- What responsibility do humans have to care for the natural world and maintain animal habitats?

JOHN 7:37–39

Holy Spirit

This text refers to the coming of the Holy Spirit at Pentecost, which takes place in Acts 2. In that story of the early church, the disciples are all together in one room; then "suddenly from heaven there came a sound like the rush of a violent wind, and it filled the entire house where they were sitting" (Acts 2:2). Tongues of fire rest on their heads, and the disciples are filled with the Holy Spirit (2:3). This allows them to speak in different languages, and they go out into the street and the temple courtyard to tell everyone the good news (2:4).

But in this passage, the author of John says that Jesus "said this about the Spirit, which believers in him were to receive" (John 7:39). The text continues: "For as yet there was no Spirit, because Jesus was not yet glorified" (7:39).[5] What does the author mean when he says that there was no Spirit? Was there a time when the Spirit did not yet exist? Or does he merely mean that the believers had not yet received the Holy Spirit at Pentecost? It is hard to reconcile the absence of the Spirit here with the witness to the presence of the Spirit throughout Scripture.

In the very beginning of Genesis, in the account of God creating the heavens and the earth, "the spirit of God swept over the face of the waters" (Gen. 1:2 alt.). In Hebrew, the word for spirit is a feminine noun that can also be translated as "wind" or "breath." This feminine aspect of God—Spirit, breath, wind—was there from the beginning. When Mary was pregnant and went to visit Elizabeth, "Elizabeth was filled with the Holy Spirit, and the child leaped in her womb" (Luke 1:41 alt.). And when John baptized Jesus, the Spirit descended like a dove and remained on him (cf. John 1:32). Like the God who protects her children under her wings in Psalm 17:8, this Spirit of God has wings.

At the same time, there may be truth in this passage for members of the congregation who do not feel the presence of the Holy Spirit. One way for a preacher to approach the text is to ask congregants to consider where God is, thinking in physical terms. When we pray on our knees, is God above us? Or below us? If we hold hands in a circle, is God in the middle of the circle? Or in the other people we touch? What does it mean to say that God is within us or in our hearts? If God is everywhere, how can we say that God is in one specific place? If we do not feel the presence of the Holy Spirit, does that mean she is not present?

The same can feel true for God's activity in the world: If God is always there, how can we say that God is at work or not? Sometimes it feels like there is no Spirit. At times it is so hard to feel the work of God in the world. Sometimes we want to cry out like the psalmist and like Jesus, "My God, my God, why have you forsaken me?" (Ps. 22:1; Matt. 27:46). The Spirit of God may sweep over the face of the deep, but we may not feel it. And other times, the presence of God is so clear. It sweeps over individuals and groups like tongues of fire, leading them to speak. This Spirit flows out like rivers of living water, quenching the thirst of all who drink.

- Have you experienced times when you felt the Holy Spirit? When it felt like there was no Spirit?
- How do you reconcile this text with other descriptions of the Spirit throughout the Bible?
- How can churches support people who are going through a time when God feels absent?

Ninth Sunday in Ordinary Time

GENESIS 2:4–9, 15–25

Woman and Man

The "Lord God" in the second creation story is described quite differently from the God depicted as creating the cosmos in Genesis 1! Instead of making broad statements that create worlds, the "Lord God" is more intimately involved in creation. The various images of God in this text include God as a potter, God as bellows, and God as a farmer.[1] Like a potter, God forms a human out of the dust of the ground (Gen. 2:7). Then God breathes the divine breath of life into the person's nostrils, like bellows (2:7). And God plants a garden for food, giving it to the human (2:8). This version of God also uses trial and error, first attempting to give the human a partner from the animals (2:18–20).

The description of the creation of humans is different from the first creation story as well. The Hebrew word for the first human can mean "a human being," "a man," or it can be the proper name Adam; ancient listeners probably would hear multiple meanings.[2] Rather than creating humankind simultaneously as male and female, as in Genesis 1:27, here God makes one human first. But very quickly, God realizes that it is not good for the human to be alone and decides to make the human a partner (2:18). Although this text has been used prescriptively to describe God's intent for a pairing of husband and wife, it is more inclusive to read it as a way to understand why people long to be together. It is also important to notice that the human is a complete human being before receiving a partner—potentially a relief to single members of the congregation!

When God sees that none of the animals will be an adequate partner for the human, God decides to make the second human out of the first (2:21–22).

This raises several questions about the initial human's gender. If we read this text in combination with the creation story in Genesis 1, the first human would have been made in the image of God, both male and female. Jewish and Christian scholars have speculated that this would make the original human nonbinary, or having both feminine and masculine traits.[3] The part of the first human that God removed is also mysterious. It has been translated as "rib," but the Hebrew word does not appear as a description of the body anywhere else,[4] and in other contexts it is translated as "side" (e.g., Exod. 25:12). Saying that the second human was created out of the first human's side suggests splitting the original human into two equal people.

It can be challenging to preach on this text because it has been one of the primary sources for arguments that women are subservient to men. People have argued that women are subservient in part because God created the man first and the woman second and by describing the woman as a "helpmeet" ("suitable helper"; Gen. 2:18 KJV alt.). However, there is no indication of hierarchy in the text. This Hebrew word, also translated as "partner," is often used to describe God, as in Psalm 121:1–2.[5] It is not a stretch to read the text as saying that the man and the woman are equal partners.

The final verses of the text indicate that this story served a purpose for its listeners: to explain why people leave their parents' homes and form new relationships.[6] The description "bone of my bones and flesh of my flesh" (Gen. 2:23) demonstrates kinship in a way that is not conveyed well in English.[7] Interestingly, this description of romantic partnership does not include any reference to procreation. The desire for union with another person is worthy in and of itself.

- What can we learn about God by comparing the differences in the descriptions of God in the first and the second creation stories?
- How does it change your understanding of this creation story to see it as descriptive rather than prescriptive?
- Do we use this text in some ways that are harmful to people in our congregations? How can we interpret Scripture so that we do not cause harm?

ACTS 5:1–11

Sapphira

The story of Ananias and Sapphira can paint a disturbing picture of God: Ananias and Sapphira sell their property and give part of the proceeds to the church, but because they held a portion back and lied about it, God strikes them dead. This story is similar to the account in Joshua 7, where Achan took some of the things that were devoted to God for destruction.[8] When Achan confessed, the Israelites stoned and burned Achan and his family (7:20–26). The parallels between these stories provide a counternarrative to the idea that the "Old Testament God" is violent and vengeful and that the "New Testament God" is loving and forgiving. The God described in Acts 5 is just as punishing as the one in Joshua 7.

One way to read this is to blame Peter for the deaths of Ananias and Sapphira. It is possible that when Peter confronts Ananias about holding back the proceeds and lying to God, Ananias dies of a heart attack.[9] Then, when Sapphira comes in and Peter coldly tells her that her husband has died and been buried without her knowledge, she may die of shock. Peter is in a difficult position here, leading this new faith community and enforcing the community norms of who is in and out. He clearly feels strongly about members lying to God and may feel motivated to protect God and the community.

Sapphira is the second woman named in Acts, after Mary (1:14): her name means "beautiful" or "good" and is the name of a gem (a sapphire). People in the early church would recognize this as the name of a wealthy woman. Sapphira's wealth raises the question of whether it was difficult for wealthy members to be part of this early church community. Sapphira knows that her husband kept back some of the proceeds from the sale of the land. She also has an opportunity to tell the truth yet also lies: she is not condemned solely for her husband's actions. If Sapphira and Ananias are truly equal partners in this decision, Sapphira may be the most "equal" woman in the New Testament.[10] But in this culture, it is more likely that Ananias as her husband has control over Sapphira.[11] She may feel obligated to do what he says. At least, she may feel pulled in different directions, between her loyalty to this new faith community and her loyalty to her husband.

The book of Acts famously describes how the community shares everything in common, sells their possessions, and distributes the proceeds to all as they have need (2:44–45). The text about Ananias and Sapphira begins immediately after the story of Barnabas selling a field that belonged to him and laying the proceeds at the apostles' feet (4:37). Many church communities try to follow the model of sharing everything in common; they see the early church as an ideal example of how the church should be. However, the story of Ananias and Sapphira is also intrinsic to the story of the early church. This is not a perfect community, but an imperfect community with imperfect people. And yet, in this story Luke names the community as "the . . . church" for the first time (Acts 5:11).

Rather than trying to smooth things over and make this a simple story, the preacher can present all the difficult aspects of the text. This is a God who is scary and punitive. Peter, the leader of the church, acts in a way that is not pastoral. Sapphira may be conspiring with her husband, or she may be making the best of a bad situation. It may come as a relief to people today to know that the early church in this text is not perfect. Just like our churches now, there are disagreements, secrets, and imperfect leaders, and God is not always easy to understand.

- What do you think caused the deaths of Ananias and Sapphira?
- How does including this story complicate the picture of the early church in Acts?
- Do you see parallels between this story and views about money in your church? Is it more difficult for wealthy church members to consider sharing everything in common?

Tenth Sunday in Ordinary Time

GENESIS 18:1–15

Sarah Laughs

This desert story feels like a mirage. Things look one way initially, and then differently at second glance, like water shimmering in the desert. Instead of trying to find definite answers, preachers can approach this text by holding on to that feeling of different ways of seeing and understanding. This text shows us how we can see and not see God at the same time, a sense of knowing and not knowing, of being outside, inside, and in between.

The first place this seeing in different ways occurs is in how the author describes God. "The LORD appeared to Abraham by the oaks of Mamre" (Gen. 18:1), but then Abraham "looked up and saw three men standing near him" (18:2). The language is ambiguous and even more so in Hebrew. When Abraham addresses one of them as "My lord," it seems as though he knows that this is God. But in Hebrew, the term is actually plural, "my lords," which is the formal way to address God.[1] So it could be that Abraham knows this is God and is using the traditional way to speak to God. Or it could be that he thinks these are three men and he is using the correct language for that!

Either way, Abraham shows great hospitality to his visitors. He convinces them to stay and hastens into the tent. This is another place where things are different from the way they initially seem. In the earlier scene, it looks as though there is only a man present, sitting in the entrance to his tent. But now it is clear that Sarah has been inside the tent all along (18:6). God is outside the tent, Sarah is inside the tent, and Abraham is in the space between. This threshold is significant: it signifies the space between people and God. Sarah and Abraham are in the space between what they have been and what they will be. God is here to tell them that their lives will change: they will have the son they have prayed for. But for now, they are in this space between, where things look one way one minute and another the next.

The next thing that seems to miraculously change is the food. When Abraham talks to the men, he suggests that "a little water be brought" and "a little bread, that you may refresh yourselves" (18:4–5). But then Abraham goes to Sarah and says, "Make ready quickly three measures of choice flour, knead it, and make cakes" (18:6); then he goes to the herd and personally picks out a calf, "tender and good," which he tells the servant to prepare (18:7). Finally, he takes curds and milk and the calf that has been prepared: he sets it before the visitors (18:8). This modest meal of a little bread and water has become a magnificent feast![2]

Then comes the biggest surprise of all: the announcement that Sarah will have a child (18:10). Looking at Sarah and Abraham, this might seem impossible: Sarah is 90 years old and her husband is 100. It should come as no surprise that Sarah laughs; when God told Abraham the same news earlier, he laughed too (17:17).[3] But Sarah quietly laughs to herself inside the tent. That is why it is so surprising when the man asks, "Why did Sarah laugh?" (18:13). Sarah thought she was reacting in the privacy of her own tent, but this stranger heard her. She suddenly knows that this stranger is no ordinary man, who would not have known what she has done.

Sarah is afraid, an understandable reaction. If she knows that this is God, the larger context is of a God who can be wrathful and unpredictable (the next chapter describes the destruction of Sodom and Gomorrah). Sarah is right to be afraid of a God who destroys entire cities for their lack of hospitality. But this is also a God who sees the unseen. Sarah is hidden away in the tent, doing unseen women's work,[4] but she is not hidden from God. God has seen her struggle and her tears; God knows what she wants more than anything; and when she denies what she has said, God repeats it back to her. This is a God who knows her, who enjoys her spirit and her laughter—a God to whom all things are revealed.

- How does this text reflect varied ways of seeing and understanding God?
- Do you think that Sarah knows she is preparing food for God?
- Is it possible to reconcile the many aspects of God in Genesis?

ACTS 9:36–43

Tabitha

The short, miraculous story of Tabitha shows many possible roles for women in the early church. Tabitha is part of the church community in Joppa, a city on the Mediterranean coast that now is present-day Yaffa, adjacent to Tel Aviv.[5] Tabitha is described as a disciple here (Acts 9:36). She is the only woman explicitly named as a disciple in the New Testament, and this is the only time that the feminine form of the Greek word appears in the New Testament.[6] However, that does not mean there were no other female disciples. Tabitha demonstrates that it was possible for a woman to be a disciple in the early church. To be a disciple means that a person is attached to a teacher or movement and follows the instruction and commitments of that teacher or movement. As a disciple, Tabitha studies and follows the teachings of Jesus. She lives out her beliefs by devoting herself to "good works and acts of charity" (Acts 9:36).

Tabitha has two names, Tabitha and Dorcas; both names mean gazelle. Like the apostle Paul, Tabitha is a Greek-speaking Jew with both a Jewish name and a Greek name. Scholars have speculated about what kind of woman Tabitha was because the text is unclear. Some assume that Tabitha was an independently wealthy woman.[7] Others note that Tabitha was a common name for enslaved women at the time and suggest that she was enslaved or a freed woman.[8] Tabitha may have been a widow,[9] supporting herself by making clothing. The community has celebrated her traditional virtues and industriousness.[10]

The community of widows in this text illustrates another lifestyle for women in the early church. The word "widow" was fairly inclusive at the time: it could mean any woman who did not have male protection or support. A widow might be a woman who had been married but her husband had died; she might be a divorced woman or an unmarried woman who no longer had her father's protection.[11] Earlier in Acts, there was a dispute because a certain group of widows was "being neglected in the daily distribution of food" (6:1). Later, the church would set up the "office of widows": the church would support widows who had no family members, and these widows would devote themselves to prayer and good works (1 Tim. 5:3–16). This community of widows in Joppa may have been a prototype for the office of widows.

When Tabitha dies, members of her community care for her body (Acts 9:37). She is a valued part of this community, so much so that they send two men to Peter—the head of the church—to ask him to come after her death. Peter comes and, in a miracle that recalls the prophets Elijah and Elisha as well as the story of Jesus and Jairus's daughter, he raises Tabitha from the dead (cf. 1 Kgs. 17:17–24; 2 Kgs. 4:18–37; Luke 8:41–42, 49–56). Ultimately, Tabitha's life becomes a sign: many people believe because they hear her story (Acts 9:42).

For preachers, the story of Tabitha provides a way to talk about all the different roles that women played in the early church, as well as the roles of women in the church now. Tabitha was a widow and engaged in the traditionally female role of producing clothing, but she was also a disciple. When she died, she was mourned by her widow community as well as the men in her community, who sent for Peter. She is also the recipient of this miracle, showing the power of God working through Peter.

- What are examples of the roles that women play in the early church?
- What makes Tabitha so central to her community?
- How do these roles of women in the text parallel roles that women occupy in the church today?

Eleventh Sunday in Ordinary Time

GENESIS 19:12–26

Lot's Wife

The unnamed woman married to Lot is a refugee, fleeing from an ecological catastrophe. In this story, Sodom has been a thriving city, with fertile vegetation. But in one day, the entire city and surrounding area are destroyed by "sulfur and fire" (Gen. 19:24). Present-day meteorologists explain the desert landscape around the Dead Sea as a product of low rainfall, due to the mountains to the west.[1] The area has sulfur and bitumen deposits and petrochemical springs, which might have been ignited by an earthquake.[2] The author of Genesis describes this landscape as God's "punishment" for the sinful actions of humans (19:15). This text is timely for preachers in an era of climate change. When we talk about environmental disasters, do we blame God? Or human decisions? The vulnerable often are the ones who suffer the most when disaster strikes.

Hebrews 13:2 instructs: "Do not neglect to show hospitality to strangers, for by doing that some have entertained angels without knowing it." For Lot's wife, the hospitality that her husband has showed to strangers brought unforeseen consequences. The previous night, she has endured the trauma of all the men in the town surrounding her house and demanding that Lot bring the strangers out so that the men can sexually assault and dominate them (Gen. 19:5). Her husband instead offers her daughters to the crowd (19:8). In the morning, the strangers physically remove her family, taking them by the hand to lead them out of the city before it is destroyed (19:16).

The most common reading of this story is that Lot's wife is punished for looking back after the angels warned the family not to look back (19:17).

Preachers can explore a more empathetic reading, seeing her as a woman who has been forced to leave her home and everything she knows. The men who were to marry her daughters refused to go with them, thinking that it was a joke (19:14). She has lost family members as well as the possibility of grand-children. Her anticipated future story has changed overnight, challenging her story of herself and the life she has built in Sodom.[3]

It also seems unfair that Lot's wife is punished so harshly for one look backward, after Lot repeatedly delays and negotiates with the angels. First, Lot lingers until the angels need to physically bring him, his wife, and his two daughters out of the city (19:16). Then, when the angels tell them to flee to the hills, Lot asks if they may instead go to the small city of Zoar (19:20). The angels (and God) put up with Lot's delay and bargaining. In that context, it seems strange that one look back from Lot's wife is worthy of death. An alternative explanation is that as they are fleeing for their lives, the fallout of fire and chemicals engulfs her.[4]

In some Jewish traditions, Lot's wife is named Edith.[5] In this telling, Edith has four daughters, two married and two betrothed. She looks back because she has lost her daughters and her sons-in-law and because she has compas-sion for the city.[6] In the ancient Near East, salt was a desirable preservative and seasoning, which could be mined from the rock formations along the Dead Sea.[7] It was also associated with destruction (e.g., Ps. 107:34). Perhaps the pillar of salt is a monument to this destruction by God and the grief that Edith felt at losing her family and everything that was familiar to her.

- How can churches respond with compassion to increasing numbers of refugees fleeing from environmental disasters due to climate change?
- What does this story about Lot's wife have to teach us about trauma and the loss of an anticipated future?
- How can we read stories like this one with empathy, instead of rushing to easy conclusions?

ACTS 12:11–16

Rhoda

The context for this text is Herod Agrippa's persecution of people in the early church, though the way those persecutions are described in Acts may not be historically accurate.[8] The preacher can provide the context within the chapter, while also letting the congregation know that this is a story, not strictly history. In the verses before this text, Peter was under arrest. While he was in jail, an angel appeared and led him out (Acts 12:6–10). When Peter realized that it was not a dream, he went to the house of Mary and knocked (12:11–12).

Features of this story are reminiscent of two earlier stories about Peter and women. In the first, after Jesus was arrested, a servant girl said that Peter had been with Jesus, but Peter denied it (Luke 22:56–57). The second is when Mary Magdalene, Joanna, Mary the mother of James, and other women told the disciples that Jesus was raised from the dead, but they did not believe the women (24:10–11). Peter ran to the tomb to see for himself and was amazed (24:12). He does not have a great history of communicating with women.

The two women in this passage are at different ends of the social and economic hierarchy. Mary is a wealthy woman who owns a large house where people in the early church would meet to pray, an example of an early house church.[9] Her son has two names (like Tabitha and Paul): this is a family that is between two cultures, the Greek culture around them and their Jewish culture. Mary is a patron of the early Christian community, one of the women who kept the church alive during times of persecution.[10]

This Mary has at least one enslaved person in her house, Rhoda, who is on the opposite end of the social spectrum (Acts 12:13 NRSV uses the euphemism "maid").[11] Rhoda is a reminder and the embodiment of the people enslaved by members of the early church.[12] It is unclear from the text whether Rhoda is a Christian. She is watching the door while the others pray, though that may be one of her duties. What is clear is that Rhoda recognizes Peter's voice: she knows Peter well enough to hear his voice and to know that he is the one knocking at the door.

The author of Acts plays this for comic effect.[13] The joke is how ridiculous Rhoda is: instead of opening the gate, she is so overjoyed that she runs back in (12:14). But Rhoda is someone at the margins: she is an enslaved woman. Rather than a ridiculous figure, she is one who speaks truth to power. When the people say that she is out of her mind, she insists that Peter really is there (12:15). It might have been easier for her to keep quiet, but she is emphatic that it is so. Instead of doubting herself, she tells the others what she has heard until they finally go to look. Then, like Peter at the tomb, they are amazed.

Preachers approaching this text might use it as an opportunity to tell the story in two ways: first as a comedy and then as an example of a marginalized person whom others do not believe, but who stands up for what she knows to be true. The preacher can draw parallels between Rhoda and those whom society considers a joke or untrustworthy, but who have important things to teach those with more wealth and authority. It is easier for a wealthy woman like Mary to be heard, but for Rhoda to continue speaking up is an act of bravery.

- What difference does it make to read this story while thinking that Rhoda is a "maid" versus knowing that she is enslaved?
- What does this text teach us about the different social roles of women in the early church?
- What are other examples of people in marginalized positions who speak truth to power?

Twelfth Sunday in Ordinary Time

GENESIS 19:30–38

Lot's Daughters

Over the course of this chapter, Lot's daughters go from being treated as objects owned by their father to characters with agency. The daughters first appear in the troubling story of Sodom, when Lot offers them to the violent crowd, saying, "Look, I have two daughters who have not known a man; let me bring them out to you, and do to them as you please" (Gen. 19:8). The following morning, the angels seize the daughters by the hand to take them out of the city before it is destroyed (19:16). In this text, the daughters are no longer passive: they speak and plan together.

These verses have many aspects of a folktale, beginning with the older daughter's repetition of their plan. This older daughter takes charge, saying to her sister, "Let us make our father drink wine, and we will lie with him, so that we may preserve offspring through our father" (19:32). There is a heightened reality to the story: each daughter needs only one attempt to become pregnant by their father, unlike many other women in the Hebrew Scriptures who are unable to conceive. Like some folktales, this story explains and dismisses the neighboring people as the product of incest.[1] For people in the U.S. South, the trope of dismissing people by accusing them of incest (i.e., marrying cousins) is familiar! Finally, there is symmetry to what happens to Lot: he has offered his daughters for rape: in the end, his daughters rape him.

For preachers, the sexual violence is troubling on all sides. Although the daughters' treatment of their father may suggest "what goes around comes around," nonconsensual sex is not a punch line, regardless of the perpetrator.

165

Rather than accepting the tidy narrative approach, preachers can take this opportunity to start a conversation about trauma and the ways that people who have unresolved trauma can harm others. These daughters have experienced a lot of trauma: the threat of sexual assault, the loss of their home, and the death of their fiancés and their mother.

Some interpreters have read this text as examples of people taking something that is good too far. Lot is committed to providing hospitality to strangers,[2] a theme throughout the Bible. But he goes too far when he puts his daughters in the way of harm instead of the strangers. The daughters are also trying to do something good: continue the family line. Yet they go too far when, to conceive, they have sex with their father without his consent.

There are several gaps in the story. It begins with Lot going up out of Zoar and into a cave with his daughters because he is afraid to stay in Zoar (19:30). The reader does not know how long Lot was in Zoar or why he left (perhaps it is because he was not accepted there).[3] Scholars have compared this story with certain events after the flood, another story with a patriarch who was drunk on wine and sexually exposed (9:18–27).[4] Like Noah's family, Lot's daughters may believe that their father is the only man alive, and thus the only possibility for them to have offspring. Yet they are working with imperfect information: there are other men nearby. Although the daughters may feel as though this is their only option when they are trapped in the cave with their father, there are other possibilities. Rather than acting alone, they could have communicated with their father or tried to find other men.

- What does this story have to teach us about sexual violence, cycles of abuse, and trauma?
- Does reading this story as a folktale enrich your understanding of it? What other literary frames do you use to understand troubling texts?
- What are other examples of people making decisions with imperfect information? How might more information lead to a better decision?

ACTS 16:11–19

Lydia and the Enslaved Girl

Paul's traveling ministry to start new Christian communities provides the context for these contrasting stories of Lydia and the unnamed enslaved girl. In the verses before this text, Paul has a vision about a man in Macedonia pleading with him to come and help them (Acts 16:9). Consequently, Luke narrates how Paul and Silas and others travel to Macedonia. The description of the journey is significant because the community in Macedonia becomes the first church founded by Paul in western Europe.[5] When Paul and the other(s) arrive, instead of meeting a man, they meet Lydia.

Philippi, in the district of Macedonia, was a diverse city in the Roman Empire; the passage demonstrates that it is not predominantly Jewish.[6] Paul and Silas need to go outside the city walls to find a place of prayer, probably a makeshift synagogue beside the river. They talk to women when they arrive, suggesting that there is not a quorum of ten Jewish males for worship.[7] Lydia lives in Philippi, but she is from Thyatira, in the district of Lydia, known for its purple cloth (16:14). Her name is the same as that district. She is an immigrant and a well-established one: she has a business and is the head of a household. It is not clear how wealthy Lydia is, but her business would put her in contact with wealthy people, and she probably is at least financially comfortable. Luke describes Lydia as "a worshiper of God" (16:14), meaning that she is not Jewish (she also has a Greek name).[8] Lydia hears what Paul has to say, God opens her heart, and she and her household are baptized. Thus, Paul's first convert in western Europe is a woman who becomes a leader in the church in Philippi.[9]

The second woman in this passage is the enslaved girl. The spirit that possesses her gives her the ability to tell fortunes, and the men who own her use that power to make money (16:16). This is an example of prophecy being seen in a negative light in the early church.[10] When Paul commands the spirit to come out of the enslaved girl, it is a strange miracle. Paul does not care about the girl herself. He does not heal her because she is suffering, but rather because he is irritated (16:18). The men who own the girl are furious with Paul and Silas, and it is unlikely that they will treat her any better. The text does not say what ends up happening to the enslaved girl, but it is possible that Paul has ruined her life by taking away her useful skill.

This seems like a perversion of the miracles that Jesus performed, such as when he called the woman he healed "Daughter" (Mark 5:34) and invited Mary Magdalene, who had seven spirits go out of her, to travel with him (Luke 8:2–3). Ultimately, this is an example of leaders of the early church treating people differently based on their social status. The wealthier, independent woman who provides hospitality becomes a leader of the church, and the truth-telling, enslaved girl is forgotten.[11] Thus, unfortunately, this church, among the first in Europe, reproduces the oppressive systems that surround it.

The preacher can point out how, as in the stories of Rhoda and her mistress, Mary (Acts 12), these women from different social classes are presented differently. In this text again, the church seems to have already strayed from the world-changing message of Jesus that the last shall be first. It is a good reminder for those in the church who have higher social status to pay attention to whether those on the margins are being ignored or even harmed by the church.

- In reading these two stories about women in the early church together, what stands out to you?
- What more would you like to know about Lydia and the enslaved girl?
- How do you see churches today treating people in higher or lower social classes differently from each other?

Thirteenth Sunday in Ordinary Time

GENESIS 21:8–21

Sarah and Hagar

The story of Sarah and Hagar is like a fairy tale about a wicked stepmother. The story is told twice: first in Genesis 16 and again in Genesis 21:8–21.[1] Sarah is an older, barren woman with power; Hagar is a younger, fertile woman who is enslaved. God has promised Abraham that he will have descendants, but Abraham and Sarah are old, so Sarah comes up with a solution: she gives the enslaved woman Hagar to Abraham as a wife to bear children for him (Gen. 16:3). After Hagar conceives, she looks on Sarah with contempt, and Sarah strikes out at Hagar (16:6). Hagar runs away to the desert but encounters an angel, who tells her to return and that she will bear a son named Ishmael (16:10–11).

But this is not a fairy tale: it is part of our Scripture. The story of Hagar is tragic and ethically challenging. In *Texts of Terror*, Phyllis Trible says, "All we who are heirs of Sarah and Abraham, by flesh and spirit, must answer for the terror in Hagar's story. To neglect the theological challenge she presents is to falsify faith."[2] Trible points out that Hagar's story depicts oppression in three familiar forms: nationality, class, and sex.[3] Hagar is an outsider: she is a foreigner, she is enslaved, and she is a woman. Hagar's body is at the disposal of the people who own her; they can decide to impregnate her and then send her away to die without consequence.[4]

Sarah dehumanizes Hagar by referring to her as "this slave woman" (21:10) rather than calling her by her name. But, as womanist theologian Wilda Gafney points out, the name Hagar is a masculine Hebrew name meaning "foreign thing" and can mean foreigner or sojourner. This is not a name, and it is not what Hagar's Egyptian parents called her.[5] Hagar is a foreign thing to Sarah and Abraham, which makes it easy for them to discard her when they no longer want or need her. Like a maiden in a fairy tale, Hagar is cast out, sent into the wilderness of Beer-sheba with her young son (21:14).

In this text Abraham's actions show the shadow side of patriarchy, a system that can, at its best, protect women. For Abraham, all that matters is the heir. Once God tells Abraham that it is through Isaac that offspring will be named for him, Abraham is willing to send his wife Hagar and his son Ishmael away with nothing more than bread and a skin of water (21:14). By contrast, Abraham makes a great feast on the day that his other son, Isaac, is weaned (21:8). Abraham fails in his role as patriarch, the one who should be protecting his wives and children.

But God has not forsaken Hagar. In the wilderness, Hagar again encounters an angel, who tells her not to be afraid, "for God has heard the voice of the boy" Ishmael (21:17). The angel shows her where there is a well of water (21:19), and the two survive. Even though Hagar was abandoned by those who should have cared for her, God remembers the enslaved woman in the wilderness. For preachers, this text gives space to remember those who are harmed by the ones who should protect them. It is a reminder that the people we often lift up in our stories can be the villains in the stories of others.

- How do Sarah and Abraham fail to protect Hagar?
- How does Hagar's story fit into the larger story of Genesis?
- What are some other examples of people who are harmed by those who have an obligation to protect them?

ACTS 18:1–4, 24–28

Priscilla

Priscilla, also called Prisca, is a leader in the early church, and she first appears here in Acts. Paul has been traveling from city to city, establishing Christian communities. He is an evangelist, teaching people about Christ and encouraging them to convert to Christianity, but he finds something different when he arrives in Corinth.

Aquila, a Jew with family ties to Pontus, and his wife, Priscilla, are living and working in Corinth because "Claudius had ordered all Jews to leave Rome" (Acts 18:2). This historical detail is corroborated by Roman historian Suetonius, who wrote that Jews were causing disturbances at the instigation of "Chrestus," which may be a corruption of "Christ."[6] Not all of the Jews were ordered to leave Rome, however. It probably was the Jews who were followers of Christ and were causing a disturbance by proclaiming the good news.[7] Thus, Priscilla and Aquila are not people whom Paul has to convert: they are already Christ followers and evangelists.

Priscilla and Aquila are also tentmakers, working together in trade as well as evangelism. Paul finds them because he is a member of a trade guild.[8] He needs to work to support his ministry, and this guild provides financial support as well as community. It must have been exciting for Paul to find others who are not only in the same trade but also fellow evangelists, who can work together in trade and ministry. Priscilla and Aquila do not only work with Paul in Corinth; they also travel with him to Ephesus (18:18–19).

Notably, Priscilla's name appears first when the couple is mentioned, both here and in Paul's Letter to the Romans (Acts 18:18, 26; cf. Rom. 16:3–4). This may be because Priscilla outranks Aquila socially or economically.[9] The passage provides Aquila's family origin, but there is no information about Priscilla's background. Paul uses a Greek word to describe her that means fellow worker, co-laborer, or companion in work (Rom. 16:3). This is a title that he uses for others like Timothy, Mark, and Luke.[10] Paul recognizes Priscilla's value as a co-laborer in Christ, just like the men who are with him in ministry.

It is possible that Priscilla is named first because she is the leader in this mission, particularly in teaching. When Apollos arrives, it is clear to Priscilla and Aquila that he has enthusiasm but does not know the full gospel (Acts 18:25). Rather than publicly confronting him, Priscilla and Aquila take Apollos aside and privately instruct him (18:26). So Priscilla is not only an evangelist herself, but also one who helps train others.[11] This is a successful approach: Apollos accepts the teaching that Priscilla and Aquila offer and goes on to be an effective preacher of the gospel (18:28). Priscilla and Aquila provide an example of a teaching team, a wife and husband who work together and train others in the work of ministry.

Preachers can use this text to point out the benefits of collaborative ministry. When Paul finds Priscilla and Aquila, they are all able to be more effective in ministry because they are supporting each other emotionally and financially. In addition, this text provides an example of strong female leadership in the church. Priscilla appears not only here; she also is named in the letters that Paul sends, showing her continuing influence in leading house churches. She is not silent but takes an active role in leading and teaching, correcting colleagues who might harm the witness of the early church.

- When have you heard about Priscilla and Aquila before? Do you associate their story with specific contexts?
- What stands out to you in this account of Priscilla and Aquila? Is anything surprising?
- How is Priscilla an example for church leaders today?

Fourteenth Sunday in Ordinary Time

GENESIS 24:10–21

Rebekah

The story that introduces Rebekah gives a variety of examples of how people hear God's voice and how different people respond to it. The first person in this story who hears God's voice is Abraham, and he hears the voice of God directly. God speaks to Abraham clearly, and Abraham makes a covenant with God (Gen. 15:1–20). Abraham does what God says: he is even willing to kill his son Isaac when God commands it (22:2–3). Here, Abraham asks his chief steward to go back the country from which Abraham came and find a wife for Isaac. Abraham assures the servant that God "will send his angel before you, and you shall take a wife for my son from there" (24:7). Abraham is confident that he has heard the voice of God and that the trip will be successful.

The next person who interacts with God is the unnamed servant. He does not hear from God directly; instead, he receives instructions from Abraham. The servant trusts that Abraham has heard God correctly, and he follows the instructions to go back to Abraham's homeland and find a wife for Isaac (24:10). But when he gets there, things are not so clear. So the servant prays. He prays specifically that the woman who says, "Drink, and I will water your camels"—that will be the wife for Isaac (24:14); he is asking God for a sign. While the servant is still praying, Rebekah appears and does exactly what he has asked for, but he still is not sure whether God has made his journey successful. He wonders in silence (24:21).

The third person in this story is Rebekah. Unlike Abraham and the servant, Rebekah does not hear a call from God, either directly or through prayer.

Instead, the text describes Rebekah's generosity; when the servant asks for water, she gives it to him and offers to water his ten camels. This is a huge amount of water: one camel can drink 20–30 gallons of water at a time![1] It suggests a scene of Rebekah running back and forth, filling the trough over and over. Rebekah is a generous person, so she responds generously, which is a sign to the servant that she is the person he seeks. Also, Rebekah is brave and resolute. Later, after the servant tells the whole story to Rebekah's family, they call Rebekah and say to her, "Will you go with this man?" She says, "I will" (24:58). Rebekah is decisive when asked if she will go.[2] It may be that God is speaking to Rebekah through her very nature: when she behaves generously, bravely, and decisively, the next step opens to her.

All the different ways that God speaks to people provide approaches for a sermon on this passage: God speaks directly, through others, through prayer, in silence, and through people's natures and gifts. Many people do not hear directly from God or receive clear answers to prayer. Preachers can use Rebekah's story to suggest that God calls us through the way we are and the choices we make. Rebekah has become a part of the story of God's people because she makes a decision to go when her family asks her wishes. The text invites us to consider how we hear the voice of God and how God speaks to those around us.

- What are some of the ways that God speaks to people in this text and elsewhere in the Bible?
- How do you experience the voice of God? Do you hear God speaking to you directly, through prayer, in silence, or through other people?
- How do you recognize when others have heard God speaking to them?

ACTS 21:7–15

Daughters Who Prophesy

As Paul nears the end of his last journey to Jerusalem, he visits the home of Philip in Caesarea and encounters Philip's four daughters, all of whom have the gift of prophecy (Acts 21:8–9). The single verse about these four unnamed women has stirred up many questions for scholars. Why include the fact that Philip has four daughters with the gift of prophecy if there is no more information about them? How does this gift of prophecy manifest itself? For preachers, this is a text that underscores the importance not only of naming but also of telling the story of people who fall outside the norms.

The last time Philip appeared in Acts was when he converted the Ethiopian eunuch (8:26–40). Thus Philip is associated with both evangelism and people who are outside the usual social structures of family and marriage. After converting the eunuch, Philip "proclaimed the good news to all the towns until he came to Caesarea" (8:40). Luke may have included the mention of his daughters to indicate how much time has passed since he founded the church and settled in Caesarea, enough time for him to have four grown daughters.[3]

The NRSV states that the four daughters are "unmarried," but this can also be translated as virgins. Many commentators have speculated on why Luke would include the detail that these daughters are unmarried or virgins. It may be a reference to their relative youth or because prophetesses in the Hellenistic region were often virgins.[4] Another possibility is that Luke associates female prophetic activity with virgins or celibate women, like Mary and Anna, or because he opposes marriage for believers (cf. Luke 20:34–36).[5] Or Luke may have mentioned the daughters' virginity to suggest that celibacy is more holy.

Some scholars have asserted that Luke includes the fact that the women have the gift of prophecy as an embodiment of the gift of the Holy Spirit at Pentecost (Acts 2:17–18).[6] This shows that the Holy Spirit is empowering the church in Caesarea as well as Jerusalem. Another possibility is that these four women prophets are reminiscent of the four female prophets named in the Hebrew Scriptures: Miriam, Deborah, Huldah, and Noadiah.[7] Maybe they proclaim what God has done, as Miriam does (Exod. 15:20–21); have wisdom to lead, as Deborah does (Judg. 4:4); warn the leaders that the people have turned away from God, as Huldah does (2 Kgs. 22:14–17); or challenge other prophets, as Noadiah does (Neh. 6:14).

Instead of describing a prophetic word from these women, Luke describes the prophecy of another, a man named Agabus, who comes down from Judea (Acts 21:11). Previously in Acts, Agabus has predicted a famine (11:27–30), and he returns here to warn Paul.[8] His prophetic act is similar to earlier prophets (e.g., Isa. 20:2; Jer. 13:1–11; Ezek. 4:1–8).[9] Agabus's prophecy raises questions about his relationship with Philip's daughters. Perhaps he is a more seasoned prophet, who would spend time in the house with these younger women. At the least, the women would witness Agabus giving his prophetic pronouncement and see how the people around him respond: while most of the people there urge Paul not to go to Jerusalem, Paul is resolved to go (Acts 21:12–13). As a prophet, Agabus has the authority to receive and deliver the prophecy, and others interpret it.[10]

Luke records very few prophecies from women: only the words of Elizabeth (Luke 1:42–45), Mary (Luke 1:46–55), and the enslaved girl through whom a demon speaks (Acts 16:16–18).[11] He is willing to state that women will prophesy (2:17; 21:9), but chooses not to tell the stories of these women who do prophesy.[12] This is a lost opportunity for the church. Instead of the specific examples of these women, readers need to speculate about what it means for a woman to have the gift of prophecy and what that looks like. In our preaching, we have the chance to mourn this loss and do our best to share the often untold stories of women prophets.

- Why did Luke include Philip's daughters with the gift of prophecy in this text?
- How do you think their gifts of prophecy were manifested? Do you think they were celebrated in the community?
- Where do you see the gift of prophecy in your congregation? What stories can you tell about people with that gift?

Fifteenth Sunday in Ordinary Time

GENESIS 25:21–28

Rebekah Gives Birth

At first glance, the story of Rebekah and Isaac seems a lot like the story of Sarah and Abraham: a woman who is barren and a patriarch who desires offspring to continue the family line. There are key differences, however, beginning with who prays to God. In this text, Isaac is the one who prays, and God answers his prayer (Gen. 25:21).[1] There is no mention of Rebekah praying, nor does the Scripture say that she desires children. In addition, the text specifies that Isaac only prays once—and Rebekah becomes pregnant after the two have been married for twenty years![2] Unlike other patriarchs, Isaac does not take another wife or have children with a servant woman. Perhaps Isaac and Rebekah were the rare couple in the Hebrew Scriptures who were content to be childless together for a long time.

Once Rebekah becomes pregnant, she is not a grateful or glowing expectant mother. Instead, Rebekah suffers in her pregnancy—likely a common occurrence at a time when pregnancy and childbirth were painful and dangerous. The Hebrew is unclear, but at least some translations suggest that Rebekah feared for her life during this time, asking, "If it is to be this way, why do I live?" (25:22). Or maybe she just wants an end to her discomfort! Rebekah goes directly to God with her inquiry. The text does not say where Rebekah goes, but the language suggests it might be a sanctuary.[3]

Then God speaks directly to Rebekah! God gives Rebekah an oracle, like the one God gave Hagar (16:11–12),[4] telling her that she is suffering because she has two nations in her womb (25:23). At this point, Rebekah embodies the tensions between two peoples: her sons will each father a nation, and those two nations will be in conflict with each other. God goes on to say that one of Rebekah's sons will be stronger and "the elder shall serve the younger" (25:23). It is unclear why God tells Rebekah this. Does God want Rebekah to help her younger son fulfill God's will? Regardless of the intent, this is one of the rare times when a woman in the Hebrew Scriptures asks God a question and receives a direct answer.

So far in this text, the usual gender roles seem reversed. Isaac is the one praying for a child, and Rebekah communicates directly with God. Isaac and Rebekah's twin sons also reflect different gender roles. When Rebekah gives birth, her sons could not be more different from each other. Esau is hairy and has traditionally masculine traits: he is a hunter and a man of the field (25:27). Jacob is a quiet man, "living in tents," places most often associated with women (25:27; cf. 18:9).[5] Isaac favors the more masculine Esau, and Rebekah prefers the more traditionally feminine Jacob (25:28).

How much does the oracle affect Rebekah's choice to love Jacob more than his brother? Isaac's preference for Esau is straightforward: he loves Esau because he is "fond of game" (25:28). Once Rebekah knows that her younger son will be stronger than the older, it must influence her decisions to help him gain power. Later, Rebekah will help Jacob trick his brother and father, gaining the blessing for himself (27:5–17). It is through Rebekah's actions that the oracle is proven right: Jacob is the younger twin yet gains his father's blessing.[6]

Tellingly, when Jacob later meets his future wife, Rachel, he says that he is "Rebekah's son" rather than Isaac's son (29:12). It is unusual for someone to identify their mother instead of their father, though this may be because his family there knows Rebekah, not Isaac. This introduction underscores how Jacob is Rebekah's son through and through. He inherits her cunning and her desire to gain power, as well as the way she bends gender through her actions and her relationships. In the end, Jacob and Rebekah ensure that Jacob will be the father of the Israelites.

- How can churches recognize that not all people want to be parents and not all pregnancies are desired or happy occasions?
- How do you feel when you read Scripture where God speaks directly to individuals about what will happen in the future?
- What other examples can you think of in Scripture where people act in ways that seem contrary to traditional gender roles?

ROMANS 16:1–7, 12–16

Phoebe

Paul's greetings at the end of Romans reveal a surprising amount about individual women in the church at the time, as well as the composition of the church in Rome. In particular, these greetings show his deep respect for women, both as members of the church and ministers of the good news.[7] Nearly half the people whom Paul names in his greetings are women.[8] Although many of the names are otherwise unknown, they reflect a wide range of social strata, with both Jews and Gentiles leading the church.[9] For preachers, this text is an excellent counter to the narrative that the early church leadership consisted of only men, and it provides an opening for churches today to be even more inclusive in language and leadership.

Paul begins by introducing Phoebe (Rom. 16:1), who most likely will deliver the letter and probably will interpret it to the believers in Rome.[10] Paul says that Phoebe is a deacon of the church in Cenchreae (16:1); "deacon" is a title that he uses for himself and others engaged in a ministry of teaching and preaching, with no gender distinctions (see that Greek term in 1 Cor. 3:5; 2 Cor. 6:4; Phil. 1:1).[11] Phoebe is an independent woman, not defined by a father, husband, or family: this implies that she is a businesswoman who is able to travel independently.[12] Paul also states that she is a benefactor (literally, a "patron") to himself and others, meaning that she is a person of influence socially and financially as well as a leader in the church.[13]

Next, Paul greets Prisca (or Priscilla) and Aquila, who have worked with him (Rom. 16:3; for more on Priscilla, see the commentary on Acts 18:1–4, 24–28). As elsewhere, Paul lists Prisca before her husband, suggesting that she is a more prominent figure (cf. Acts 18:18, 26; 2 Tim. 4:19).[14] It is unclear how they "risked their necks" for Paul's life (Rom. 16:4). Since working with Paul, they have moved back to Rome and are now leaders of a house church (16:5). Paul emphasizes their influence, saying that "all the churches of the Gentiles" give them thanks (16:4).

The third significant woman in Paul's greetings is Junia; he says she is a "relative," which may mean a fellow Jew or a blood relative, who was in prison with him (16:7).[15] Paul designates Junia as an "apostle" (16:7), meaning that she is an early witness to the resurrection.[16] Until at least the Middle Ages, church writers interpreted Junia as a female name, but later interpreters assumed that a woman could not have been an apostle and instead used the masculine name Junias.[17] However, there is ample evidence that the name Junia was common for women and no evidence that the name Junias was ever used among men.[18] Modern scholars have recognized that this is a female apostle.

In addition, Paul refers to several other women, including Mary, Tryphaena and Tryphosa, Persis, and Julia, as well as the mother of Rufus and the sister of Nereus; he commends them for their work in the church.[19] It appears that many of these women are leaders of house churches in Rome, and nothing suggests that their work is different from their male counterparts.[20] Here in this text, Paul assumes that women will engage in ministry.

While this description of the church is much more inclusive than often thought, there is another way that preachers can make the language in this text even more inclusive. Where the NRSV and other translations say, "brothers and sisters," the original Greek was "brothers." By including "sisters," the translators are trying to make this more inclusive (and in places, more accurate, because Paul is referring to women as well as men). However, preachers can take the next step to change "brothers and sisters" to "siblings," to include nonbinary people and people of other genders.

- How do Paul's greetings expand your understanding of the early church?
- Why do you think Paul would choose Phoebe to deliver his letter to the church in Rome?
- What can the church do now to be more inclusive in its language and leadership?

Sixteenth Sunday in Ordinary Time

GENESIS 29:15–28

Rachel and Leah

As many scholars have pointed out, this story about Rachel and Leah mirrors many of the themes in the story of Jacob and Esau, including disputes between older and younger siblings, lack of sight, and deception.[1] These similarities begin with the descriptions of Leah and Rachel. Like Jacob and Esau, they are described by their physical attributes, but with one key difference. The physical descriptions of Jacob and Esau reveal something about their personalities (Gen. 25:27). By contrast, the descriptions of Leah and Rachel focus solely on the traits that make them attractive to men: Leah's eyes, which may be translated as either "lovely" (NRSV) or "weak" (NIV); and Rachel being "graceful and beautiful" (29:17). Like so many sisters, these two are compared based on their physical attractiveness rather than their character. This part of the Bible has a lot of sibling rivalry, but the conflict between these sisters is particularly feminine in tone.

The focus on the women's appearance is fitting for a text that treats them as bargaining pieces in negotiations by men. Leah and Rachel have agency before and after this passage, but here, they are merely objects to be bought and sold. Laban asks Jacob what he wants as payment for his wages (29:15), and Jacob asks for Laban's younger daughter, Rachel, in exchange for seven years of work (29:17). Jacob's work is a bride-price, a way of compensating the family for the loss of its daughter and maybe assuring funds for the daughter's dowry.[2] Later, Rachel and Leah will be very upset that their father sold them and used up the money given for them (31:15). At the end of the seven years of work, Jacob asks for his payment: "Give me my wife that I may go in to her" (29:21). The language demonstrates that Jacob feels entitled to Rachel's body as payment for the work he has done.

Then comes the dramatic twist: instead of giving Rachel to Jacob, Laban deceives him by bringing Jacob his other daughter, Leah (29:23). There is a frustrating lack of detail in this description, leaving the reader to wonder who knew what when.[3] Do Rachel and Leah know about their father's plan? All the people in the place go to the marriage ceremony—are they all in on it? What do Rachel and Leah think about this exchange? Jacob has been living with this family for seven years; surely he should have been able to tell the difference between the sisters! Regardless, Jacob ends up with both sisters as his wives in one week,[4] leading to more conflict and heartbreak that will continue in the next generation.

There are two other women mentioned parenthetically in this text: Zilpah and Bilhah. When Laban gives Leah and Rachel to Jacob, he also gives Zilpah and Bilhah to Leah and Rachel as "maids" (29:24, 29). Zilpah and Bilhah will play an important role in the family when Leah and Rachel begin to have children. Leah gives birth to four sons, but Rachel is unable to conceive until later, so she gives Bilhah as a wife to Jacob; Bilhah has two sons, Dan and Naphtali, whom Rachel names (30:3–8). Then when Leah is no longer able to have children, she gives Zilpah to Jacob as a wife; Zilpah has two sons, Gad and Asher, whom Leah names (30:9–13). Bilhah appears one more time: Leah's eldest son Reuben has sex with her (35:22).

In a text where women are treated as property, there are still layers of privilege and autonomy. Leah and Rachel have power over Zilpah and Bilhah. They use these women's bodies for offspring, giving them to their husband and then claiming and naming their children. For preachers, this is a reminder that even in the most patriarchal cultures, some women have more power than others. Bilhah and Zilpah are mentioned only as property, to be used for work and sex. Unlike the other women, they have no distinguishing characteristics, and churches have largely forgotten them.

- How does this passage reinforce the idea that women are only valued for their appearance and bodies?
- This is often remembered as the story of Rachel and Leah; how can our churches make space to remember women like Zilpah and Bilhah?
- When people say that they believe in "biblical marriage," is this what they have in mind?

1 CORINTHIANS 1:10–18

Chloe

Paul writes this letter to the believers in Corinth because he has heard that they are quarreling among themselves (1 Cor. 1:11). He hears this news from "Chloe's people," literally, "[those] of Chloe."[5] There is no more information about Chloe or her people, but the designation indicates that Chloe is the head of this household (like Lydia in Acts 16:14–15), which typically would include relatives, enslaved people, and freed people.[6] Chloe and her people must be in good standing with Paul and the church in Corinth to be a credible source for Paul about the divisiveness in the church.[7] What in other circumstances might be considered gossip is, in this case, the impetus for a letter from Paul to that church.

In response, Paul implores the church to be "united in the same mind and the same purpose" instead of dividing into competing groups (1 Cor. 1:10). The divisions within the church seem to be caused by groups, each of which claims to belong to one of the various leaders. This follows practices in the city of Corinth, where discrete groups joined to specific wealthy patrons would compete against each other.[8] Paul gives the examples of people saying that they "belong" to Paul, Apollos, Cephas, and Christ (1:12), though these probably are examples rather than the historical reality.[9] While Apollos seems to have spent time in Corinth and been popular there (cf. Acts 18:27), there is no indication that Cephas (Paul's Aramaic name for Peter) has ever been to Corinth.[10]

Paul argues that there is no basis for the idea that the person who baptizes new believers wins their exclusive loyalty.[11] In a comical series of verses, Paul demonstrates how little it matters who performs the baptism: he cannot even remember whom he baptized! He first states that he only baptized Crispus and Gaius (1 Cor. 1:14), but then remembers that he also baptized the household of Stephanas and possibly others (1:16). Regardless, Paul reminds them that they were not baptized in his name, but in Christ's name (1:13).

In this text, Paul makes both implicit and explicit arguments that the church should be united. Throughout, Paul uses family language to convince the church that they should act like family members toward each other. Although in the original Greek, Paul is writing to "brothers," he clearly assumes that women are included, so the NRSV translation of "brothers and sisters" is appropriate.[12] His explicit argument is that the "message about the cross" is the interpretive solution to the problem of factions in Corinth (1:18).[13] For Paul, the cross stands for the larger story about the death and resurrection of Jesus Christ.[14] By reminding them of the cross, he is imploring the people in the church in Corinth to remember what is central about their faith instead of being distracted by human leaders.

For pastors, this text can serve as a reminder that there are varied gifts in pastoral leadership and pastors are called to different aspects of ministry. Paul states that Christ did not send him to baptize but to preach the gospel (1:17). He is not minimizing the importance of baptism but saying that it is not his primary calling. Paul also makes a distinction between clever or wise speech ("eloquent wisdom") and simply proclaiming the gospel, and he points to the inherent power of the cross (1:17). This may be a relief for preachers: it is not necessary to come up with the perfect words in every sermon, but rather more important to tell the story of God's saving work in the world.

- What more would you like to know about Chloe and her people?
- Do the divisions among believers in Corinth seem like divisions in the church today? Why or why not?
- What are things that Christians have in common? Does focusing on telling the story of our faith bring us together?

Seventeenth Sunday in Ordinary Time

GENESIS 31:14–35

Rachel Steals the Gods

At the beginning of this text, Leah and Rachel are unusually unified in their response to Jacob. Despite all their conflict and competition in bearing children, here they speak in one voice, telling Jacob to leave and "do whatever God has said to you" (Gen. 31:16). The sisters have a common enemy: their father, who has treated them poorly. Leah and Rachel use legal language to describe what their father has done,[1] saying that he has sold them, treated them like foreigners, and wasted all their money.[2] Even in a system where women are routinely treated as objects, Laban has gone too far, and Leah and Rachel advise their husband to follow what he has heard from God.

However, the exchange between Jacob and Laban after Laban overtakes the fleeing party demonstrates how both men still see the women as objects. First, Laban says that Jacob has "carried away my daughters like captives of the sword" (31:26). Laban's description reveals how he sees his daughters like the spoils of war, and it reflects the precarious position of women in times of conflict. Then Jacob responds by saying that he fled in secret "because I was afraid, for I thought that you would take your daughters from me by force" (31:31). Like Laban, Jacob sees his wives as objects that can be taken away rather than as people with their own thoughts, feelings, and autonomy.

Finally, Laban comes to the point of his pursuit, asking Jacob, "Why did you steal my [household] gods?" (31:30), and Jacob says, "Anyone with whom you find your gods shall not live" (31:32). This creates dramatic tension because the reader knows what Jacob does not: his beloved wife Rachel has "stolen the gods" (31:32). Why does Jacob make this pledge? Perhaps because it establishes him as a patriarch who controls the life and death of the people under his care.[3] Or likely he is certain that no one in his party has taken the gods. But his words have potentially deadly consequences. A current-day analogy might be drawn to white people who call the police about noise complaints by people of color. With a few words, someone in a more privileged position can unthinkingly put marginalized people at risk of deadly violence.

Fortunately for Rachel and Jacob, Rachel is the trickster who outwits both Laban and Jacob. In a comical account, Rachel puts the household gods in the camel's saddle and sits on them (31:34). Laban goes through each tent, giving us a glimpse into the day-to-day life of these people as they travel: Jacob, Leah, and Rachel each have their own tents, and Zilpah and Bilhah share a tent (31:33). When Laban searches Rachel's tent, she tells him: "Please don't be angry that I can't stand up before you, father, for I am having my period" (31:35).[4] Rachel uses this ruse to keep the household gods, which are a sign of the family blessing and would usually be inherited by Laban's firstborn son.[5]

It is unclear why Laban leaves Rachel alone. Maybe he is concerned for her well-being, or he might be embarrassed. Another possibility is that he is staying away from her because she is ritually unclean. Regardless of the reason, the result is that Rachel gets away with her deception. She tricks the tricksters—Jacob and Laban—and neither of them ever know that she is the one who stole the gods. And she does so in way that seems like a feminine cliché: by using the excuse of her period.

- Leah and Rachel are angry that their father has treated them unfairly within a patriarchal system. How would this story be different if they were to challenge that system?
- In news stories, what language do writers use that makes women injured in conflict seem like objects?
- Is Rachel the hero in this story?

1 CORINTHIANS 7:25–40

Unmarried and Widows

Paul begins this text with the statement "I have no command of the Lord" (1 Cor. 7:25). This is a good reminder for pastors that not all of Scripture was written as a direct command from God. Instead, this portion of the letter is that of a pastor responding to questions from a church and giving his own opinion "as one who by the Lord's mercy is trustworthy" (7:25). He ends the text with "I think that I too have the Spirit of God" (7:40), suggesting that there are others making different claims than the ones he does here, and these others may also be invoking the Spirit of God.

Earlier in the chapter, Paul sets out his sexual ethic: he thinks it is better for everyone to remain unmarried, as he is (7:8), but if they cannot practice self-control, it is "better to marry than to be aflame with passion" (7:9). In this text, Paul explains he has this advice: "I want you to be free from anxieties" (7:32). From Paul's perspective, people who are married are divided: they need to pay attention to both the affairs of the Lord and the affairs of the world (7:32–34). By contrast, he believes that people who are not married only need to pay attention to the affairs of the Lord (7:32–34). Even though Paul clearly thinks that it is better for people to be unmarried and celibate, he knows that is not possible for everyone and reassures them that marriage is not a sin.

Next, Paul specifically addresses a man who is "not behaving properly toward his fiancée," literally, "his virgin" (7:36).[6] In Jewish and Roman marriages at the time, there were two stages: a betrothal, or binding pledge; and nuptials, or consummation.[7] Paul's focus solely on men here is a strange contrast to the earlier verses that talk about the rights of both husbands and wives (7:3–5). Commentators have suggested that Paul may be addressing engaged couples who have sworn to remain celibate, or couples who have entered into celibate relationships, or "spiritual marriages."[8] One explanation is that Paul addresses men because men had the active role in making marriages.[9] However, the lack of concern for the virgins' choice is troubling and suggests that Paul is making the women compromise; they are in a more socially vulnerable position.[10]

One of the bases for Paul's advice here is to remain as they are "in view of the impending crisis" (7:26). This can be translated in two ways: either the troubles that Christians are experiencing, or the tribulations Paul expects as the present age passes away (7:31).[11] Paul's belief that he is living in the end of the age frames all of his suggestions—particularly that they remain as they are (7:26), because he believes that Christ will soon return.[12] Accordingly, Paul suggests that people live in structures and relationships "as if not" (7:28–31), finding their value in God instead of the structures of the world.[13] For pastors in an age of climate change, this may seem familiar. It can be difficult to see the point of making individual changes when it seems likely that the world as one knows it is in impending crisis.

Finally, Paul addresses whether widows should remarry after their husbands die (7:39–40). Paul is consistent: he says that a widow is free to marry, but "more blessed if she remains as she is" (7:39–40). The way Paul addresses each of these groups individually gives the reader a sense of how the church in Corinth has framed their questions to him. Paul takes the approach of setting forth a general principle—it is better not to marry, but marriage is not a sin—and then he applies it to each individual situation. Through his repetition, the reader gets a sense of Paul as a pastor who wishes his church would respond in one way, but who is making space for those who, as he knows, will make different choices—certainly something with which modern preachers can identify.

- What questions do you think the church in Corinth asked Paul to get these responses?
- How does this text show how our ethical responses are framed by our understanding of what is happening in the world?
- Do you see similarities between Paul's concerns about the end times and concerns in your congregation?

Eighteenth Sunday in Ordinary Time

GENESIS 34:1–29

Dinah

Many of the themes in the tragic and disturbing story of Dinah will be familiar to people who grew up in purity culture, beginning with how little Dinah is present. In a text that is ostensibly about her, Dinah only appears in the first two verses—when she goes out to visit the women of the land and encounters Hamor (Gen. 34:1–2)—and later, when her brothers take Dinah out of Shechem's house (34:26). The text never reveals how Dinah feels about any of the things that are happening to her, instead focusing on the reactions and emotions of the men around her: Shechem, his father Hamor, Dinah's brothers, and her father, Jacob.

This removal of Dinah from her own story is unfortunate because her perspective would help to clear up the central mystery in the text: what happened between Dinah and Shechem? There are two opposing interpretations, and both have support within the language of the text.[1] The traditional understanding is that Shechem raped Dinah. The NRSV translation takes that approach, saying that Shechem "lay with her by force" (34:2). However, this can be translated as Shechem "slept with her, and humiliated her," as in the CEB translation. The word can mean rape or when a man puts a woman in a difficult social situation by having consensual sex with her before marriage.[2] In that situation, the proper recourse is for the man to marry the woman (Deut. 22:29), which Shechem attempts to do (Gen. 34:4).

This text may be intended as a warning against intermarriage between Israelites and Canaanites. The text begins by saying that Dinah "went out

188

to visit the women of the region" (34:1), implying that Dinah is trading with Canaanite women. Some scholars have suggested that by becoming close to these women, Dinah put herself in danger because the Canaanite women have brothers.[3] In U.S. purity culture, girls and young women receive similar messages: to only date and spend time with other Christians, or they may be in danger (and any sexual violence perpetrated against them if they fail to follow these rules is their own fault). The way Dinah disappears after her encounter with Shechem echoes in purity culture as well. Famously, Elizabeth Smart said that after she was abducted and raped, she felt like a "chewed-up piece of gum."[4] She had been taught that those who have sex before marriage had lost their value, and that is how she saw herself in the wake of the crime against her. Like Dinah, victims of rape in purity culture disappear from their own stories.

The text instead turns to the reactions of Dinah's brothers and how two of Dinah's full brothers (Simeon and Levi) engage in violence in response. Like their deceitful father, Dinah's brothers trick Shechem, Hamor, and all of the men of the city to be circumcised (34:13–17). Then, when the men of the city are still in pain and recovering from the circumcision, the brothers attack, killing all the males. Perhaps the brothers see circumcision as equivalent sexual violence to the violence done to their sister, but they go much farther in their retribution. Horrifyingly, they capture all the women of the city and make them their prey (34:29)—strongly implying that they, in turn, rape all these women.[5]

The final exchange between Jacob and his sons reveals how little they care about the lives of those they have killed and raped. Jacob says to his sons that they have gone too far and made him "odious to the inhabitants of the land." He fears that the Canaanites and the Perizzites will work together to attack him and his household (34:30). In the final verse, Simeon and Levi respond simply, "Should our sister be treated like a whore?" Regardless of what happened between Dinah and Shechem, she was not treated like a sex worker (given money in exchange for sex). The brothers' words show that they care more about the perceived slight to their honor and reputation than about what actually happened to Dinah.

- This story provides examples of terrible ways to respond to sexual violence. What are some ways that churches can be supportive of people who have experienced sexual violence?
- How would this story be different if it had been told from Dinah's perspective?
- What are the ways that churches implicitly or explicitly perpetuate purity culture when talking about stories like this?

1 CORINTHIANS 14:26–40

Women Speaking

This text and others like it have been used as a weapon against women for centuries. Despite all the evidence in the New Testament of women speaking, prophesying, and leading in the church, people have pointed to these verses to silence women and say that they cannot preach. For those who care about women preaching, this text is unavoidable. Rather than ignoring it, preachers should address it directly, put it in context, and face the harm that it has done and continues to do in the church.

The verses about women speaking in the church are part of a larger framework that Paul is providing for the church in Corinth, about how to organize their worship. He suggests that a variety of people lead parts of the worship, including "a hymn, a lesson, a revelation, a tongue, or an interpretation" (1 Cor. 14:26). He is concerned with the disorganized worship in Corinth, and he wants to limit the speaking in tongues and prophecy to two or three at the most, with people speaking one by one (14:27–31). Paul is concerned that otherwise the disorderly approach will invite criticism from outsiders.[6]

Many commentators have suggested that the verses on women being silent in the church were added later, as a marginal gloss (comments added in the margin of a manuscript by a later reader that eventually are incorporated into the text).[7] There are some stylistic differences to suggest this, such as the way the writer authoritatively appeals to "the law" in a prescriptive way, unlike the way Paul elsewhere refers to the law or uses the law as an illustration (e.g., 9:8; 14:21).[8] However, there is no manuscript evidence to support this claim.[9]

Other commentators have argued that this is in response to a specific problem (and group of women) in Corinth. The Greek word translated as "women" can refer to either adult women or wives.[10] Accordingly, 14:34 could be translated as "wives should be silent in the churches." This translation makes sense in context, when the author goes on to say, "If there is anything they desire to know, let them ask their husbands at home" (14:35). With this reading, the specific problem Paul is addressing is of wives interrupting worship to ask their husbands questions. What is shameful is the interruption—the type of speech—not women speaking in general.

A narrow reading of these verses also fits in the larger context of 1 Corinthians. Earlier, Paul assumes that women will pray and prophesy—two things that people do during worship—and he says only that women should wear head coverings during worship (11:2–15).[11] Paul also frequently refers to women he has worked with in ministry, such as Phoebe, whom he names as a deacon; Prisca, a leader of a church; and Junia, an apostle (Rom. 16:1–5,

7). Within the text, in addition, women are the third group of people—after those speaking in tongues and those prophesying—that Paul has called to exercise restraint or be silent (14:27–31).[12]

Ultimately, it does not really matter whether this was part of the original text or what Paul meant when he wrote this; what matters is the harm that it has caused. There is clear evidence in the Bible that God calls women to lead and to speak in public (e.g., Acts 2:1–18). Arguments against the language in these texts represent an effort to deal with our embarrassment with them, but they are part of the biblical canon.[13] Christians must decide whether they will trust God to call whomever God wishes to call to speak, preach, and lead. Who are we to point to a few sentences in letters to individual churches and say that trumps God's calling?

- Which of the arguments about this text are most compelling for you? How do you wrestle with the text?
- How have you seen gifts of preaching and leadership in women in the church?
- How do you respond to difficult texts in the Bible?

Nineteenth Sunday in Ordinary Time

GENESIS 39:1–20

Potiphar's Wife

The story of Joseph and Potiphar's wife is part of the Joseph novella, and it comes immediately after the chapter on Joseph's brother Judah and Tamar, Judah's daughter-in-law. This placement is important because the two stories have similar themes: both involve sexually aggressive foreign women, a common trope in the Hebrew Scriptures (cf. Prov. 5:3–4).[1] In their reception history, however, Tamar is celebrated as a heroine while Potiphar's wife is considered a villainess.

There are complicated power dynamics in this story. Joseph is enslaved in Potiphar's house, but he is also in control of everything. The passage begins by describing Joseph's handsome physique (Gen. 39:6). The Hebrew repeats itself to emphasize how handsome Joseph is.[2] This gives Joseph a kind of sexual power. Potiphar's wife is theoretically in a position of power, as the lady of the house, but when she tells Joseph to lie with her, he refuses by pointing out that she belongs to Potiphar (39:7–9). Even though she is free and he is enslaved, he sees her as an object owned by her husband.

For several reasons, what follows can be challenging for present-day preachers. It is a story of a false accusation of rape. Joseph and Potiphar's wife are alone in the house, so it becomes his word against hers. It seems clear that an attempted sexual assault occurred: the text states that Potiphar's wife tried to assault Joseph, but he escaped.[3] This may be more complicated than a simple assault, however. Many other passages in the Hebrew Scriptures demonstrate that enslaved women were sexually available to their masters (e.g.,

Gen. 16; 30:3–13); in this case, Joseph refused to be sexually available to the wife of the man who enslaved him.

The dynamics between Joseph and Potiphar's wife reveal some cultural fears about women. It underscores the idea of a righteous man and a seductive woman. This text may be an example of female sexual agency, but the idea that women use their agency to falsely accuse men of rape is troubling. These fears about women are not limited to an ancient Near East audience. This is a story that has captured people's imagination for millennia, and it has been portrayed in various ways. For example, the way the story is retold in the musical *Joseph and the Amazing Technicolor Dreamcoat* shows a fear of "free love" and independent women.

One way to approach this text is to pay attention to who is ultimately harmed the most. After this accusation, Joseph is thrown into prison (39:20). In the end, the enslaved foreigner with the least amount of power is the one who suffers the most harm. As far as Potiphar is concerned, Joseph can stay there indefinitely. Yet Joseph eventually wins his way out of prison. In that way, this text is reminiscent of lynching stories from the U.S. South, where white mobs claimed to protect the sexuality of white women by lynching black men. Although the white women in that culture had less power than the white men, the women participated in their own objectification by accusing black men. As a result, the black community—the people with the least power—suffered the most harm.

- What are the power dynamics at play in this text? Who has the most power and who has the least?
- What more would you like to know about what occurred between Joseph and Potiphar's wife?
- How have stories about false rape accusations harmed victims of sexual assault?

MARK 10:2–16

Divorce

At first glance, the two parts of this text do not seem to go together: Jesus' teaching on divorce and his invitation to the children appear to be separate stories. It might be tempting for the preacher to skip over the verses on divorce and focus instead on Jesus' call to let the little children come to him. That would be understandable, given the ways that the portion on divorce has been used in harmful ways: both to make people stay in miserable or even abusive marriages and also as justification for excluding queer people. But reading these passages together, in the political context of the time, gives the reader a more expansive and inclusive view of God's plan for the ordering of creation.

When these Pharisees ask Jesus whether it is lawful for a man to divorce his wife (Mark 10:2), that question does not seem like much of a test. Jesus turns the question back on them because it has an obvious answer: a man may write a certificate of dismissal and divorce his wife (Deut. 24:1–4).[4] This is a much more fraught question, however, given the political context. Not much earlier, John the Baptist had been arrested and executed for telling Herod that it was not lawful for him to have his brother's wife (Mark 6:17–18). By asking the more straightforward question about divorce, the Pharisees are trying to trick Jesus into making a similar statement about divorce and remarriage in Herod's family.[5]

Jesus does not take the bait. Instead, he appeals to God's desire for the ordering of creation in Genesis (Mark 10:6). Although some people have used this verse restrictively, to argue that Jesus himself says that marriage should be limited to a man and a woman, Jesus' intention here is not to create a new marriage statute. Instead, he is pointing to the way God put people into relationships with each other in the beginning of creation.[6] In this created order, there is mutuality between the genders: "God made them male and female" (10:6). God blesses the unions that people make, and breaking relationships is not part of that ideal (10:9). In a brilliant legal argument, Jesus sidesteps the political culture war that the group of Pharisees want him to address and instead points to God's ideal for creation.

When the disciples privately push him for more explanation on the matter, Jesus makes a surprising statement about the mutuality between husband and wife. Rather than following the patriarchal tradition that only a woman can commit adultery against her husband, Jesus puts husband and wife on the same level: if a man divorces his wife and marries another, he commits adultery against her, and if a woman divorces her husband and marries another, she commits adultery against him (10:11).[7] This is in line with his earlier statements about the equality of genders in God's ordering of creation.

The move from this teaching on divorce to Jesus' interaction with children demonstrates how expansive and inclusive God's ideal for the kingdom is. At the time, children were not considered persons in their own right, and they had no power.[8] But when Jesus learns that his disciples are sending the children away, he counters that by telling them to bring the children to him. By including the children, Jesus also invited those caring for the children (most likely women) to hear his teaching.[9]

For those preaching on this text, it is essential to know the congregation and to think through how the words of Jesus will sound. If there are people who have suffered abuse or are grieving the ends of their marriages, they may not be able to hear anything other than the literal meaning of what Jesus has said. If there are queer people in the congregation who have had these words used against them, the language may be re-traumatizing. With care, however, the preacher may be able to point to God's hope for healthy relationships and an expansive, inclusive view of humanity, like the one in God's original creation.

- These Pharisees are using hot-button political issues of the day to try to trick Jesus. What kinds of arguments might they make today?
- When Jesus speaks about divorce, does it seem like his intention is to create a new law?
- What kinds of people might the disciples try to keep away from Jesus if he were speaking today?

Twentieth Sunday in Ordinary Time

EXODUS 1:8–2:10

Shiphrah and Puah

Who are Shiphrah and Puah? They do not appear anywhere else in Scripture, but they serve an important purpose in this story. These two women are midwives, though their ethnicity is unclear. The Hebrew can be translated to show them as Hebrew midwives or as Egyptian midwives to the Hebrews.[1] They act the way they do because they fear God; this is the first mention of God in the book of Exodus (Exod. 1:17). In their profession, these women interact with the highest person in the land, the king; and the lowest, enslaved Hebrew women. They are young enough to have children, and God gives them families because of what they do (1:21).[2] They are unafraid when they stand before the king. And, unlike the king, they are named.

By contrast with the brave midwives, the unnamed king of Egypt acts out of fear. Pharaoh is introduced as a king "who did not know Joseph," which could mean that he did not care about Joseph (1:8).[3] He is afraid that the numerous Israelites will side with Egypt's enemies in a war and escape, so he oppresses them with forced labor (1:9–11). But once the king begins down this path, he has to continue oppressing the Israelites more and more: with hard service (1:14), by attempting to secretly kill the boys through the midwives (1:16), and then through open genocide (1:22). But by doing so, he creates the conditions that he fears: the Israelites will rise up and leave.

Pharaoh singles out the boy babies because in early ancient Israel, ethnicity was patrilineal. Eliminating the males would wipe out the people in a generation.[4] Ironically, women and girls undermine his plan.[5] First, the mid-wives see to it that the baby boys are not killed (1:17). Later, Moses' mother and sister hide the baby Moses (2:3–4). Finally, Pharaoh's own daughter saves the baby and raises him as her own (2:5–10). Pharaoh might have done better if he had targeted the baby girls!

When Pharaoh asks the midwives why they allowed the boys to live, the midwives respond, "Because the Hebrew women are not like the Egyptian women; for they are vigorous and give birth before the midwife comes to them" (1:19). Evidently the king believes Shiphrah and Puah; he does not punish them. Why would he believe this? One explanation is that he and the other Egyptians have dehumanized the Hebrew women. To them, the Israelites are like animals and do not have the same physiology as the superior Egyptians. Another explanation is that midwifery is women's work, which the king does not bother to try to understand.

The unnamed mothers in this text also act heroically by continuing to give birth in the face of oppression and danger. It is unclear whether the midwives have communicated to the Israelite mothers that the king has ordered them to kill the baby boys. Even if they do not know it, these mothers are bringing new life into a hostile and oppressive regime, where the best that they can hope for their sons is hard labor. But they persist and continue their lineage. Some commentators have suggested that God is giving them the vigor to give birth in the face of such hardship.[6]

Later, Moses will directly confront Pharaoh and lead his people to freedom. The midwives do not engage in this kind of direct confrontation. Instead, they work within the system and use cunning to achieve their goals. This text demonstrates that their approach is valid: it is because of Shiphrah and Puah that Moses is later able to resist Pharaoh. These midwives keep the Israel-ites alive for a generation. We should remember their names as examples of people who resist oppression and abuse of power wherever it occurs.

- How do you read this story if Shiphrah and Puah are Israelites? If they are Egyptians?
- What are other examples of resistance from people working within an oppressive system?
- What are some examples of times when people in power have dehuman-ized oppressed people and believed that they do not have the same bio-logical or emotional responses?

GALATIANS 4:21–30

Hagar and Sarah

In this text, where Paul writes to the church in Galatia and uses the story of Hagar and Sarah to make his argument, context is key. Taken out of context, Paul's argument may seem anti-Jewish, but the context for this argument is actually a fight between Christian missionaries. Paul is responding to a report that Christian missionaries have been telling the Gentile Christians in Galatia that they must be circumcised (i.e., "subject to the law," Gal. 4:21) to be true descendants of Abraham.[7] Accordingly, Paul reads the story of Abraham to lead to the opposite conclusion: it is the uncircumcised Gentile Christians who are "children of the promise, like Isaac" (4:28).[8]

This letter is essentially a sermon, and the allegorical reading of the story of Sarah and Hagar is its climax: Paul is using the Scripture to show that "the law" supports his position. He first explains that the story of Abraham's two wives is an allegory (4:24). The free woman (Sarah, though she is never named) corresponds to "the promise" and the Jerusalem above; the enslaved woman (Hagar) corresponds to "the law" and the present Jerusalem (4:25–26). Taken out of context, this can be a pitfall for Christian interpreters, who assume that Paul means the Hebrew Scriptures/Judaism versus the New Testament/Christianity. This is not what Paul intends. In Galatians, these two women represent two ways of "begetting" converts: through the flesh (circumcision) or through the promise.[9] Ultimately, he argues that "the law" in Genesis 21:10 is telling the Galatians to "drive out the slave and her child" (Gal. 4:30)—by which he means the rival missionaries![10]

In some ways, this sermon from Paul is extremely effective. He is preaching to a church that is insecure about its connection to its new faith. Through this allegorical retelling of the story of Sarah and Hagar, he gives the church in Galatia a way, through Scripture, to feel confident in its connection to the covenant between God and Abraham. He also successfully argues that they should throw out his rivals and instead listen to him. When the text is read in the specific context Paul intends for it, the sermon is persuasive and moving.

Unfortunately, read out of context, it has done much harm. As noted above, interpreters have used this to argue that Jews are part of the "old covenant" and Christians are the "new covenant." These arguments have led to supersessionist interpretations of Scripture (that Christians replace Jews as God's people) and Christian violence against Jews.[11] In addition, Christians have used the stories of Hagar in Genesis and this retelling in Galatians to legitimize the enslavement, sexual exploitation, and forced motherhood of black women in the United States and elsewhere.[12]

Although on its surface this is a text about women in the Bible, it is not actually about the women or their stories. Paul uses these women for his own purposes. The force of his allegory depends on the institution of slavery and an understanding that women can be used sexually.[13] Paul completely leaves out the divine promise to Hagar and her descendants and the rescue of her son.[14] He also uses Sarah's words out of context. Contrary to his assertion, it is not "law" when Sarah commands Abraham to send Hagar and Ishmael away (Gal. 4:30; Gen. 21:10). Paul's sermon shows the danger of trying to convert narrative into a command: it twists Scripture and strips the text of context and nuance.

This is a useful text for preachers, however, because deconstructing Paul's sermon in this text gives the reader or listener practice for critically reflecting on other sermons. The preacher can use this text as an example to show how a preacher's understanding of Scripture influences the outcome of an argument. Paul's use of Scripture demonstrates the importance of understanding the original context of Scripture and the intent of the writers. Finally, it shows that Scripture was written in and for a specific time and place and, taken out of that context, it may not make sense or may lead to harm.

- How is Paul's sermon effective? How does it set up the potential for harm?
- How does Paul use Scripture to make his point? What are the differences between his description of the story of Hagar and Sarah and the stories in Genesis?
- What questions does this text raise for you to consider when you are listening to sermons?

Twenty-First Sunday in Ordinary Time

EXODUS 4:18–26

Zipporah

This strange story about Zipporah and Moses feels like a dream. It also bears similarities to other times when God appears in the night, unknowable and threatening. The closest parallel is the story of Jacob wrestling with the angel at Peniel (Gen. 32:22–32). Both encounters occur at night, with no explanation for the attack. But unlike Jacob, who sent his wives across the ford ahead of him (Gen. 32:22), Moses has his wife, Zipporah, with him (Exod. 4:25). This leads to a quite different outcome!

We know a little about Zipporah's life and family from other passages. Her father, called Jethro here (he is called Reuel and Hobab in other passages),[1] is a priest of Midian (2:16). Zipporah has six sisters, and these seven women first appear together, filling troughs to water their father's flock (2:16). When some local shepherds drive them away, Moses comes to their defense and waters their flock (2:17). Jethro tells his daughters to invite Moses to break bread with them, and he gives Zipporah to Moses in marriage (2:20–21). Zipporah and Moses have two sons: Gershom and Eliezer (18:3–4).

In the lead-up to the attack, God instructs Moses to return to Egypt and tell Pharaoh to let the Israelites go. For the first time, God says, "Israel is my firstborn son" (4:22). Previously, God has referred to the Israelites as "my people" (cf. 3:7), but here, God has an explicitly parental relationship with the people.[2] Likely this is to draw a parallel between the suffering of the Israelites and the coming deaths of the firstborn sons of Egypt (4:23). However, it also reminds us of God's command to Abraham to sacrifice his son,

Isaac (Gen. 22:1–19). Firstborn sons are especially precious and vulnerable in these books.

After this pronouncement comes the attack in the night, while Moses and his family are on their journey back to Egypt. The Lord meets Moses and tries to kill him (Exod. 4:24). This portion of the Hebrew is unclear: the pronouns could mean that God attacks either Moses or his son.[3] Either way, Zipporah knows what to do. She is the daughter of a priest, and she engages in a blood ritual, cutting off her son's foreskin with a flint (4:25).[4] Again, the Hebrew is ambiguous: Zipporah either touches the foreskin to Moses' feet, saying, "You are a bridegroom of blood to me," or she throws it at God's feet, saying, "You are a blood father-in-law to me."[5] (The repetition of her words in 4:25–26 makes it seem important, but the meaning has been lost.[6] In addition, as in other texts, feet may be a euphemism for genitals.)[7] By doing so, Zipporah is triumphant! She has used this ritual to protect her family, and Moses is safe to continue on his journey to Egypt.

The ambiguity and strangeness of this passage may make preachers wary about preaching it, but these characteristics also lead to riches for reflection. One way to approach it could be through the relationship between Zipporah and Moses. They have experienced a terrifying and traumatic event together. For some spouses, that kind of experience leads to deeper closeness: this is one possible interpretation of Zipporah's pronouncement. But for others, traumatic events lead to separation. After this, Zipporah largely disappears from the narrative. Another approach could be to compare this to other stories of night encounters with God, in the Bible and in people's lives. Although many things are unclear in this narrative, at its heart it points to the deep mystery of God.

- What explanation of this story is most compelling? Why?
- This part of the Bible includes many stories threatening firstborn sons. How does that context inform how you read the text where God says Israel is God's firstborn son?
- How can we engage with texts where God is threatening?

EPHESIANS 5:21–33

Wives and Husbands

The household code in this text (and others like it) presents a challenge for Christians today. This text is part of our Scripture, which we read as continuing to speak to the church, but it reflects a cultural system, hierarchy, and understanding of humanity that is very different from our culture now. While many scholars have tried to cast this text in a feminist light or explain how it is superior to other contemporary household codes, a better approach is for the preacher to read the text in the context in which it was written and address the ways that it has been and continues to be harmful when taken out of that setting.

A household code, or pattern of instruction on duties of household members, was a well-established genre for Stoic, Greco-Roman, and Hellenistic Jewish writers at the time of the early church.[8] These codes would describe the relationships between people in the household: husband and wife, parents and children, and masters and enslaved people.[9] Within this genre, the household code in Ephesians follows the typical structure with one key difference: the author uses the structure of the household to describe how the church should ideally operate, comparing the relationship between Christ and the church to marriage.[10] One reason this text and others focus so much on the household is that the early church began as a household movement. Believers met in private households for meeting spaces for the first two centuries CE.[11] Thus the household served as a model for the church.

Arguments that the author is calling for a more just social ordering than other household codes are rather unconvincing and seem more like a way of apologizing for the text. Much has been made of the first verse, with scholars asserting that the command to "be subject to one another" (Eph. 5:21) describes an egalitarian relationship between the spouses. However, the following verses show a clear hierarchy, with the husband as the head of the wife, "just as Christ is the head of the church" (5:23).[12] Despite the calls for husbands to love their wives and care for them, this text has provided husbands with justification for dominating and abusing their wives.[13]

Ephesians is one of the letters that has disputed authorship, and some scholars have argued that this text is contrary to the ways in which Paul describes working with women in ministry elsewhere; none of the undisputed letters by Paul call for wives to be subject to their husbands.[14] Whether someone other than Paul wrote this letter would not make it any less Scripture, but it could place the text in a different historical and religious context than Paul's ministry.[15] It is possible that this reinforcement of the traditional family structure is rooted in the desire to reassure outsiders that people in the church can live peaceably in society.[16] For modern readers, it can be disappointing to see the church move toward fitting the culture of the Roman Empire instead of continuing the trend of the earlier church's move toward more liberating roles for women.[17]

In addition to the sermon providing context for the household code, a potential avenue for preaching on this text is for the speaker to examine the various metaphors at work. The primary metaphor is of Christ as married to the church (5:32), which draws on Hebrew Scriptures, such as Hosea, which use the metaphor of husband and wife.[18] But here, unlike in Hosea, the church is not an unfaithful spouse.[19] The author also calls on the metaphor of the church as the body of Christ (5:30). Another analogy is that the husband is like Christ, who gave himself up for the church (5:25). And the wife is like the husband's own body (5:28). Each of these metaphors is useful to an extent, but they also break down when stretched too far.

- How does understanding the context of household codes impact the way you read this text?
- How should preachers and congregations approach texts that describe a different historical and social context than ours?
- What metaphors in this text spark your imagination?

Twenty-Second Sunday
in Ordinary Time

EXODUS 15:1–11, 20–21

Miriam

Miriam is the first woman named as a prophet in the Bible.[1] She sings the Song of the Sea in this text immediately after the people of Israel have escaped from Pharaoh, singing to God about how God "has triumphed gloriously," throwing the Egyptian horse and rider into the sea (Exod. 15:21). Miriam's song—along with the Song of Moses in the preceding verses—is thought to be among the earliest compositions in the Bible, and some scholars believe that the Song of Moses was originally attributed to Miriam.[2]

Miriam is the sister of Aaron and Moses. Although she is not named in Exodus 2, she traditionally has been known as the older sister in that story.[3] She hid in the reeds when Moses' mother placed him in a basket in the river, after Pharaoh ordered the midwives to kill all the Jewish baby boys. Miriam "stood at a distance, to see what would happen to him" (2:4). When the daughter of Pharaoh saw the basket and the baby, Miriam stepped out and said, "Shall I go and get you a nurse from the Hebrew women to nurse the child for you?" (2:7). She then went and called her own mother to be a nurse for her brother.

In Exodus, Miriam leads her people. After this passage (in Exod. 15), the next time Miriam appears in the biblical text is in Numbers, where she and Aaron are in conflict with Moses.[4] They speak out against Moses "because of the Cushite woman whom he had married" (Num. 12:1). The meaning of this verse is unclear: Are Miriam and Aaron xenophobic? Or is this merely descriptive, and the issue is unrelated to Moses' wife's national origin? In this conflict, Aaron and Miriam say, "Has the LORD spoken only through Moses? Has [God] not spoken through us also?" (Num. 12:2). God has spoken through Miriam the prophet, when Miriam was led to sing the Song of the Sea. But this angers God, who comes to speak to them in a pillar of cloud (Num. 12:5–9). When God leaves, Miriam has become leprous (Num. 12:10). Aaron asks Moses to pray for Miriam, and he does. Miriam is cured in seven days, and this is the last time she appears in Scripture until her death (Num. 20:1–2).

Regardless of what would happen to Miriam later, in the moment reported in Exodus 15, she is a leader and a prophet. She names what has happened to her people: they have been liberated from the oppression of slavery and are free. Miriam bursts into song, praising God,[5] and the Israelites are prepared for this. Even though they are running for their lives, the women have tambourines with them! So, when the prophet Miriam takes a tambourine in her hand and sings, all the women go out after her with tambourines and dancing (15:20). Filled with the Holy Spirit, Miriam sings about what the Lord has done for her and for her people.

Miriam is often overshadowed by her two famous brothers, but preachers can use this text to show that she is a leader in her own right. Her story also raises the question of what makes someone a prophet. Readers know that Miriam is a prophet because the Scripture says so, but her story does not include specific examples of prophetic acts. In this song, however, she speaks about what God has done on behalf of her people. This is a prophetic act—to name how God is at work amid people. Through her story, Miriam provides a feminine prophetic figure, who will be echoed in other women named as prophets, such as Deborah, Huldah, and Anna.

- What are characteristics of a prophet? How is Miriam prophetic?
- How do you envision the conflict between Miriam and Aaron and Moses? Who do you think is in the right?
- What would the story of the exodus be like if it had been told from Miriam's point of view?

PHILIPPIANS 4:1–9

Euodia and Syntyche

Near the end of his letter to the church in Philippi, Paul names two women, Euodia and Syntyche, and urges them "to be of the same mind in the Lord" (Phil. 4:2). There is little information about these women, and they do not appear elsewhere. Based on this text, we do know a few things about Euodia and Syntyche: (1) they are women in the church in Philippi, (2) they are in some sort of conflict, and (3) their conflict is important enough for Paul to name it specifically (4:2). In addition, Paul wants his "loyal companion" to help them (4:3); this companion is most likely Epaphroditus, who was with Paul when he wrote this letter (2:25–30), is about to travel to Philippi, and will be present when the letter is read.[6] Paul says that Euodia and Syntyche have "struggled beside me in the work of the gospel" (4:3). Thus, Paul considers them coworkers, making them leaders in the church in Philippi. Finally, Paul says that their "names are in the book of life" (4:3), which records the names of every person destined for heaven.[7]

Beyond this, scholars have speculated about Paul's message regarding Euodia and Syntyche. Some suggest that the women's dispute is the purpose of the letter, which generally urges the church to be in agreement, using the same language as here (2:2), but now addresses the specific conflict.[8] The usual interpretation of these verses is that Euodia and Syntyche are in conflict with each other. It seems that Paul is being careful not to take sides: thus he uses the same verb and structure, "I urge," with each of the women.[9]

However, another possibility is that these women, Euodia and Syntyche, are in conflict with Paul. When Paul makes a similar plea to the church in Corinth to "be united in the same mind and the same purpose," he means the same mind as himself (1 Cor. 1:10; 4:14–21).[10] This reading makes Paul's exhortations in the following verses more pointed; he is encouraging the church to think on good and excellent things and to keep doing the things "that you have learned and received and heard and seen in me" (Phil. 4:9). In other words, he is instructing the church to follow him and the example of his life instead of these women. Otherwise, this merely appears to be a series of commands that do not seem to be connected.[11] By naming the women in a letter that will be read aloud in congregations, Paul may be trying to quash the women's disagreement with himself.[12]

Some commentators have suggested that Paul's rebuke of the women is gentle: he mentions them briefly and speaks warmly of their work. In addition, Paul addresses them by name, which he often does for his friends and fellow workers, but rarely for those with whom he disagrees.[13] It is hard to say how intense this conflict is or what Paul's take on it is because there is so little information for the women. Accordingly, they become a place for scholars, commentators, and preachers to project their own ideas about who these women are and what the conflict might be.

The gender of Euodia and Syntyche has impacted the way that this text has been read, leading to gender stereotyping and erasure. Some readers have seen them as bickering women and thereby missed or ignored their leadership in the church.[14] In the third century, Theodore, bishop of Mopsuestia, changed the name of Syntyche to Syntyches, a masculine name.[15] He claimed that this character was Euodia's husband and the jailer of Paul in Acts 16:27–34.[16] It may have seemed impossible to him that two women would be working together in ministry—one must be a man! But it is possible that he was right in seeing them as partners in life and ministry. Here they are named together, like Prisca and Aquila, or Tryphaena and Tryphosa (Rom. 16:3, 12).[17] In addition to highlighting the ministry of Euodia and Syntyche, preachers can use this text to talk about conflicts between church members. This text demonstrates how certain language we use to describe conflicts can be gendered. The preacher can draw on other examples of gendered language, as well as offering suggestions for conflict resolution.

- What else would you like to know about Euodia and Syntyche?
- What evidence suggests that they were in conflict with each other? That they were united and in conflict with Paul?
- Do you think that Euodia and Syntyche were a missionary couple like some of the other linked pairs that Paul names?

Twenty-Third Sunday
in Ordinary Time

NUMBERS 27:1–11

Mahlah, Noah, Hoglah, Milcah, and Tirzah

The story of Mahlah, Noah, Hoglah, Milcah, and Tirzah seems to be largely forgotten in Christian churches today, but it is very important in the Hebrew Scriptures. These sisters appear in five places in the Bible (Num. 26:33; 27:1–11; 36:1–12; Josh. 17:3–6; 1 Chr. 7:15).[1] They are women who sought justice in a male-dominated system, and through their persistence, they obtained it. Their story creates a legal precedent for daughters to inherit property, which comes directly from God. It also gives us a glimpse into the legal system of Israel at the time, as well as the theological underpinnings for that system.

When preaching this text, the best approach may be to retell the story, which probably is unfamiliar to most congregations. Immediately before this text is the census of the new generation (Num. 26:2–65), in which Moses names the men in the tribes of Israel and God instructs Moses on how to allocate the promised land among the families of the second generation.[2] But before Moses can allocate the land, the daughters of Zelophehad appear before Moses, Eleazar the priest, the leaders, and all the congregation (27:2). In this religious court, these sisters stand together to bring their case.

The legal issue is that their father, Zelophehad, died without sons (27:3). In Israel, only sons could inherit property; thus these daughters are left without an inheritance. However, the sisters' legal argument is not based on their inheritance rights. Instead, they argue that it is not right for their father's name to be taken away from his clan (27:4): perpetuating a man's name through sons was vital to the continued existence, or afterlife, of the deceased.[3] They note that their father was not part of the Korah rebellion; he died merely for the general sin of unfaithfulness (27:3).[4]

This legal issue is new for Moses, and he brings the case directly to God (27:5). God speaks to Moses and says that Mahlah, Noah, Hoglah, Milcah, and Tirzah are right (27:7). God tells Moses to allow these women to possess an inheritance from their father (27:7) and makes a general law from this specific case: "If a man dies, and has no son, then you shall pass his inheritance on to his daughter" (27:8). In addition, God says that this is "for the Israelites a statute and ordinance" (27:11), a designation that only occurs one other time (cf. 35:29).[5]

The sisters have won their case! But as so often happens in law, solving one problem leads to other legal issues. The sisters appear again a few chapters later, when the men of Manasseh come to Moses with the worry that these women will marry into another tribe and the inheritance would go to that tribe (36:1–4). Moses solves the problem by declaring that the sisters must marry within their father's tribe, so that the inheritance will not be transferred from one tribe to another (36:6–7). He makes this a general rule as well, for any other daughters who inherit from their fathers (36:8–9). Mahlah, Noah, Hoglah, Milcah, and Tirzah comply with this ruling and marry men in their own tribe (36:10–12).

The story is not completely over; the sisters appear one more time. After Moses' death, the sisters go to Joshua, the priest Eleazar, and the leaders and remind them, "The LORD commanded Moses to give us an inheritance along with our male kin" (Josh. 17:4). Without more discussion, Joshua gives the women their inheritance (17:6). After all these arguments and appearances, they finally have their inheritance. These women have challenged a legal system that was written without them in mind, God affirms that they are in the right, and with persistence, they receive the inheritance they are entitled to. They know they are in the right, state their case clearly, and are vindicated for their bravery and tenacity.

- Did you know the story of Mahlah, Noah, Hoglah, Milcah, and Tirzah? If so, in what context have you heard this story?
- What questions do you have about the legal system and patrilineal property rights in Israel after reading this text?
- How do you relate to these sisters?

COLOSSIANS 4:2–15

Nympha

Scholars do not agree whether the apostle Paul wrote this letter; there are differences in style, tone, and theological emphasis between Colossians and the undisputed letters of Paul.[6] If someone else wrote it, that author maintains the fiction that it is from Paul, written during one of his many imprisonments.[7] If Paul is the author, he probably wrote it not long before his death; if someone else wrote it, the author most likely wrote it shortly after his death.[8] The author refers to being in prison, hoping that God will "open a door" for him to share his ministry (Col. 4:3–4). He instructs the church in Colossae to "devote yourselves to prayer" and asks for prayers from the community (4:2).

Immediately before this text, the author instructs the church with a household code, telling wives to be subject to their husbands, children to obey their parents, and enslaved people to obey their masters (3:18–24). This context is important because it shows how much the church by this point had assimilated into the norms of the Roman Empire (for more on household codes, see the commentary on Eph. 5:21–33). The author is focused on how the church appears to outsiders (4:5). He even tells them to season their conversation with salt—that is, make it witty, attractive, and gracious (4:6).[9] The author clearly wants outsiders to recognize that the church is not a threat to society.[10] This move toward respectability is a far cry from the prophetic zeal and reimagined social structures of Pentecost and the early church in Acts!

The letter ends with a series of introductions and greetings to a remarkably diverse group, including Jews and Gentiles, a physician (Luke), and an enslaved man (Onesimus) (4:7–15).[11] The final greeting is to "Nympha and the church in her house" (4:15). This is the only place where Nympha appears in the Bible, but there are many things a reader can glean from this brief reference to her. The name Nympha means "bride."[12] As the host of a church in her house, she is a leader and authority.[13] She is probably a relatively wealthy woman, with a house large enough for the church members to meet in it.[14] She also appears to be an independent woman and not associated with a father, husband, or son.[15] Depending on the authorship of the letter, she may be someone living at the time of the writing and known to the writer.[16]

As with other female leaders in the New Testament, later scholars obscured her name and gender by changing the pronoun to a masculine "he" and calling her "Nymphas" (cf. Junia in Rom. 16:7). This is because both the masculine Nymphas and the feminine Nympha are written as Nymphan when used as a direct object.[17] However, there are no examples of Nymphas as a masculine name in Roman inscriptions, but the feminine Nympha is attested to over sixty times.[18] Most modern English translations of the Bible have corrected this error.

For preachers, this text is ripe with possibilities for preaching on how the church bends toward the surrounding culture for self-preservation. The author is so focused on how outsiders will see the church community that it dampens the gospel message. In churches today, many try to avoid difficult texts like the household codes (which do not appear in the Revised Common Lectionary!). But people in minority groups know the pressure of respectability politics and needing to behave in certain ways because otherwise it might reflect poorly on one's group or put them in danger. Those who are in the majority need to pay attention to how they are perpetuating and enforcing cultural norms. As the example of Nympha shows, if churches only expect leaders to look a certain way (i.e., as male), then the church will fail to recognize gifted leaders when they do not fit the expected mold.

- What are modern-day versions of household codes?
- How does the church perpetuate and enforce cultural norms?
- What can congregations do to fight back against these dominant narratives and encourage people from minority groups to grow in ministry?

Twenty-Fourth Sunday
in Ordinary Time

JUDGES 4:1–7

Deborah

The story of Deborah comes from two places: the narrative account in Judges 4 and the older poetry in Judges 5. Like the Song of the Sea, the song about Deborah is one of the oldest writings in the Bible.[1] The narrative account is the only part of Judges included in the Revised Common Lectionary. Perhaps this choice is because Deborah is the only judge that the Bible does not criticize. Or it may be because this story is near the beginning of the book and, unlike many of the stories of the judges, it has a triumphant ending.

The text begins with the cycle repeated throughout Judges: the people do what is evil in the eyes of the Lord, God punishes them, the people repent and cry for help, and God sends a judge to save them.[2] These "judges" generally fall into two categories: leaders who settle disputes or military leaders. Deborah is both, as well as a prophetess. She is the only judge in the book of Judges to be both a judge and a prophet, and she is the only female judge.[3] When Deborah sits under the palm of Deborah, she is in the center of Israel; the later battle takes place in the northern part of the country. This shows that people from all over Israel would come to her to ask for help. Other details about Deborah are unclear. Some translations say that she is the "wife of Lappidoth," but that can also be translated as "woman of the town Lappidoth," or "woman of torches / fiery woman."[4] It is also unclear whether she had children. The poem says that Deborah "arose as a mother in Israel" (Judg.

5:7), but that could mean that she is a metaphorical mother or leader rather than a literal mother.

In this passage, Deborah summons Barak and tells him to fight Sisera. She prophesies that the Lord will give Sisera into his hand. But immediately after this, Barak says that he will not go unless Deborah goes with him. Deborah agrees but says that God will sell Sisera into the hand of a woman (4:9). This leads into the story of Jael, who kills Sisera with a tent peg while he is taking refuge in her tent (4:21). Many interpreters have seen this as shameful for Barak—he would not go into battle without Deborah, so a woman killed his adversary—and shameful for Sisera to be killed by a woman. But it is an injustice to Deborah and to Jael to make their story all about men's shame. This is a story about a woman who is the leader of her people, and the better approach is for the preacher to keep her at the center of her own story. Rather than focus on Barak's theoretical weakness, the preacher can see this as an example of collaborative leadership.

The story of Deborah can also seem to create impossible expectations for a woman in leadership. Not only is Deborah a judge, but she is also a prophet and (possibly) a wife and mother, and the Bible doesn't say anything negative about her. But Deborah was not all things to all people, and she did not do everything by herself.[5] She calls to Barak, who leads the troops into battle, where God is victorious. She is not the one to take down Sisera: Jael accomplishes that. Deborah is faithful to what God calls her to be: a judge and a prophetess. And through the actions of all these faithful people, God is triumphant.

- How does the story of Deborah reflect collaboration in leadership?
- What are other examples of the expectation that women in leadership will be perfect examples? How does that impossible standard harm women?
- How would it change the story if Deborah had some flaws, like many of the male judges? Would that make her seem stronger or weaker?

1 TIMOTHY 2:1–15

Women Silent/Saved

This text is familiar to anyone who cares about women preaching in the Christian church. It is in the context of the letters to Timothy and Titus, which are known as the Pastoral Letters because they discuss issues that concern a pastor: the expectations for life in a Christian community and how the church should behave.[6] Scholars have questioned the authorship of these letters since the nineteenth century, and very few believe that Paul is their author.[7] The immediacy of Christ's return that appears in Paul's Letters is absent. Instead, the author focuses on how to preserve the reputation of the church, which is a small minority in the larger culture.[8]

The text begins with instructions on prayer, which include praying for kings and all who are in high positions "so that we may lead a quiet and peaceable life" (1 Tim. 2:2). This sets the context for the rest of the text: the author asserts that it is God's desire for believers to live quietly and peaceably (2:3). The way to do this is by being socially conservative, obedient to the state, and conforming to the Roman ideal of a patriarchal household.[9] The author follows a typical household code (for more on household codes, see the commentary on Eph. 5:21–33) and applies this to the church as a whole as a model for congregational behavior.[10] This approach is understandable because all the early churches met in private homes.[11]

The author has three sets of instructions to respond to behavior that threatens the goals of prayer and a quiet life. First, he addresses the men, saying that they must avoid anger and conflict (2:8). Second, he says that the women must dress modestly and decently because that is proper for those who revere God (2:9). This suggests that there may have been some wealthy women in the congregation, who had money to spend on fine clothing and jewelry.[12] Third, the author gets to the point that has been used against so many women: women must be silent and may not teach or have authority over a man (2:11–12).

Scholars have pointed out that the words "man" and "woman" here also mean "husband" and "wife," so it is likely that this is about the relationship between individual husbands and wives rather than men and women in groups.[13] This makes sense in the context of the household codes, which place the patriarch at the head of the household, as well as the expectation in the early church that husbands would teach their wives about the Christian faith at home (cf. 1 Cor. 14:34–35).[14]

The author supports his position by citing the creation story of Adam and Eve, arguing that because God formed Adam first, he has natural dominance, and that "the woman" was the one who was deceived and the transgressor (1 Tim. 2:13–14). However, this reading of Genesis ignores the creation story's declaration that God created humankind in God's image, male and female (Gen. 1:27), as well as Adam's culpability (3:17).[15] The author also makes the strange statement that women will be saved through childbirth (1 Tim. 2:15), the only place in the New Testament where gender factors into salvation.[16] Even though the author says, "The saying is sure" (cf. 3:1), he seems to be bending theology and Scripture to support cultural norms rather than the other way around.[17]

This may be a daunting subject for preachers, yet putting the text in its cultural context goes a long way. In addition, the preacher can remind their congregation that this text describes the author's ideal for Christian communities, not the reality of the early church. Indeed, the fact that the author felt the need to instruct women to be silent suggests that women were speaking and teaching![18] This text can also serve as a caution for congregations that are feeling pressure to conform to cultural norms instead of following the leading of the Spirit.

- Does God want us to have a quiet and peaceable life?
- How has the church used this text against women who feel led to preach and teach? Does this reflect God's will?
- How do churches bend theology and Scripture to fit cultural norms today?

Twenty-Fifth Sunday
in Ordinary Time

JUDGES 4:12–22

Jael

For those who expect a biblical heroine to be a certain way—a loyal wife, a nurturing mother, or even a victim of sexual violence—Jael subverts all those expectations. The first description of Jael is as a wife: she is the wife of Heber the Kenite (Judg. 4:17). As the descendants of Moses' father-in-law, the Kenites might be expected to be allies to the Israelites, but Heber has separated from the other Kenites and migrated far to the north.[1] Jael convinces Sisera to come into her tent because of the peace between his king and the clan of Heber (4:18), but she later turns on Sisera. It is unclear why she attacks her husband's ally, and Heber never appears.

As in other texts in the Hebrew Scriptures, Jael's tent is a place of feminine domesticity, and in this text, Jael takes on the role of nurturing mother. She covers Sisera with a rug, like a mother tucking a child into bed (4:18). When he asks her for water to drink, she instead gives him milk (4:19). As he drifts off, Sisera proves that he trusts Jael by sleeping in her presence and telling her to keep watch (4:20). He even tells her what to say if someone approaches, trusting that she will do as he says (4:20).

But Sisera has put his trust in the wrong woman. Jael softly approaches Sisera like a lover, then uses a tent peg and hammer—symbols of domesticity and tools that a woman would use to pitch a tent—to kill him (4:21).[2] The description of Jael's attack is visceral: she drives the peg into his temple until it goes into the ground (4:21). It is even more graphic in the song in the following

216

chapter, where it says, "She crushed his head, she shattered and pierced his temple" (5:26). And this poetic version contains more mother imagery: Sisera falls "between her feet" (5:27 ESV), like a bloody child that she has birthed.[3]

The older, poetic version of the text puts this story in a different light by introducing another woman, Sisera's mother. In the song, Sisera's mother waits for her son and wonders why he is taking so long to return (5:28). She assumes that it is because he has been triumphant in battle and speculates that he and his men are dividing the spoil, including "a girl or two for every man" (5:30). Sisera's mother expects her son to rape the women of the land that he has conquered; she allows time for that.[4] But instead, a woman penetrates Sisera: Jael prevents him from committing future sexual violence by hammering a stake through his skull.

Jael is difficult to categorize. Is she a seductress, inviting an unknown man into her tent to sleep? Or is she responding to the shift in power with the Israelite victory? The text does not pay attention to Jael's point of view or motivation; it merely reports what Jael says and does. When Barak comes in pursuit of Sisera, she goes to meet him as she met Sisera, then brings Barak into her tent to see his enemy with a tent peg in his temple (4:22). The author does not record Barak's response.

In the Bible, there are many celebrated stories of men engaging in extreme violence, but not many about women. This story of Jael may seem shocking in its violence, but she is celebrated in one of the earliest poems in the Bible: "Most blessed of women be Jael, the wife of Heber the Kenite, of tent-dwelling women most blessed" (5:24). This outsider fulfills Deborah's prophecy that "the LORD will sell Sisera into the hand of a woman" (4:9), and she secures the victory.

- The text does not give Jael's motivation for killing Sisera; what seems like the most likely reason that she decided to kill him?
- How does it feel to read about a woman engaging in this type of violence?
- Do you think that Jael was justified in killing a man who probably routinely raped women as spoils of war?

1 TIMOTHY 5:1–16

Widows

In this text, the author of 1 Timothy turns his attention to a specific group of people in the early church community: widows. At the time this text was written, the definition of widows was broader than modern readers might expect. At the time, the term described any woman who lacked a husband's protection and support, including those whose husbands had died, who were divorced, or whose husband was away for an extended period of time (such as soldiers).[5] In addition, these women were not necessarily economically disadvantaged; women owned one-third of all property and had revenue from the return of their dowry after their husbands' death or other forms of inheritance.[6]

Taking this context into account, it becomes clear why the author wants to distinguish between widows generally and those who are "really widows" (1 Tim. 5:3). The early church continued the Hebrew tradition of providing for widows (Deut. 24:17–22), and the author wants to provide support for those who are genuinely in need.[7] Accordingly, the author states that widows who have family members to support them should go there first (1 Tim. 5:4). If family members do not support the widows in their family, they are "worse than an unbeliever" (5:8). Wealthy widows provide another potential source of support; the author urges them to assist other widows, possibly by bringing them into their households (5:16; e.g., Acts 9:39).[8]

The author defines widows more narrowly in this text than in the broader culture: only particular widows are on the list that the community supports (5:9). These are the widows who have no family support, are over sixty, have only been married once, and are known for their good deeds (5:9–10). The author is skeptical about younger widows and describes them in gendered stereotypes, saying that they are gadabouts, gossips, and busybodies (5:13). He also fears that they will give in to their sexual desires and marry, violating their first pledge (5:11–12), which suggests that the widows on the list make a vow of celibacy.[9] This suspicion of younger women may stem from the author's concern about women spreading rival teachings (see 2 Tim. 3:6–7).[10] He would rather see them marry, bear children, and manage households (1 Tim. 5:14).

Some scholars have suggested that this regulation of widows constitutes a separate office of widows within the church, with parallels to the office of bishop (3:2–4). This type of office of widows is found in other church writings and inscriptions from the second and following centuries.[11] Widows in these communities were celibate Christians who engaged in teaching, prayer, hospitality, and other forms of ministry.[12] It is possible that the author of this letter is putting restrictions on who qualifies as a widow because he wants to limit the power and authority of these women, keeping the office only as a charity that provides for destitute women.[13] Women who have been engaging in "good works, hospitality, and caring for the afflicted" might be restricted to a life of prayer (5:5, 10).[14]

One of the author's primary concerns in this letter is how the church appears to outsiders.[15] He worries that widows who do not behave appropriately will give "the adversary"—probably hostile outsiders—an opportunity to revile the church (5:14).[16] He notes that some have already left to follow

Satan (5:15), referring to false teachings.[17] For preachers, this text gives an example of how the groups of people in the church most in need of support can also stimulate concerns about what the church will look like to outsiders. The various widows described in the text seem threatening because they fall outside the standard patriarchal structure of society at the time. Accordingly, preachers can use this text to talk about the people in society today who do not fit into the typical patterns, the anxieties they create in communities, and the gifts they have to offer the church.

- Who is the author of this text trying to protect? What are his concerns?
- What kinds of things do you envision these mentioned widows doing?
- What structures do our communities have in place to protect the vulnerable, like the widows in this text?

Twenty-Sixth Sunday
in Ordinary Time

JUDGES 11:29–40

Jephthah's Daughter

Feminist scholars have brought the tragic story of Jephthah's unnamed daughter to light over the past few decades. This text raises as many questions as it answers. Readers wonder why Jephthah makes his vow, why the daughter goes along with it, and why God remains silent instead of saving the daughter from slaughter, as God saved Isaac. Rather than trying to find easy answers to these questions, the text offers pastors an opportunity to lament abuse and make space for the stories of those who suffer at the hands of those who should protect them.

There is no clear answer to the question of why Jephthah makes his vow to kill whoever comes out of the doors of his house to meet him (Judg. 11:30–31). In *Texts of Terror*, Phyllis Trible argues that in making the vow, Jephthah is unfaithful. The spirit of the Lord is already upon Jephthah, but he does not trust it and instead attempts to manipulate God into victory.[1] Others have asserted that Jephthah does not intend to kill a *person*. The Hebrew is ambiguous: it could mean "whoever" or "whatever" first comes out of the house, and houses at the time typically had animals on the first level.[2] Yet the courtyard is also used for cooking and other domestic chores, a typical place for women to work.[3] Perhaps Jephthah is simply thoughtless, deciding to worry about the sacrifice later if it gets him the victory he wants in the moment.

Upon Jephthah's return, his daughter comes out to meet him with timbrels and dancing (11:34). Jephthah should have foreseen this because it is a customary way for women to celebrate victory in battle (cf. Exod. 15:20–21; 1 Sam. 18:6–7).[4] Jephthah does not tell his daughter directly about his vow, but she knows (Judg. 11:35–36). The daughter's response suggests that this is a familiar pattern in their family: her father makes impulsive decisions, and she bears the consequences. She takes his vow seriously and asks for two months with her friends before her death (11:37). It may seem strange to modern readers for her to "bewail [her] virginity," but this is not merely missing out on sex: the daughter is mourning the life that she will not have, including marriage and children. Her father's careless words have become a death sentence for her.

True to form, Jephthah's response is less thoughtful. First, he blames his daughter for being the first one out of the house, saying, "You have brought me very low; you have become the cause of great trouble to me" (11:35). As commentators have pointed out, this is a tragedy for him as well: she is his only daughter, and without her he will not have children to carry on his memory and family line.[5] But he offers no words of comfort to his daughter, instead focusing on himself, like an abusive father who tells his child, "You made me do this."

In the end, this turns into a yearly ritual of lament: the daughters of Israel go out for four days every year to lament Jephthah's daughter (11:39–40). In preaching this text, pastors can take their cue from these daughters of Israel. Sadly, there are still parents abusing their children today. This story creates an opening for the church community to lament the abuse that takes place, to mourn for children who suffer the consequences of their parents' terrible decisions. Like the daughters of Israel, we can create a liturgy of lament, a time to recognize that this happens, and to mourn as a community.

- Why would Jephthah make this kind of vow?
- Was Jephthah's daughter faithful in her response? Would it have been better for her to run away?
- How can churches create space and ritual to mourn abuse together?

2 TIMOTHY 1:3–7

Lois and Eunice

As noted in the commentaries for 1 Timothy, the Pastoral Letters most likely were written not by Paul but by an author writing in Paul's voice after his death (possibly as late as the mid-second century CE).[6] Because this text is so clearly meant to be in Paul's voice, I will refer to the author as Paul in this commentary. The setting for 2 Timothy is a letter from Paul in prison, probably in Rome. He has been abandoned by all but a few of his friends and is facing his imminent death.[7] Paul considers Timothy like a son to him; he is one of the most loyal members of his mission team (Phil. 2:22).[8]

Paul begins with gratitude to God and states that he worships God "as my ancestors did" (2 Tim. 1:3). This reference to his ancestors serves two purposes. First, it suggests that Christianity is an ancient religion. Romans had higher respect for older religions than for new cults.[9] Second, this shows the continuity of the Christian faith from Judaism. Paul's ancestors worshiped the same God that he does, and he sees his ministry as a continuation of his Jewish faith. This is notable, considering some of the anti-Jewish sentiment in parts of the New Testament.[10]

In a parallel move, Paul describes Timothy's faith as the faith that "lived first in your grandmother Lois and your mother Eunice" (1:5). According to Acts 16:1, Timothy's mother was a Jewish woman and Christian believer (though she is unnamed), and his father was a Greek.[11] Paul does not name any further male forebears, suggesting that they are not known. The historicity of these women is questionable: both ancient Jewish and Christian writers tended to provide additional information about people they venerated, including adding proper names.[12] Regardless of whether these women really existed, their inclusion illuminates some of the characteristics of the early church. It is unclear whether the faith of Timothy's grandmother Lois is Christian or Jewish faith.[13] If she was a Christian, Timothy is in the third generation of Christianity.[14] Alternatively, if she was Jewish, this reinforces Paul's earlier discussion of his ancestors and the continuity between Judaism and Christianity. Later in the letter, Paul says that Timothy has known the sacred writings from childhood (2 Tim. 3:14–15), which some scholars have understood to mean that Lois and Eunice were responsible for Timothy's childhood education in Scripture.[15] Although this potentially presents these women as knowledgeable in Scripture, it also occurs within a series of writings that have a lot to say about appropriate women's roles (typically, raising children in the home).[16]

Next, Paul encourages Timothy to "rekindle the gift of God that is within you through the laying on of my hands" (1:6). In the biblical tradition, the laying on of hands transfers authority or power, and this may refer to when the council of elders laid hands on Timothy (1 Tim. 4:14; see also Num. 27:18–23). Paul's description of rekindling the gift brings to mind the image of a campfire that is fanned into flame every morning.[17] This imagery of fire connects to the next verse, which describes the Spirit that God gives, not a Spirit of cowardice (or timidity), but a Spirit of power, love, and self-discipline (or good judgment and moderation).[18]

A preacher can go in a variety of directions with this text, depending on what is happening within the congregation. One possibility is to use this text to encourage the congregation during difficult times, reminding the church of the Spirit that God gives. Another route is to focus on the women carrying on the faith. The preacher can draw out this passing of the faith from one generation to the next, recognizing the gifts of previous generations. Or the preacher can speak about the fire of the Holy Spirit and how that moves from person to person, through the laying on of hands, ordination, and gifts of the Spirit.

- What gifts have you and your congregation received from earlier generations?
- How are the gifts of the Spirit passed from person to person?
- What are the characteristics of the Spirit, in this text and elsewhere?

Twenty-Seventh Sunday
in Ordinary Time

RUTH 1:1–22

Ruth and Naomi

In the beginning of the book of Ruth, Naomi is like a female Job: she has lost nearly everything. She had to leave her home due to a famine, and then her husband and sons die, leaving her without social status and support. She ultimately loses her sense of identity, telling the women of Bethlehem not to call her Naomi but Mara, "for the Almighty has dealt bitterly with me" (Ruth 1:20). Yet, like Job, Naomi continues to engage with the God who seems to have turned against her.

But unlike Job's friends, Naomi's daughter-in-law Ruth commits to Naomi. When Naomi tells her daughters-in-law to go back to their mothers' houses, Ruth gives the most famous speech in the book: "Where you go, I will go" (1:16). This passage is often read at weddings, and that may be an appropriate setting for it. The Hebrew calls on the language of marriage: when Ruth clings to Naomi, it is the same word as when a man leaves his mother and father and cleaves to his wife, and they become one flesh (Gen. 2:24).[1] In the strongest possible language, Ruth is by Naomi's side.

The book of Ruth is one of only two books in the Bible named after a woman and the only one named after a foreign woman.[2] Since the book focuses so much on women's voices, some scholars speculate that it was written by a woman. It also provides a contrast to the violence (especially toward women) in Judges.[3] The first chapter shows interactions between a variety of women. There are three women who make different choices: Naomi, who decides to leave the country where she has lived; Orpah, who follows Naomi's instructions to return to her mother's house; and Ruth, who chooses to go with Naomi. Then, when Naomi and Ruth arrive in Bethlehem, the women in the town ask whether this could be the Naomi they knew (1:19).

Because the story of Ruth ultimately has a happy ending, it may be tempting to give short shrift to Naomi's lament. There are many women in the Bible who cry out to God for a son, but Naomi's cries are different. She has had sons and a husband, and she knows that she is too old to bear more. She had an idea of what her life would be—securely surrounded by her children and grandchildren—but her story has changed. Late in life, she needs to start over and find ways to protect herself and her daughter-in-law. But there is hope, even in Naomi's despair. Naomi and Ruth arrive in Bethlehem at the beginning of the barley harvest. This provides an immediate source of food; it foreshadows the blessings that will come to Naomi and Ruth.[4] Like Job, Naomi will have security (and even a son) restored to her by the end of the book. There is no way to replace what she has lost, but the harvest is a sign that Naomi has hope for the future.

Often in sermons, the story of Ruth is told whole, without considering the pieces of it individually. Preaching on the first chapter alone gives congregations an opportunity to reflect on the grief and loss that Naomi experiences before moving on too quickly to the happy ending of the book. Even though there will be more to Naomi's story, that does not erase the pain that she has experienced in the loss of her husband and sons. Especially if there are people grieving in the congregation, Naomi's story may speak to their condition.

- What are some of the parallels between Naomi and Job?
- Why is Ruth's speech so often read at weddings? How does it change the meaning to put this speech back in its original context, between a mother-in-law and daughter-in-law?
- How can churches support those who have experienced loss like Naomi?

2 TIMOTHY 3:1–7

Silly Women

In this text, the author begins with a warning about the "last days" and the distressing times that will come (2 Tim. 3:1), but this is not a prediction of the future: the author sees these predictions being fulfilled in the churches of his day.[5] For early Christians, Christ's resurrection and Pentecost were the beginning of the end times, which would culminate in "the last day" of resurrection and judgment.[6] Accordingly, the author is using this understanding of the depravity of the end times to attack unnamed false teachers (cf. 1 Tim. 4:1–5).[7]

The author follows this with a list of vices (2 Tim. 3:2–5), thereby insulting the false teachers indirectly. By saying that these are the ways in which people will act in the last days, the author suggests that this is how the false teachers are currently behaving. This type of vice list was common in Hellenistic writings of the time.[8] Other than monetary greed and disobedience to parents, this list does not include specific wrongdoing, but rather the kinds of behavior that most people would consider wrong, like slander and abuse (3:2–3).[9] The author's point is that these teachings are corrupt and lead to social disorder.[10]

The culmination of this list of unacceptable behaviors is that the false teachers "captivate silly women" (3:6). The word translated as silly literally means "little women" and has the connotation of women who are gullible.[11] By saying that these women are "overwhelmed by their sins and swayed by all kinds of desires" (3:6), the author plays on cultural stereotypes of the time, which considered women as easily manipulated, flighty, and not rational like men.[12] There is a tension between the stereotype of the immature and naive women and the fact that the majority of women at the time had little or no education and thus would be hungry for knowledge.[13]

Not only are these false teachers swaying the women; they also "make their way into households" (3:6). The language here suggests that these false teachers are "creeping" or "worming their way" into households, and once there, winning over the women.[14] This evokes two characteristics of the early church that made it vulnerable: (1) early churches would meet in homes, where these false teachers have infiltrated; and (2) the early church was made up of converts, who might be converted again by a more convincing teacher. The author has effectively built up these false teachers as monsters who are in male church members' very homes, influencing their wives.

This text provides a clear example of some of the rhetorical approaches that people take to discredit those with whom they disagree: fearmongering about the last days, a list of terrible things (not necessarily describing the Other), playing into stereotypes about marginalized groups, and suggesting that one's enemies are invading their homes. Preachers can use this text as an example of how even those with good intentions can fall into these scare tactics. This text provides an opportunity to think about who is harmed by these types of arguments: here, it is the "silly women," when the author perpetuates stereotypes about them. Conflict is inevitable in the church, but there are better and worse ways to make arguments, and the approaches in this text are not ideal.

- How does the author use the vice list in 3:2–5 to discredit the false teachers?
- What are the images of women in the early church in this text? How do they compare to other examples of women in the early church?
- What makes this type of argument effective? What are the downsides of using this kind of rhetoric?

Twenty-Eighth Sunday
in Ordinary Time

1 SAMUEL 2:1–10

Hannah

This is Hannah's prayer and song when she brings her son, Samuel, to the temple to be raised by Eli the priest. Although it seems that giving up her only son would be a hard event for Hannah, she responds with a prayer of thanksgiving. Samuel has just been weaned, so he is probably about three years old. The reference to the king and God's anointed at the end (1 Sam. 2:10) suggests that this prayer was originally written for a different context, possibly a royal birth.[1] However, the themes of barrenness, childbirth, and reversals fit in the context of Hannah's story.

Her prayer describes enemies twice: "My mouth derides my enemies, because I rejoice in my victory" (2:1); and "[God's] adversaries shall be shattered" (2:10). It is common in psalms for the psalmist to use war imagery and describe God as defeating enemies, but this may also have a personal meaning for Hannah. Before she became pregnant with Samuel and because she did not have children, her husband's other wife, Peninnah, would provoke her every year when they would go to worship and sacrifice at Shiloh (1:6–7). As with the psalms, the reader can think about the specific situation of the psalmist, or the reader can apply the psalm to their own life, praying along with Hannah.

This is not the first time a prayer of Hannah's is recorded, though her first prayer did not take the form of a psalm. Instead, she silently poured her heart out to God, asking for a son (1:11). Hannah vowed that, if God granted her petition, she would set him before God as a nazirite (1:11). In Hannah's second prayer, after God has answered her prayer, Hannah describes God. The God whom Hannah describes is holy and a rock, a God of knowledge, weighing actions (2:2–3). This is a God who is in control of lives: "The Lord kills and brings to life; [God] brings down to Sheol and raises up" (2:6). And this is a God in control of the entire universe: "For the pillars of the earth are the Lord's, and on them [God] has set the world" (2:8).

The prayer reveals a God of surprising reversals. The strong are weak and the weak are strong; the full are hungry and the hungry are fat with spoil (2:5); God raises the poor from the dust (2:8). Another reversal describes barren women: "The barren has borne seven, but she who has many children is forlorn" (2:5). This may seem like a personal insult to Peninnah, but it also reflects that God cares about women's bodies. God has heard the prayer of a childless woman, and Hannah's concerns are God's concerns.[2]

Hannah's prayer is important in its own right, but it is also significant for Christians, especially because it is the basis for Mary's prayer in Luke 1:46–55.[3] Using the same form, Mary exalts the Lord and describes how God "has brought down the powerful from their thrones and lifted up the lowly" (Luke 1:52). Hannah's earlier example of a praying mother makes Mary's prayer possible: Hannah's prayer gives Mary a model to describe her own experience of God. Preachers can compare the two prayers, showing how the example of one person gives a structure for someone else. Following this, the preacher can invite the congregation to create their own prayers like the prayers of Hannah and Mary, or to simply pray along with these women, letting their words speak for everyone.

- What is surprising to you about Hannah's prayer?
- How is Hannah's prayer similar to Mary's prayer in Luke 1:46–55?
- What would you include in your own prayer, using Hannah's prayer as a model?

2 TIMOTHY 4:9–22

Claudia and Prisca

As noted in the other commentaries on 1 and 2 Timothy, the author of this text most likely was not Paul, but someone writing as Paul. There are hints that this is written for a community instead of Timothy as an individual, such as the final blessing to a plural "you" (2 Tim. 4:22).[4] However, these final exhortations and requests also seem like something a person would write under pressure—written quickly and without the careful composition found elsewhere.[5] It is possible that these are the last words from Paul, written in his final imprisonment.[6]

The author paints a bleak picture of Paul's final days. Most of his ministry companions are gone, either having deserted him, like Demas, or going on other missions (4:10). Paul says that no one came to support him at his first defense (4:16), which may have been an earlier trial or a phase of his current trial.[7] He longs to see Timothy one last time (4:9, 21), suggesting that he has a little more time before the end.[8] Paul is consumed with loneliness, remembering those who worked with him in ministry in the past.

To describe his current plight, Paul calls on Scripture, saying that he "was rescued from the lion's mouth" (4:17). This evokes Psalm 22:21 ("Save me from the mouth of the lion!") as well as the story of Daniel being delivered from the lions (Dan. 6:10–23).[9] It is most likely a metaphor because Roman citizens were not thrown to the lions, but it vividly illustrates the peril that Paul finds himself in.[10] Like the psalmists, Paul turns to God for strength and rescue (2 Tim. 4:17–18). In addition to describing what is happening to him, Paul makes some personal requests that further show what his life is like. He asks Timothy to bring him a cloak along with books and parchments (4:13). It is unknown what these books and parchments might contain, but these depict Paul as anticipating a cold winter and longing for something to read.[11]

As in other epistles, this one ends with a series of greetings, beginning with Prisca (a nickname for Priscilla) and Aquila (4:19; for more on Prisca, see the commentary on Acts 18:1–4, 24–28). Prisca is named first here (and elsewhere), suggesting that she has greater importance in the Christian community than her husband, who would customarily be named first.[12] The frequent naming of Prisca and Aquila in these letters suggests the success of the churches they hosted in their homes and that they probably were Paul's favorite hosts.[13] Finally, Paul includes a woman named Claudia as one of the people who are with him and sending greetings (4:21). She is named in a list with Eubulus, Pudens, and Linus, but nothing else is known about her or her relationship with these men.[14] Given the uncertainty of the authorship of this book, it is unclear whether Claudia was a historical person that Paul knew, a person that the later author knew, or a creation of the author to lend authenticity.[15] However, the fact that she is included is a reminder that women were important to Paul's ministry (despite indications to the contrary earlier in 2 Timothy) and that women were vital members of the early Christian church.

For preachers, this text provides a place to reflect on the loneliness that sometimes accompanies leadership. Even the most effective leaders struggle and have feelings of sadness and isolation. Here, Paul—arguably the most effective leader in the early church—is depicted as deserted by his friends and companions. He is drawing on God for strength in literal times of trial. This is a realistic picture of the difficulties that Paul and others experienced in trying to follow the way of Jesus (who also faced arrest and execution!). But although Paul feels alone, he is not. The greetings in the end of the letter are a reminder of the community of the church, both near and far.

- What details make it seem like Paul is the author of this letter? Why would another author write this from Paul's perspective?
- How can churches provide support for people who are feeling lonely and deserted by their friends?
- How does it feel to stay in Paul's sense of isolation and knowledge of the end instead of trying to come to a happy resolution?

Twenty-Ninth Sunday
in Ordinary Time

1 SAMUEL 19:11–17

Michal

Michal is trapped in a web of competing loyalties and men who treat her badly, beginning with her father, Saul, who sees Michal and her sister Merab as pawns to use for his own political gain. Saul first offers Merab to David as a wife, thinking that the Philistines will kill David for him (1 Sam. 18:17). But Saul later gives Merab to another man and instead offers David his younger daughter, Michal (18:20–21). Later, after David has escaped, Saul gives Michal to another man, Palti, or Paltiel (25:44). Saul sees Michal only as a valuable object that he can give to the man of his choice (even when she is already married!): he does not care that Michal loves David.

Michal does love David; the author says so twice (18:20, 28). Sadly for Michal, the text does not say that David loves her in return. Instead, he loves her brother, Jonathan (2 Sam. 1:26). Thus, Michal finds herself in a marriage with a man she loves, who in turn loves another man. After David escapes, he has two secret meetings with Jonathan, but he does not meet with Michal then.[1] Although many have celebrated the love between David and Jonathan, this is a tragedy for Michal.

This text, 1 Samuel 19:11–17, is probably out of chronological order; it appears to have occurred on Michal and David's wedding night and likely originally came right after the story of their marriage (18:27).[2] Michal has one night with her beloved, then has to send him away in the morning to

232

save him from her murderous father. In her actions, Michal evokes two other heroic women in the Bible: Rachel, who tricked her father and hid the family gods (Gen. 31:34–35); and Rahab, who lowered the Israelite spies out of her window so that they could escape (Josh. 2:15).

By helping David escape, Michal makes it clear that she chooses him over her father. Michal is not merely an object or a scorned wife: she has agency and a mind of her own. She is the one who learns that David is in danger and tells him that he must escape (1 Sam. 19:11). She devises the plan for David to get away and puts herself at risk by fooling Saul's messengers: in the bed she places an idol with goats' hair on its head (19:13). Her plan is a success! David escapes, and Michal thus buys time for him while the messengers go back and tell Saul that David is sick (19:14–15).[3] When Saul finally discovers the trick, Michal convinces him that she did it because David has threatened her (19:17).[4]

David seems to forget about Michal until it is politically convenient for him, and then he asks for her back (2 Sam. 3:14). Michal's second husband, Paltiel, weeps and walks behind her as she is taken away (3:15–16). Is it any wonder that Michal begins to despise David? In the final encounter between Michal and David, she vents all her anger about his self-centeredness and the way he exposes himself (6:20).

Scripture says that Michal has no children (6:23), but there is no explanation why. Some have speculated that this is a punishment from God. Perhaps David rejects Michal, or perhaps Michal will have nothing to do with David.[5] It is easy for preachers to see Michal only as a tragic figure, but that would be to deny her of her agency and voice. Instead, preachers can remember Michal as the woman in love, who tricks the king to save the life of the man she loves.

- How did the patriarchal system oppress Michal? In what ways did she fight against it?
- What parts of the story would you like to know more about?
- How would this story in 1 and 2 Samuel be different if it were told from women's point of view?

TITUS 2:1–10

Household Roles

In some ways the instructions in this text follow the typical pattern of the household codes (for more on the household codes, see the commentary on Eph. 5:21–33). However, after one sentence about older men (Titus 2:2), the author spends a disproportionate amount of space prescribing the roles of women.[6] The author only encourages younger men to be self-controlled (2:6). In addition, instead of the traditional pairings—husband and wife, parent and child, master and slave—the author focuses almost entirely on the people in those pairs with less power, without mentioning either husbands or masters. The effect is to demonstrate the tenuous position of the early church and the author's need to control those with less power.

The instructions for older men and older women mirror those of bishops and deacons and women deacons (or deacon's wives) in 1 Timothy 3:2–13. Like that description, the older women must not be slanderers or indulge in too much wine (Titus 2:3; cf. 1 Tim. 3:11). Where Titus 2:3 NRSV says that the older women should be "reverent," a better translation is "as befits a priest."[7] The author envisions the older women as engaging in priestly ministry in teaching what is good to younger women (2:3–4). This both expands the role of older women and confines it. They are teachers, but only in the private sphere, teaching younger women about how to manage a household (2:4–5).[8]

The description of younger women reflects an ideal Roman wife, who loves her husband and children and is a matriarch within the household (2:4–5). The author's goal is to make sure that these younger women behave so that the church will not be discredited in the public eye (2:5).[9] At this point in the church, the home serves as a model for church management; if women behave in ways that are destructive of that model, they might harm the reputation of the gospel.[10] The fact that the author spends so much time exhorting these women suggests that they are not embodying these ideals of the broader culture.[11] Rather than following the model of more liberating words of Scripture, the author instead feels the need to bring the women back in line.

Finally, the author turns to those who are enslaved, telling them to be "submissive to their masters," "not to talk back . . . but to show complete and perfect fidelity" (2:9–10). The result of this is for them to "be an ornament to the doctrine of God our Savior" (2:10). The historical context of these verses is essential to understand them. Enslaved people were members of the early church. Some Christian masters forcibly baptized enslaved people; other enslaved people voluntarily joined the church.[12] For the author, the obedience of enslaved people is essential for the survival of the Christian community, as a vulnerable minority.[13] Although it is still an abuse of power, it is different for a person with relatively little power to tell enslaved people to behave than for a person with all the power to use that power to dominate enslaved people.

Texts like this one can be uncomfortable for churches today, and it may be tempting to skip over them. Yet they are an important reminder of the cultural context of the early church, as well as the ways that Christians have used the Bible to oppress people. One approach that preachers of this text can take is to repent of the ways that Christians have used this text and others like it to justify enslaving people. As the church went from a vulnerable minority to a political power, Christians failed to put these words into context and instead used them to oppress other vulnerable groups. Preachers now can encourage their congregations to be aware of how the Bible continues to be used against vulnerable groups; they can work toward using the Bible to preach liberation and good news for the oppressed.

- How do these instructions protect people in the early church?
- How have they been taken out of context?
- How can churches use the Bible as a liberating force instead of a weapon that oppresses vulnerable minorities?

Thirtieth Sunday in Ordinary Time

1 SAMUEL 25:2–3, 18–31

Abigail

When Abigail first appears, the author says that she is clever, an unusual description for a woman; it also says that she is beautiful, a way women are frequently described in the Hebrew Scriptures (1 Sam. 25:3). The focus on a woman's physical attractiveness will not come as a surprise for feminist preachers. Commentators have given explanations for why Abigail is described this way. One is that it contrasts her with her husband, Nabal, who is described as "surly and mean" (25:3); but the description of Nabal does not focus on his appearance. Another justification is that it more closely aligns Abigail with David, who is "handsome" (16:12).[1] That kind of physical description of a man is rare; the use of similar terms is typical for women. Yet Abigail is so much more than her physical appearance: she is a leader, a trickster, a peacemaker, and ultimately a prophet.

It becomes clear that Abigail is a leader when the young man who works in her household comes to her to save them (25:14). Although Nabal is technically the head of the household, both the young man and Abigail know that he is "so ill-natured that no one can speak to him" (25:17). The young man trusts Abigail to understand the scope of the problem and to come up with a solution, which she does. Her solution shows that she is a trickster. Like another famous trickster, Jacob, she prepares gifts to send ahead to a potentially deadly adversary (25:18; cf. Gen. 32:13–21). The text spends a lot of time describing the provisions that Abigail sends to David, possibly to show

236

the wealth of Abigail and Nabal, or to demonstrate her care and generosity. Abigail's trick is her body: immediately after David vows to kill all the men in Nabal's household (literally, anyone who urinates against a wall; cf. KJV),[2] a woman from that household appears in front of him (1 Sam. 25:22–23)! Abigail uses her female body to stop David.[3]

At this point, Abigail also uses her gifts of speech and diplomacy to save the men in her household. In a long speech, Abigail takes the guilt for what has happened (25:24), dismisses her husband as a "fool" (the meaning of his name; 25:25), and reminds David that the Lord has sent him (25:28). Most importantly, Abigail tells David not to take vengeance against her household because it would give him bloodguilt (25:26), which would be an impediment to his ascendancy to the throne. Cleverly, Abigail suggests that David has already decided not to do this evil and that God has restrained him from it (25:26), when she is the one who is stopping him! Although Abigail describes herself as David's servant, she also implies that God is working through her.

Then Abigail takes on the role of the prophet. She says that David's life "will be bound in the bundle of the living," or the book of life (25:29).[4] Abigail tells him that anyone who rises against him will fail, thus alluding to Saul without naming him (25:29).[5] She reminds David of his defeat of Goliath by saying that his enemies "shall sling out as from the hollow of a sling" (25:29). And she foresees the future when the Lord will appoint him "prince over Israel" (25:30). This text comes after the death of Samuel and before David has Nathan as an advisor; here Abigail serves in the role of prophet for David. By the end of her speech, David is convinced.[6] He blesses her good sense and that she has kept him from bloodguilt, agreeing not to fulfill his vow (25:32–35).

There are several directions that a preacher could take this sermon. One is to contrast the description of Abigail's physical beauty with the overwhelming description of her cleverness and diplomacy in saving the members of her household. It may not occur to people in the congregation how often a woman's appearance is commented upon, and this story shows how unnecessary it can be. Another approach is to stress the image of Abigail as a peacemaker—the woman who stops two groups of people who want to do violence by putting her body between them.

- After reading this story, how would you describe Abigail?
- In what ways does Abigail subvert the authority of the men around her?
- What are the potential dangers of associating beauty with goodness?

PHILEMON 1–7

Apphia

This text comes from one of Paul's undisputed letters, which he writes from an unknown prison.[7] He refers to himself as a "prisoner of Christ" and notes that Timothy is with him and helping to send the letter (Phlm. 1). The reason for the letter is that he is sending a man named Onesimus back to Philemon, the primary recipient of the letter (vv. 10–12). From the face of the letter, it is not clear what the relationship between Onesimus and Philemon is, but most scholars think that Philemon enslaved Onesimus and that Paul is sending Onesimus back to Philemon, his master.

After greeting Philemon as "our dear friend and co-worker," Paul greets two others: Apphia, whom he names as "our sister" or "the sister"; and Archippus, "our fellow soldier" (v. 2). It is unusual for Paul to address a woman in the openings of his letters (cf. 1 Cor. 1:11; Rom. 16:1, 3, 6, 7), so her inclusion suggests that Apphia is prominent in the church.[8] Paul also greets "the church in your house" (Phlm. 2), using a singular "your." This church may be in the household of Philemon, Apphia, or Archippus.[9] When Paul says, "Grace to you," this is with a plural "you" (v. 3).[10] Thus, the letter is both to an individual and to the larger church community.

This is the only place where Apphia is named, so scholars have speculated about her and her relationship with Philemon and Archippus for millennia. In the fourth century, John Chrysostom in a homily asserted that she was Philemon's wife.[11] The term "sister" sometimes has marital connotations, but it was also common for people in the early church to refer to each other with familial language.[12] Because Paul refers to Philemon as "beloved" (v. 1 KJV; cf. NRSV, "dear friend"), some scribes added "the beloved" after Apphia's name as well.[13] Alternatively, she may be the female partner in a female-male missionary team, leading this house church.[14]

Unfortunately, the rest of the letter does not help to clarify who Apphia is or her role. The "you" in verses 4–7 is singular, addressing Philemon. Before getting to his main point, Paul says that he is grateful for Philemon's "love for all the saints," his "faith toward the Lord Jesus," and how "the hearts of the saints have been refreshed" through him (vv. 4–5, 7). Then Paul makes his argument that Philemon should welcome Onesimus (v. 17). Paul states that Onesimus is "no longer . . . a slave but more than a slave, a beloved brother" (v. 16), but he does not suggest that Philemon should free Onesimus. The fact that Apphia is named in the beginning of the letter suggests that she has influence, possibly as a witness, or that she may bear some of the responsibility for the enslaved members of this household church.[15]

This text illustrates some of the frustrations of trying to preach on women in the epistles: some of these women get only a mere mention! This has led scholars and preachers to speculate on their role in the early church, often linking the women to men in marriage. But read in another light, this text shows the complex nature of privilege in the early church and today. Although women in the early church were often under the authority of men, some also had power over enslaved people in their households. Apphia seems to be in such a position of power here.

In addition, the book of Philemon is a reminder that Christians must reckon with our history of slavery and oppression. In the nineteenth century, proponents of slavery in the United States used this book in support of the 1850 Fugitive Slave Act (Missouri Compromise), arguing that the Bible instructs people to return enslaved people to slavery.[16] For white women in particular, it is not good enough to focus only on the ways that Christians have used the Bible to oppress women: women have also been (and continue to be) complicit in such oppression.

- Based on this text, what is your impression of Apphia? What else would you like to know about her?
- How is Philemon a liberating text? How does it continue to uphold systems of oppression?
- In what ways do white women benefit from white supremacy and patriarchy in the United States today?

All Saints' Day

PROVERBS 31:10–31

Capable Wife

The opening lines of this acrostic poem about a "capable wife" encapsulate some of the tensions within the text. The text echoes the wisdom poem in Job 28: the narrator here asks who can find "a capable wife" (Prov. 31:10), like the narrator in Job asking where wisdom can be found (Job 28:12). Both are more precious than jewels (Prov. 31:10; Job 28:16). But even though the author is saying that a capable wife is valuable, in doing so he objectifies her. The author sees the wife as a valuable asset, like jewels, who brings gain to her husband (Prov. 31:11).

The majority of the poem is a list of the good things that the wife does to bring wealth and care for her family. It becomes increasingly clear that this is not one woman, but a compilation of the qualities of many women. She does not seem to sleep, but rather "rises while it is still night" (31:15), and "Her lamp does not go out at night" (31:18).[1] Each of the tasks that she does is enormous individually, such as planting an entire vineyard with her own hands (31:16). If taken literally as a model for womanhood, this sets up expectations that no woman can fulfill.

There is no distinction in Hebrew between the words for "woman" and "wife," so the poem could be translated either way, but here she is both a woman and a wife. Commentators have noted that this "ideal" woman is heterosexual, cisgender, married, and a mother.[2] However, it is interesting to see what is not included in the picture of the perfect woman: there is no comment on her physical attractiveness and, although she is a mother, the poem does not describe the work of mothering as one of her many tasks.[3]

Some of the ways the author describes her seem more traditionally masculine than feminine, such as buying a field for a vineyard (31:16) in a time when most women could not own property.[4] The word "competent" can also be translated as "strong."[5] She is not only mythic in the amount of tasks she accomplishes, but also in her association with warriors. The word "gain" is usually associated with the booty a warrior would bring back from victories, and girding her loins with strength (31:17 KJV) is an act that men would do to prepare themselves for warfare (e.g., 2 Sam. 22:40; 1 Kgs. 18:46).[6] This praiseworthy woman is blurring gender lines!

There are many parallels between the competent wife and the feminine embodied Wisdom who appears throughout Proverbs. The two are framing devices for the book as a whole: Wisdom is in the first chapter, and the competent wife in the last. When Wisdom calls out to the people, she says that she has stretched out her hand (Prov. 1:24), like the prophets. The competent wife is also like the prophets when she "opens her hand to the poor" and "reaches out her hands to the needy" (31:20): the call of the prophet is to protect the vulnerable, and the competent wife responds to that call.

One of the purposes of Wisdom throughout Proverbs is to reveal God's order in the cosmos. Wisdom was with God in the creation of the heavens and the earth, working alongside God as a master craftswoman (8:22–31). Then Wisdom creates a smaller version of God's created order when she builds her house (9:1). Here, the capable wife reflects that wisdom through the order of her household. She is not silent, but "opens her mouth with wisdom" (31:26), speaking as well as doing. The fortunate husband need only look to his wife and her works to see how God intends creation to be ordered. Even through this patriarchal lens, the glory of God is made known through a woman.

- If you were to make a list about a praiseworthy woman, what would you include? What would you leave out?
- Many women feel pressure to do everything for everyone, like the woman in this text. How can churches encourage self-care and community care?
- How do women reflect the glory of God?

JAMES 2:14–26

Rahab

"Faith without works is . . . dead" (Jas. 2:26). Scholars have spent more time on this text than any other part of James,[7] but too often they focus on things that have little to do with the actual message. First, the issue here is not really about salvation; James has already said that the "implanted word" of God "has the power to save . . . souls" (1:21).[8] The text is not about how to be saved, but how to live as a Christian. If you have faith but do nothing to help others, what good is it?

The second issue that has proven a distraction for scholars and preachers is whether this letter contradicts Paul (cf. Rom. 3:19–5:1; Gal. 2:11–3:24).[9] But James and Paul have different concerns, and it is unlikely that either is responding to the other.[10] Paul is focused on salvation, and he asserts that it is not obtained through works of the Jewish law. By contrast, James is talking about the works that come out of obedience to God's word and therefore demonstrate faith.[11] When James speaks about those lacking food, he mirrors the language of Isaiah 58:7 on the fasting approved by God: "Is it not to share your bread with the hungry?"[12] This is a faith grounded in the deep morality of God as reflected in the Hebrew Scriptures.

This text also includes people of different genders when describing those in need and people of faith. Throughout the book, James refers to both men and women as his brothers and sisters, and he specifies here that the person in need may be "a brother or a sister" (2:15).[13] But the other siblings that James addresses respond by dismissing those in need with platitudes: "Go in peace; keep warm and eat your fill" (2:15). Then James gives both Abraham and Rahab as examples of people whose faith is demonstrated by their actions (2:21–25).[14]

By choosing Rahab, James provides an example of a woman who is revered for her own actions and not because of her relation to a patriarch.[15] James presents Rahab as one who cares for the messengers in distress, unlike those who fail to care for the needy (2:15). She embodies hospitality. The inclusion of Rahab may also be a reminder of Abraham's hospitality in inviting in the strangers and caring for them (Gen. 18:1–15). James draws on the tradition of hospitality in the Hebrew Scriptures to make his point about faith and works.

However, James's inclusion of Rahab makes a deeper point: Rahab is an example of deep faith as well as works. In Joshua (2:10), Rahab gives what may be the longest prose speech by a woman in the Bible,[16] reminding the spies of what God has done for Israel by bringing them out of Egypt and leading them to triumph in battle against other kings. In addition, the author of Hebrews remembers Rahab as a person of faith (11:31). Thus, James is not arguing that only works are important; he instead chooses a person of faith who also engages in works of hospitality.

For preachers, this text will mean different things in different contexts. In congregations where people are concerned with personal salvation, it is a call to demonstrate that faith in the world through acts of hospitality and justice. In congregations that are more focused on works, the text serves as a reminder that social justice is rooted in faith. This text also provides a reminder of the story of Rahab, a woman who embodies both faith and works.

- How have you heard people preach about the statement "Faith without works is dead"?
- How does Rahab embody both faith and works?
- Does your congregation tend to focus more on faith or works?

Thirty-First Sunday in Ordinary Time

2 SAMUEL 13:1–21

Tamar and Amnon

The horrific story of Amnon raping his sister Tamar is one that many preachers and congregations would probably prefer to avoid. But it is part of our sacred text, and the way it plays out reflects many of the realities that are common in sexual assaults today. Tamar is not raped by some stranger, but by a family member in a familiar place.[1] She does her best to convince her brother to do the right thing, explaining how this will have terrible consequences for both of them, but he is stronger and overpowers her. And afterward, the men in her family respond poorly, further traumatizing Tamar.

The trap that Amnon sets for Tamar takes advantage of her goodwill toward him, as well as their father David's goodwill. At the suggestion of his cousin, Amnon pretends to be ill and asks his father to send Tamar to him to prepare cakes for him (2 Sam. 13:5–6). Tamar does what her father asks and follows each of the steps that Amnon has laid out: making dough, kneading it, and baking cakes (13:8). For the reader, this is like watching a horror movie because we know what will come next, but Tamar does not. Amnon asks everyone to leave and says to Tamar that he wants to eat from her hand, bringing her close enough to be within his grasp (13:10).[2]

In many texts about rape in the Bible, there is no indication of how the victim responds, but that is not the case here! When Amnon makes it clear what he intends to do, Tamar responds eloquently, trying to convince her brother to change his mind. She argues that this is against the ways of their people and would bring shame to them both (13:12–13). Tamar comes up with a better solution: go to their father and ask for his blessing (13:13). As a woman, Tamar knows that she cannot stop Amnon indefinitely, but there is a way for him to have her sexually that will not ruin her life.

But Amnon is determined and overpowers Tamar physically (13:14). Despite the violence that Amnon has just done to her, Tamar continues to advocate for herself. She reminds Amnon that sending her away is against the law (Deut. 22:28–29),[3] but he does so anyway (2 Sam. 13:17–18). After the servant bolts the door behind her, Tamar raises her voice in lament (13:19). Tamar will not silently accept what has happened to her; she tears the dress that designates her as a virgin and puts ashes on her head, a visible reminder of the pain that her brother has caused.

The ways in which the other men in Tamar's family respond only compound her trauma. First, Tamar's cousin Jonadab conspires with Amnon and comes up with the plan (13:5–6). Although Jonadab never explicitly says that the goal is rape, the intent is clear.[4] When Absalom, Tamar's full brother, learns what has happened, he says to Tamar, "Be quiet for now" and "Do not take this to heart" (13:20)—attempting to silence her. Even when he later "avenges" her by killing Amnon, he advances his own prospect to the throne and does nothing to help Tamar out of her despairing state; she remains "a desolate woman" in his house (13:20). Finally, Tamar's father, David, does nothing. Rather than protect his daughter, he sides with his son "because he loved him, . . . his firstborn" (13:21). David's anger is useless for Tamar, who probably wonders whether her father purposely sent her into violence. In a patriarchal system, these are the men who should be protecting Tamar, but they only cause her further harm.[5]

Unfortunately, the narrative centers on Amnon and his feelings. The author focuses on how Amnon "loved" Tamar (13:1–4) and then how that turns to "great loathing" after he violates her (13:15). After this text, Tamar disappears from the story, which turns instead to the rivalry between Amnon and Absalom.[6] As challenging as this story is, it reflects the experiences of many people in the church who have suffered sexual assault, rape, and silencing. Like Tamar, preachers can lament this violence and hopefully help their congregations provide more support to people who have suffered sexual violence than the men in this text, who fail to care for Tamar.

- How do Amnon and Jonadab objectify Tamar? What would their conversation be like if they saw her as a full person?
- What questions would you like to ask Tamar?
- How can our churches better support people who have experienced sexual abuse by a family member?

REVELATION 12:1–6, 13–17

Woman and Earth

This text makes many references to the Hebrew Scriptures and encompasses all the cosmos; at the center of it is the image of a woman in heaven (Rev. 12:1). She is a portent, a sign of deeper symbolic meaning, instead of a literal woman.[7] It is not clear what this meaning is, and there are many debates about whom she might represent. She is a cosmic queen, like Isis; the earliest Christians interpreted her as the people Israel, who gave birth to the Messiah.[8] By the sixth century, the church associated her with the Virgin Mary, which is reflected in iconography depicting Mary with stars in her crown and the moon under her feet (12:1).[9] This woman cries out in birth pangs (12:2)—one of the few places in Revelation where a woman has a voice.[10] The woman echoes God's crying out like a woman in labor in Isaiah 42:14 and may symbolize the dawning of a new age.[11]

But the woman is not the only portent in this scene. There is also a great red dragon, standing before the woman and waiting to devour her child as soon as she gives birth (Rev. 12:3–4). This dragon is a symbol of blood, violence, and kingship.[12] He destroys the cosmos with his tail (12:4). The child he tries to consume is the awaited Messiah (see Ps. 2:8–9),[13] but the child is miraculously snatched away and taken to the throne of God before the dragon is able to act (Rev. 12:5). The dragon then follows the child into heaven, where the angel Michael defeats him and throws him back to earth (12:7–9).

Meanwhile, the woman flees to the wilderness, where God has prepared a place for her (12:6). Safety in the wilderness evokes many stories in the Hebrew Scriptures, such as the Israelites after the exodus (Ps. 78:52) and Elijah in flight (1 Kgs. 17:2–6).[14] The story that is closest to this one, however, is the story of Hagar in the wilderness, protected by God and the angel after Abraham has cast her and her son out (Gen. 21:14–19). Here the woman goes to this place of protection twice: first, for 1,260 days for nourishment after giving birth (Rev. 12:6); second, for "a time, and times, and half a time" (three and a half years) after the dragon returns (12:14). This second time, the woman is "given the two wings of the great eagle," evoking God lifting the Israelites on eagles' wings (Exod. 19:4; Isa. 40:31).

There is another explicitly feminine figure in this text: the personified Earth (12:16).[15] When the dragon, possibly modeled on the sea serpent Leviathan,[16] pours water after the woman to sweep her away (12:15), Earth helps the woman by opening "her mouth" and swallowing the river (12:16 KJV). In other places, a terrifying earth swallows the enemies of God (Exod. 15:12;

Num. 16:32–34), but here Earth is a friendly presence, helping the woman in her time of need.

The powerful imagery in this text lends itself to sermons about how, in the battles between good and evil, those who are most vulnerable are at risk.[17] The news is filled with headlines about war zones and refugees; for people giving birth or facing having their children taken away, this text is terrifyingly close to home. The text also paints a picture of a God who prepares a safe, if unexpected, place in the wilderness. A preacher may use this text to highlight those who are in such desperate situations and ask who are the ones—like Earth in this text—helping those in need.

- When you read the description of the woman, what does she symbolize?
- What threats today are like the dragon?
- How can congregations help those who vulnerable, like the woman and her child in this text?

Thirty-Second Sunday
in Ordinary Time

1 KINGS 10:1–13

Queen of Sheba

The queen of Sheba is a powerful woman! Although the goal of this text is to demonstrate the height of Solomon's reign,[1] it also reflects the power of this unnamed woman who travels from a distant land. The region of Sheba (or Seba) was large and wealthy place that scholars think may have been in what is now Yemen, or possibly in ancient Ethiopia.[2] Solomon hoped to establish trading relationships with this region.[3] In addition to the power associated with her title and country, the queen of Sheba shows her power through her wit and understanding. She comes to test Solomon with "hard questions" (1 Kgs. 10:1). The text does not say what those hard questions are, and commentators have speculated that they might be riddles, like the ones that Samson used in his contest with the Philistines (Judg. 14:12–18).[4] Another possibility is that she is coming as a fellow ruler, to consult with Solomon about diplomatic issues.[5] She sees Solomon as an equal and respects his answers to her questions; in fact, his answers leave her breathless (1 Kgs. 10:4–5).[6]

The queen of Sheba also demonstrates her power with the extravagant gifts that she brings to Solomon. This probably is a historic trade mission,[7] and the narrator describes the queen's gifts in detail: 120 talents of gold, precious stones, and spices that will never come in such a quantity again (10:10). Solomon responds in kind, giving the queen of Sheba "every desire that she expressed, as well as what he gave her out of Solomon's royal bounty" (10:13)—again marking her as his equal. The queen also provides surprising religious wisdom. She and her people most likely worship Astarte (or Ishtar), the "queen of heaven and mother of all deities."[8] But the queen comes to visit because of Solomon's "fame due to the name of the LORD" (10:1), and when she sees Solomon's wisdom and prosperity, she blesses God and says that God is the one who has set Solomon on the throne of Israel (10:9). She also reminds Solomon of his duty as king "to execute justice and righteousness" (10:9).

In the end, one of the most powerful things that the queen of Sheba does is to leave (10:13). She is a ruler in her own right, and she is able to trade with Solomon without marrying him. The queen also provides a contrast to the foreign women that Solomon marries who lead him away from God (11:1–8).[9] Unlike those other unnamed women, this is a queen who interacts with Solomon as an equal and leads him back to his own religious tradition. She also demonstrates that seduction is not the only option for women to be influential.

The image of this wise queen visiting Solomon has cultural resonance. Even Jesus refers to this woman, whom he calls "the queen of the South" (Matt. 12:42; Luke 11:31). Jesus clearly has heard the story of this queen: he says she "will rise up at the judgment with this generation and condemn it, because she came from the ends of the earth to listen to the wisdom of Solomon, and see, something greater than Solomon is here!" (Matt. 12:42). Some interpreters also associate her with Candace of Ethiopia (Acts 8:27).[10] The tradition of having strong female leaders in other regions has sparked the imagination of Israelites and perhaps showed them another way to be.

For preachers, this text provides an example of strong female leadership and diplomacy. It expands the world of the ancient Near East and demonstrates that the Israelites are aware of women in positions of power. In preaching this text, one approach is to compare the queen of Sheba with other rulers, of any gender. Another possible approach would be to compare this text with the account in 1 Kings 3:16–28, about the two women fighting over the baby. These two texts provide examples of women at extreme ends of the social spectrum.[11]

- What is the most powerful aspect of the queen of Sheba in this text?
- What is surprising about this account?
- How is Solomon's response to the queen of Sheba like or unlike the way he treats the women fighting over the baby (3:16–28)?

REVELATION 17:1–6

The Great Whore

The Great Whore, or the Whore of Babylon, is a metaphor that the author of Revelation uses to describe the Roman Empire. The text begins with one of the seven angels, each with a bowl (Rev. 15:7), that have poured out God's wrath on the earth, taking the writer in the Spirit (or in a trance) to see the judgment of the Great Whore (17:1). In this context, Babylon is a coded name for Rome,[12] and the author follows the prophets in the Hebrew Scriptures by using the metaphor of prostitution for godless cities.[13] The beast that the Whore rides has seven heads, suggesting the seven hills of Rome (Rev. 17:9),[14] and the angel explains that the ten horns on the beast represent ten kings to come (17:12).

The Whore is beautiful and terrifying;[15] she wears luxurious clothes and jewels, and she is seductive. The mark on her head may be a reference to the mark of the beast (cf. 13:11–18). Alternatively, it could signify the lowest form of prostitute, an enslaved and tattooed woman.[16] The Whore drinks from "a golden cup full of abominations and the impurities of her fornication" (17:4), and she "was drunk with the blood of the saints and the blood of the witnesses to Jesus" (17:6). This reference to the blood in the cup has several potential meanings, including fear of persecution and showing that the Whore violates Jewish dietary regulations. The image has inherent misogyny, suggesting menstrual blood in the hand of this dangerous, sexually aggressive woman.[17]

Over the next few chapters, the Whore is punished. The horns (kings) and the beast hate the whore: "They will make her desolate and naked; they will devour her flesh and burn her up with fire" (17:16). The Whore is not only killed; she is also stripped naked, devoured, and burned. Burning is a punishment for whoredom in the story of Judah and Tamar (Gen. 38:24; cf. Lev. 21:9). When the Whore is destroyed, the heavenly choir sings, "Hallelujah! The smoke goes up from her forever and ever" (Rev. 19:3).

This text draws on many of the tropes throughout the Bible of dangerous and evil women, especially the story of Jezebel: whoredom (infidelity to God), wearing fine things, and meeting a gruesome end (cf. 2 Kgs. 9:30–37). But unlike many of the stories of evil women, this is not a historical account. It is a metaphor. John of Patmos chose to describe Rome as an unfaithful woman along with the gendered violence that follows. How do we grapple with these depictions of violence against women in our sacred text?[18] Is there good news here?

This text also provides an example of a place to argue against the text. It reveals the anxieties about women that occur throughout the Bible: that women are beautiful and seductive, prostitutes, unfaithful, and will lead men away from God. The author does real violence by choosing to portray the empire as a woman and then punishing her in such gendered ways. This text is a clear example of how the metaphors we choose to use matter. It gives preachers an opportunity to think about what stories we choose to tell, how we tell them, and the images we use. Who is harmed by these stories? Whom do these stories raise as examples? All these decisions have consequences.

- What makes this gendered violence effective as a metaphor? How is it problematic?
- If you were to retell this story, what would you use as an alternative metaphor?
- How can preachers place this kind of violent imagery in context without doing further harm?

Thirty-Third Sunday in Ordinary Time

2 KINGS 9:30–37

Jezebel

Jezebel is the ultimate trope of the "threatening foreign woman" in the Hebrew Scriptures. Her name has become synonymous with an evil temptress. This text about her death occurs in the larger context of her life and leadership. Jezebel is first introduced as Ahab's wife in a verse suggesting that Jezebel leads Ahab into sin and worshiping Baal (1 Kgs. 16:31). However, marrying a foreign woman is also a way for the king to ensure peace with neighboring countries; Solomon had hundreds of foreign wives![1] For a king to marry a foreign woman is not in and of itself sinful.

The next verses about Jezebel mention in passing that she is "killing off the prophets of the LORD" (18:4, 13). This sets up the confrontation between Jezebel and the prophet Elijah, when Elijah has four hundred prophets of Baal killed (18:40). When Ahab tells Jezebel what Elijah has done, she sends a messenger to Elijah with her oath: "So may the gods do to me, and more also, if I do not make your life like the life of one of them by this time tomorrow" (19:2). Elijah is terrified and flees (19:3). At this point, Elijah and Jezebel are going toe to toe: Jezebel worships her gods, Elijah worships his God; Jezebel kills prophets, Elijah kills prophets.[2] What began as a confrontation between Elijah and Ahab becomes a direct confrontation between Elijah and Jezebel. She does not send word through her husband: she sends her own messenger to Elijah to tell him that she plans to kill him.

Jezebel grows in power, which eventually surpasses the power of her husband. After Ahab tries to get a vineyard from Naboth, but Naboth refuses, Jezebel arranges to get the vineyard for him. The passage describes Ahab as "resentful and sullen" and says that he "lay down on his bed, turned away his face, and would not eat" (21:4). Jezebel writes letters in Ahab's name, telling nobles to sit Naboth opposite two scoundrels who would bring charges against him. After the people stone Naboth to death, Jezebel gives Ahab the vineyard. Jezebel is a political force, more powerful than the king. In addition, the characterization of Ahab signifies a gender reversal: he is pouting, like an ineffectual woman, and she is the powerful, masculine leader.[3] Notably, Jezebel is the only woman in the Hebrew Scriptures recorded as writing.[4] Jezebel is educated and intelligent, and she gets what she wants.

The idea that Jezebel was a prostitute seems to come from two places. First, we notice a comment that Jehu makes to Jezebel's son Joram: "What peace can there be, so long as the many whoredoms and sorceries of your mother Jezebel continue?" (2 Kgs. 9:22). But this reference to "whoredoms" does not mean literal prostitution; it is the kind of language used to describe people who are unfaithful to God. Jezebel is never unfaithful to God because she has never followed God; she is completely faithful to her own gods and never wavers from them.[5] Second, a verse says that Jezebel "painted her eyes" and "adorned her head" (9:30). But here Jezebel is not trying to seduce Jehu. Rather, she immediately insults him by comparing him to Zimri, who ruled for only seven days (1 Kgs. 16:15). By adorning herself, Jezebel faces death on her own terms, as a queen.

In the end, Jezebel is completely destroyed. She is thrown from a window by her own officials, trampled by horses, and eaten by dogs—unclean animals.[6] This vivid description of her death reflects the animus of the writer and the height of Jezebel's power. She must be killed before Jehu can establish his rule, even though her husband and sons are already dead.[7] The story of Jezebel creates space to reflect on the biblical trope of the threatening foreign woman. She is a memorable, complex person; to the biblical author, she presents a threat that must be completely destroyed.

- What makes Jezebel so threatening?
- How have you heard people use the name "Jezebel" to dismiss or degrade women?
- Is it possible for the church to have an understanding of Jezebel that does not paint her as a villain?

REVELATION 2:18–29

Jezebel

In the letter to the church in Thyatira, John of Patmos, the author of Revelation, focuses on a teacher whom he calls Jezebel (Rev. 2:20–24). Scholars studying the seven cities named in Revelation 2–3 know the least about Thyatira, located between Pergamum and Ephesus. It was known in Roman times for its numerous trade guilds producing metalworking and wool.[8] Membership in the trade guilds involved participation in religious ceremonies.[9]

The author describes this "Jezebel" as one who is a false prophet and a teacher (2:20). It is not clear whether this woman's name is Jezebel, but it is more likely that the author is using this name to associate the woman with Queen Jezebel (for more on Jezebel, see the commentary on 2 Kgs. 9:30–37).[10] By using this name, the author is casting the woman as a villain, reminding the church of the foreign queen who led Israel away from God.[11] The author uses this name to signal that he will dismiss this woman and shame her.[12]

The main disagreement that the author has with the woman is that she has been telling people in the church that they may eat food sacrificed to idols (Rev. 2:20). Whether to eat food sacrificed to idols (which people could buy in ordinary markets) was a matter of debate among early Christians. Many early church leaders do forbid eating such meat, but Paul allows it (Acts 15:20, 29; 1 Cor. 8:4–8; 10:23–27).[13] Evidently the author here follows the stricter approach. But rather than state this directly, the author uses the metaphor of fornication (Rev. 2:20). It is possible that the woman's teachings also includes less restrictive sexual practices, but more likely the author is using fornication as slander. He follows the tradition of prophets in the Hebrew Scriptures who describe worship of other gods as sexual immorality (e.g., Jer. 2; Hos. 2). He continues the metaphor by calling her followers adulterers (Rev. 2:22).[14] This charge of fornication may also refer to her positive relations with others in the prevailing Greco-Roman culture, which the author would see as a compromise.[15]

The punishment for this woman and her followers is severe, reflecting the violent death of Queen Jezebel.[16] The author, speaking on behalf of Christ, says that he will throw her onto a sickbed and strike her children (her followers) dead (2:22–23). At the beginning of the letter, the author says, "These are the words of the Son of God," whom he describes as having "eyes like a flame of fire" (2:18). This is a disturbing image of Christ, destroying a woman and killing her children.

For preachers, this text provides a clear example of the power of imagery and gendered rhetoric to dismiss a woman in ministry. The author humiliates his rival by accusing her of sexual promiscuity and uses the name of Christ to violently oppose her. There were legitimate differences of opinion in the early church, as there are now, but this text shows the cost of trying to win an argument by any means possible. Unfortunately, we do not know any more about this woman, who was an early teacher in the church. She is never allowed to speak for herself,[17] and her side of the story is lost.

- What do you think the woman he calls Jezebel was teaching people in the church?
- How does the author's description of the Son of God here compare to other images of Christ in the Bible?
- What are some modern examples of people using similarly gendered language to dismiss powerful women?

Christt the King Sunday

2 KINGS 22:3–20

Huldah

When King Josiah tells his high priest to inquire of the Lord for him, the high priest takes a group to see the prophetess Huldah. The context of this passage is the restoration of the house of the Lord: when Josiah was eighteen, he ordered his secretary Shaphan to repair the house of the Lord and pay the workers who repaired it. While doing this, the high priest Hilkiah found "the book of the law" (probably a scroll).[1] Josiah could have sent his men to Jeremiah or Zephaniah (prophets who were contemporaries of Huldah), but instead they go to see Huldah (2 Kgs. 22:14).

Who is Huldah? She appears in the Bible only in this passage and in the parallel story in 2 Chronicles 34:21–28. The Scripture locates her within her family and in Jerusalem: it names her husband and the part of Jerusalem where she lives (2 Kgs. 22:14). She does not live in the palace, but in another part of the city, where people need to go to consult with her. Scholar Wilda Gafney suggests that Huldah serves as a kind of second mother to Josiah, saying that Josiah's mother Jedidah "and the prophet Huldah deserve the credit for raising the eight-year-old Josiah to be the man he becomes after his father's death."[2]

Huldah is not the only female prophet in the Hebrew Scriptures. Others include Miriam (Exod. 15:20), Deborah (Judg. 4:4), and Noadiah (Neh. 6:14).[3] Notably, this passage does not highlight the fact that Huldah is a female prophet, suggesting that this is a commonly accepted role for women. When she speaks, Huldah uses the standard language of the prophets: "Thus says the Lord, the God of Israel" (2 Kgs. 22:15). In the first part of her prophecy,

Huldah confirms that God will "bring disaster on this place" and on all its inhabitants because they have not followed the book of the law. In doing so, Huldah verifies the book of the law as Scripture,[4] confirms Josiah's fears, and speaks to the terrible consequences that Judah faces because it did not follow God's commands.

In the second part of the prophecy, Huldah says that because Josiah has been penitent and humbled, he will be gathered to his ancestors in peace. Considering that Josiah does not die a peaceful death (see 23:28–30), was Huldah wrong? Scholars disagree. Some argue that being "gathered to your grave in peace" refers to burial, not death.[5] Others point to the violent death in battle with Pharaoh Neco (23:30) to say that the second part of Huldah's prophecy was incorrect. This raises larger questions about prophecy: Is the purpose of prophecy to correctly predict the future? Or to turn people back toward God? Huldah's prophecy may be like the message that Jonah brought to Nineveh: "Forty days more, and Nineveh shall be overthrown!" (Jonah 3:4). Nineveh is not overthrown in forty days, but Jonah's prophecy brings about a reform, and God has a change of mind. Here, Huldah's words bring about a reformation in Judah. King Josiah and all the people make a covenant to follow the Lord and keep all of God's commandments that are written in the book (2 Kgs. 23:3). If the purpose of prophecy is to speak on behalf of God and turn people toward God, then Huldah's prophecy is extremely effective.

- Why would King Josiah send his men to Huldah instead of the other prophets?
- What else would you like to know about Huldah and other prophetesses in the Hebrew Scriptures?
- Is the purpose of prophecy to predict the future? Or to turn people toward God? Does prophecy have other purposes?

REVELATION 19:4–9; 22:17

Bride

It can be easy to read this text in terms of binaries (good versus evil) and outdated stereotypes of women (the virgin and the whore); yet with a little imagination, it can be a text of liberation and welcome a new understanding of God's kingdom and witness in the world. The text begins with celebration, but it is the celebration of the death of the Whore of Babylon (Rev. 18; 19:2–4). The twenty-four elders and the four living creatures that appear first in 4:4–8 fall down in worship before God, who is seated on the throne (19:4). This is one aspect of the text that can be difficult for feminist preachers: the cries of "Hallelujah" are at the death of an evil, sexually immoral woman, who is contrasted with the pure, virginal Bride.[6]

In the next verse, a voice comes from the throne (19:5). The author does not specify that this voice is God's; the fact that it comes from the throne suggests that this voice and the multitude that respond to it are an aspect of God, the angelic host, or God's servants.[7] This is a place where preachers can talk about the impact of different voices, possibly bringing in members of the congregation to read the lines. The words sound different coming from the mouths of people of different genders, speaking on behalf of God and God's servants.

These voices announce the marriage of the Lamb and the Bride (19:7). This marriage is a metaphor for the union of Christ as the bridegroom and the church as the Bride, drawing on the images in the Hebrew Scriptures of Israel as God's bride (e.g., Isa. 54:6; Ezek. 16:7–8; Hos. 2:16).[8] Unlike the illicit sex of the Whore, the marriage between the Bride and her bridegroom is acceptable sexuality, representing the communion between the Son of Man and the churches.[9] The Bride is ready for her bridegroom, who has given her fine, bright linen (Rev. 19:8). In an unusual turn, the author explains the significance of this image: "The fine linen is the righteous deeds of the saints" (19:8).[10]

Later the author reveals that the Bride is "the holy city, the new Jerusalem" (21:2). This is where God will dwell with humanity, with the throne of God and the Lamb in the midst of the city (21:3, 22:3). Feminist scholars have criticized this image, saying that it focuses on the woman's physical attributes (when the author describes her wealth and adornments) and that the Bride is the most passive female character in Revelation.[11] They suggest that this creates a limited role for femininity in God's new realm, with space for only those who are beautiful, submissive, and self-sacrificing.[12]

The final place where the Bride appears is with the Spirit (22:17). In Greek, the word for "Spirit" is a neuter noun, though throughout the Bible, "spirit/ Spirit" has feminine associations. Here, the nonbinary femme Spirit and the Bride declare the words of Jesus, offering the living water to everyone (22:17): "everyone who hears," "everyone who is thirsty," and "anyone who wishes [to] take the water of life as a gift" (22:17). This is a beautiful image of those who are inviting others to receive God: it not just a message from men, but one from the mouths of women and nonbinary people as well. Together, the Bride and the Spirit preach, sharing the good news of this water that is for everyone.

- Are the depictions of the Whore and the Bride disappointing? What are some other examples of women being pitted against each other as good and evil?
- What else do you envision the Bride saying in her sermon?
- How does this depiction of the Spirit expand your understanding of God?

Notes

Introduction

1. For much more on the ways Christians have stereotyped Judaism, see Amy-Jill Levine, *The Misunderstood Jew: The Church and the Scandal of the Jewish Jesus* (San Francisco: HarperSanFrancisco, 2007), 119–66.
2. Gale A. Yee, *The Hebrew Bible: Feminist and Intersectional Perspectives* (Minneapolis: Fortress Press, 2018), viii.

ADVENT-CHRISTMAS-EPIPHANY

First Sunday of Advent

1. Onan's sin was shirking his duty to impregnate his wife, not masturbation.
2. Susan Niditch, "Genesis," in *Women's Bible Commentary*, ed. Carol A. Newsom, Sharon H. Ringe, and Jacqueline E. Lapsley, 3rd ed. (Louisville, KY: Westminster John Knox Press, 2012), 42.
3. Terence E. Fretheim, "The Book of Genesis," in *The New Interpreter's Bible Commentary*, ed. Leander Keck, vol. 1 (Nashville: Abingdon Press, 2015), 231.
4. Harold W. Attridge, Wayne A. Meeks, and Jouette M. Bassler, *HarperCollins Study Bible: New Revised Standard Version with the Apocryphal/Deuterocanonical Books* (San Francisco: HarperOne, 2006), 62–63.
5. Amy-Jill Levine and Marc Zvi Brettler, *The Jewish Annotated New Testament: New Revised Standard Version Bible Translation* (New York: Oxford University Press, 2017), 11.
6. Attridge, Meeks, and Bassler, *HarperCollins Study Bible*, 1762.
7. Carol Howard Merritt, "Thoughts on I Am Mary," December 11, 2018, https://.facebook.com/carolhowardmerritt/posts/10156134555225863.
8. Joel B. Green, ed., *The CEB Study Bible* (Nashville: Common English Bible, 2013), 106 NT.
9. Cf. Jane D. Schaberg and Sharon H. Ringe, "Gospel of Luke," in *Women's Bible Commentary*, ed. Carol A. Newsom, Sharon H. Ringe, and Jacqueline E. Lapsley, 3rd ed. (Louisville, KY: Westminster John Knox Press, 2012), 502.

Second Sunday of Advent

1. Harold W. Attridge, Wayne A. Meeks, and Jouette M. Bassler, *HarperCollins Study Bible: New Revised Standard Version with the Apocryphal/Deuterocanonical Books* (San Francisco: HarperOne, 2006), 313.
2. Joel B. Green, ed., *CEB Study Bible* (Nashville: Common English Bible, 2013), 330 OT.

3. Amy C. Cottrill, "Joshua," in *Women's Bible Commentary* (Louisville, KY: Westminster John Knox Press, 2012), 105.

4. Richard Hess, "Joshua," in *The New Interpreter's Bible One-Volume Commentary* (Nashville: Abingdon Press, 2010), 147.

5. Priests for Equality, *The Inclusive Bible: The First Egalitarian Translation* (Lanham, MD: Rowman & Littlefield Publishers, 2009), 125.

6. Green, *CEB Study Bible*, 331 OT.

7. Karl Jacobson, "Commentary on Luke 1:39–45 (46–55)," *Working Preacher*, December 23, 2012, https://www.workingpreacher.org/preaching.aspx?commentary_id=1500.

8. R. Alan Culpepper, "The Gospel of Luke," in *The New Interpreter's Bible Commentary*, vol. 8 (Nashville: Abingdon Press: 2015), 42.

9. Jane D. Schaberg and Sharon H. Ringe, "Gospel of Luke," in *Women's Bible Commentary* (Louisville, KY: Westminster John Knox Press, 2012), 502.

10. John T. Carroll, "Luke," in *The New Interpreter's Bible One-Volume Commentary* (Nashville: Abingdon Press, 2010), 681.

11. Amy-Jill Levine and Marc Zvi Brettler, *The Jewish Annotated New Testament: New Revised Standard Version Bible Translation* (New York: Oxford University Press, 2017), 110.

Third Sunday of Advent

1. Eunny P. Lee, "Ruth," in *Women's Bible Commentary* (Louisville, KY: Westminster John Knox Press, 2012), 147.

2. Patricia Tull, "Commentary on Ruth 3:1–5; 4:13–17," *Working Preacher*, November 11, 2012, https://www.workingpreacher.org/preaching.aspx?commentary_id=1336.

3. Alphonetta Wines, "Commentary on Ruth 3:1–5; 4:13–17," *Working Preacher*, November 8, 2015, https://www.workingpreacher.org/preaching.aspx?commentary_id=2617.

4. Katharine D. Sakenfeld, "Ruth," in *The New Interpreter's Bible One-Volume Commentary* (Nashville: Abingdon Press, 2010), 185.

5. Brent Strawn, "Commentary on Ruth 3:1–5; 4:13–17," *Working Preacher*, November 8, 2009, https://www.workingpreacher.org/preaching.aspx?commentary_id=414.

6. Harold W. Attridge, Wayne A. Meeks, and Jouette M. Bassler, *HarperCollins Study Bible: New Revised Standard Version with the Apocryphal/Deuterocanonical Books* (San Francisco: HarperOne, 2006), 1763.

7. See, e.g., Amy-Jill Levine and Marc Zvi Brettler, *The Jewish Annotated New Testament: New Revised Standard Version Bible Translation* (New York: Oxford University Press, 2017), 111.

8. R. Alan Culpepper, "The Gospel of Luke," in *The New Interpreter's Bible Commentary*, vol. 8 (Nashville: Abingdon Press, 2015), 42.

9. Jane D. Schaberg and Sharon H. Ringe, "Gospel of Luke," in *Women's Bible Commentary* (Louisville, KY: Westminster John Knox Press, 2012), 504.

Fourth Sunday of Advent

1. Harold W. Attridge, Wayne A. Meeks, and Jouette M. Bassler, *HarperCollins Study Bible: New Revised Standard Version with the Apocryphal/Deuterocanonical Books* (San Francisco: HarperOne, 2006), 450.

2. Joel B. Green, ed., *CEB Study Bible* (Nashville: Common English Bible, 2013), 486 OT.

5. Christopher R. Seitz, "The Book of Isaiah 40–66," in *The New Interpreter's Bible Commentary*, vol. 4 (Nashville: Abingdon Press, 2015), 428.

6. Karl Kuhn, "Commentary on Matthew 2:1–12," *Working Preacher*, December 25, 2013, https://www.workingpreacher.org/preaching.aspx?commentary_id =1962.

7. Harold W. Attridge, Wayne A. Meeks, and Jouette M. Bassler, *HarperCollins Study Bible: New Revised Standard Version with the Apocryphal/Deuterocanonical Books* (San Francisco: HarperOne, 2006), 587.

8. Amy-Jill Levine and Marc Zvi Brettler, *The Jewish Annotated New Testament: New Revised Standard Version Bible Translation* (New York: Oxford University Press, 2017), 13.

9. M. Eugene Boring, "The Gospel of Matthew," in *The New Interpreter's Bible Commentary*, vol. 7 (Nashville: Abingdon Press, 2015), 78.

10. Jan Schnell Rippentrop, "Commentary on Matthew 2:1–12," *Working Preacher*, January 6, 2018, https://www.workingpreacher.org/preaching.aspx ?commentary_id=3523.

11. Stephen Westerholm, "Matthew," in *The New Interpreter's Bible One-Volume Commentary* (Nashville: Abingdon Press, 2010), 633.

12. Mark Allan Powell, *HarperCollins Bible Dictionary* (New York: HarperOne, 2011), 300.

First Sunday in Ordinary Time

1. J. Clinton McCann Jr., "The Book of Psalms," in *The New Interpreter's Bible Commentary*, vol. 3 (Nashville: Abingdon Press, 2015), 674.

2. Rolf A. Jacobson, "Psalms," in *The New Interpreter's Bible One-Volume Commentary* (Nashville: Abingdon Press, 2010), 345.

3. Nancy L. deClaissé-Walford, "Psalms," in *Women's Bible Commentary* (Louisville, KY: Westminster John Knox Press, 2012), 230.

4. DeClaissé-Walford, "Psalms," 230.

5. Joel B. Green, ed., *CEB Study Bible* (Nashville: Common English Bible, 2013), 110 NT.

6. Harold W. Attridge, Wayne A. Meeks, and Jouette M. Bassler, *HarperCollins Study Bible: New Revised Standard Version with the Apocryphal/Deuterocanonical Books* (San Francisco: HarperOne, 2006), 1765.

7. Green, *CEB Study Bible*, 110 NT.

Second Sunday in Ordinary Time

1. Callie Plunket-Brewton, "Commentary on Isaiah 60:1–6," *Working Preacher*, January 6, 2016, https://www.workingpreacher.org/preaching.aspx ?commentary_id=2745.

2. Joel B. Green, ed., *CEB Study Bible* (Nashville: Common English Bible, 2013), 1192 OT.

3. Charles L. Aaron Jr., "Commentary on Isaiah 60:1–6," *Working Preacher*, January 6, 2019, https://www.workingpreacher.org/preaching.aspx?commentary _id=3941.

4. Christopher R. Seitz, "The Book of Isaiah 40–66," in *The New Interpreter's Bible Commentary*, vol. 4 (Nashville: Abingdon Press, 2015), 528.

5. R. Alan Culpepper, "The Gospel of Luke," in *The New Interpreter's Bible Commentary*, vol. 8 (Nashville: Abingdon Press, 2015), 59.

6. Culpepper, "Gospel of Luke," 59.

7. Ginger Barfield, "Commentary on Luke 2:41–52," *Working Preacher*, December 27, 2009, https://workingpreacher.org/preaching.aspx?commentary_id=484.

Third Sunday in Ordinary Time

1. Patricia K. Tull, "Isaiah," in *Women's Bible Commentary* (Louisville, KY: Westminster John Knox Press, 2012), 257.
2. David L. Petersen, *The Prophetic Literature* (Louisville, KY: Westminster John Knox Press, 2002), 92.
3. Anathea Portier-Young, "Commentary on Isaiah 62:1–5," *Working Preacher*, January 17, 2010, https://www.workingpreacher.org/preaching.aspx?commentary_id=495.
4. Christopher R. Seitz, "The Book of Isaiah 40–66," in *The New Interpreter's Bible Commentary*, vol. 4 (Nashville: Abingdon Press, 2015), 532.
5. Tull, "Isaiah," 264.
6. Amy-Jill Levine and Marc Zvi Brettler, *The Jewish Annotated New Testament: New Revised Standard Version Bible Translation* (New York: Oxford University Press, 2017), 178.
7. Gail R. O'Day, "The Gospel of John," in *The New Interpreter's Bible Commentary*, vol. 8 (Nashville: Abingdon Press, 2015), 458; cf. Levine and Brettler, *Jewish Annotated New Testament*, 178.
8. Eliseo Pérez-Álvarez, "Commentary on John 2:1–11," *Working Preacher*, January 17, 2016, http://www.workingpreacher.org/preaching.aspx?commentary_id=2748.
9. Gail R. O'Day, "Gospel of John," in *Women's Bible Commentary* (Louisville, KY: Westminster John Knox Press, 2012), 520.

Fourth Sunday in Ordinary Time

1. Joel B. Green, ed., *CEB Study Bible* (Nashville: Common English Bible, 2013), 1255 OT.
2. Patrick D. Miller, "The Book of Jeremiah," in *The New Interpreter's Bible Commentary*, vol. 4 (Nashville: Abingdon Press, 2015), 733.
3. Green, *CEB Study Bible*, 1255 OT.
4. Carol Meyers, *Women in Scripture* (Grand Rapids: Wm. B. Eerdmans Publishing Co., 2001), 324.
5. Miller, "Book of Jeremiah," 734.
6. Miller, "Book of Jeremiah," 735.
7. M. Eugene Boring, "The Gospel of Matthew," in *The New Interpreter's Bible Commentary*, vol. 7 (Nashville: Abingdon Press, 2015), 201.
8. Boring, "Gospel of Matthew," 210.
9. Amy-Jill Levine and Marc Zvi Brettler, *The Jewish Annotated New Testament: New Revised Standard Version Bible Translation* (New York: Oxford University Press, 2017), 13.
10. Daniel J. Harrington, *The Gospel of Matthew* (Collegeville, MN: Liturgical Press, 2007), 191.
11. Harold W. Attridge, Wayne A. Meeks, and Jouette M. Bassler, *HarperCollins Study Bible: New Revised Standard Version with the Apocryphal/Deuterocanonical Books* (San Francisco: HarperOne, 2006), 1690.
12. Amy-Jill Levine, "Gospel of Matthew," in *Women's Bible Commentary* (Louisville, KY: Westminster John Knox Press, 2012), 472.
13. Thomas Bohache, "Matthew," in *Queer Bible Commentary* (London: SCM Press, 2006), 507.

14. Boring, "Gospel of Matthew," 210.
15. Boring, "Gospel of Matthew," 210.

Fifth Sunday in Ordinary Time

1. Priests for Equality, *The Inclusive Bible: The First Egalitarian Translation* (Lanham, MD: Rowman & Littlefield Publishers, 2009), 472.
2. Joel B. Green, ed., *CEB Study Bible* (Nashville: Common English Bible, 2013), 1303 OT.
3. Harold W. Attridge, Wayne A. Meeks, and Jouette M. Bassler, *HarperCollins Study Bible: New Revised Standard Version with the Apocryphal/Deuterocanonical Books* (San Francisco: HarperOne, 2006), 1087.
4. Kathleen M. O'Connor, "Lamentations," in *Women's Bible Commentary* (Louisville, KY: Westminster John Knox Press, 2012), 280.
5. Attridge, Meeks, and Bassler, *HarperCollins Study Bible*, 1087.
6. Kathleen M. O'Connor, "The Book of Lamentations," in *The New Interpreter's Bible Commentary*, vol. 4 (Nashville: Abingdon Press, 2015), 892.
7. C. Clifton Black, "Commentary on Mark 6:14–29," *Working Preacher*, July 12, 2015, https://www.workingpreacher.org/preaching.aspx?commentary_id=2503.
8. Carol Meyers, *Women in Scripture* (Grand Rapids: Wm. B. Eerdmans Publishing Co., 2001), 93.
9. Attridge, Meeks, and Bassler, *HarperCollins Study Bible*, 1735.
10. Attridge, Meeks, and Bassler, *HarperCollins Study Bible*, 1735.

Sixth Sunday in Ordinary Time

1. Joel B. Green, ed., *CEB Study Bible* (Nashville: Common English Bible, 2013), 1341 OT.
2. Katheryn Pfisterer Darr, "The Book of Ezekiel," in *The New Interpreter's Bible Commentary*, vol. 5 (Nashville: Abingdon Press, 2015), 124.
3. Darr, "Book of Ezekiel," 119.
4. Darr, "Book of Ezekiel," 125.
5. Carol Meyers, *Women in Scripture* (Grand Rapids: Wm. B. Eerdmans Publishing Co., 2001), 427.
6. Elizabeth Struthers Malbon, "Gospel of Mark," in *Women's Bible Commentary* (Louisville, KY: Westminster John Knox Press, 2012), 484.
7. Green, *CEB Study Bible*, 81 NT.
8. Leah Clemmons, Sermon on Mark 7:24–37, Candler School of Theology, Atlanta, May 5, 2018.

Seventh Sunday in Ordinary Time

1. Katheryn Pfisterer Darr, "The Book of Ezekiel," in *The New Interpreter's Bible Commentary*, vol. 5 (Nashville: Abingdon Press, 2015), 121.
2. Harold W. Attridge, Wayne A. Meeks, and Jouette M. Bassler, *HarperCollins Study Bible: New Revised Standard Version with the Apocryphal/Deuterocanonical Books* (San Francisco: HarperOne, 2006), 1128.
3. Carol Meyers, *Women in Scripture* (Grand Rapids: Wm. B. Eerdmans Publishing Co., 2001), 536.
4. Meyers, *Women in Scripture*, 537.
5. Jacqueline E. Lapsley, "Ezekiel," in *The New Interpreter's Bible One-Volume Commentary* (Nashville: Abingdon Press, 2010), 464.
6. Attridge, Meeks, and Bassler, *HarperCollins Study Bible*, 1128.

7. Joel B. Green, ed., *CEB Study Bible* (Nashville: Common English Bible, 2013), 1352 OT.

8. Corrine L. Carvalho, "The Challenge of Violence and Gender under Colonization," in *The Hebrew Bible: Feminist and Intersectional Perspectives* (Minneapolis: Fortress Press, 2018), 111.

9. Meyers, *Women in Scripture*, 537.

10. Teresa Hornsby, "Ezekiel," in *Queer Bible Commentary* (London: SCM Press, 2006), 423.

11. Jane D. Schaberg and Sharon H. Ringe, "Gospel of Luke," in *Women's Bible Commentary* (Louisville, KY: Westminster John Knox Press, 2012), 507.

12. Attridge, Meeks, and Bassler, *HarperCollins Study Bible*, 1785.

13. Amy-Jill Levine and Marc Zvi Brettler, *The Jewish Annotated New Testament: New Revised Standard Version Bible Translation* (New York: Oxford University Press, 2017), 136–37.

14. Cf. John T. Carroll, "Luke," in *The New Interpreter's Bible One-Volume Commentary* (Nashville: Abingdon Press, 2010), 694.

15. Meyers, *Women in Scripture*, 114–15.

16. Meyers, *Women in Scripture*, 114–15.

Eighth Sunday in Ordinary Time

1. Gale A. Yee, "The Book of Hosea," in *The New Interpreter's Bible Commentary*, vol. 5 (Nashville: Abingdon Press, 2015), 429.

2. Corrine L. Carvalho, "The Challenge of Violence and Gender under Colonization," in *The Hebrew Bible: Feminist and Intersectional Perspectives* (Minneapolis: Fortress Press, 2018), 110.

3. Michael Carden, "The Book of the Twelve Minor Prophets," in *Queer Bible Commentary* (London: SCM Press, 2006), 445.

4. Yee, "Book of Hosea," 426.

5. Yee, "Book of Hosea," 436.

6. Carol Meyers, *Women in Scripture* (Grand Rapids: Wm. B. Eerdmans Publishing Co., 2001), 85–86.

7. David G. Garber Jr., "Commentary on Hosea 1:2–10," *Working Preacher*, July 28, 2013, https://www.workingpreacher.org/preaching.aspx?commentary_id =1802.

8. Yee, "Book of Hosea," 429.

9. Yee, "Book of Hosea," 430–31.

10. Gale A. Yee, "Hosea," in *Women's Bible Commentary* (Louisville, KY: Westminster John Knox Press, 2012), 305.

11. Yee, "Book of Hosea," 437.

12. R. Alan Culpepper, "The Gospel of Luke," in *The New Interpreter's Bible Commentary*, vol. 8 (Nashville: Abingdon Press, 2015), 326.

13. Culpepper, "Gospel of Luke," 326.

14. Amy-Jill Levine and Marc Zvi Brettler, *The Jewish Annotated New Testament: New Revised Standard Version Bible Translation* (New York: Oxford University Press, 2017), 157, 616.

15. Levine and Brettler, *Jewish Annotated New Testament*, 616.

16. Harold W. Attridge, Wayne A. Meeks, and Jouette M. Bassler, *HarperCollins Study Bible: New Revised Standard Version with the Apocryphal/Deuterocanonical Books* (San Francisco: HarperOne, 2006), 1803.

17. Culpepper, "Gospel of Luke," 326; Luke Timothy Johnson, *The Gospel of Luke* (Collegeville, MN: Liturgical Press, 1991), 312.

18. Joel B. Green, ed., *CEB Study Bible* (Nashville: Common English Bible, 2013), 154 NT.
19. Green, *CEB Study Bible*, 154 NT.
20. Richard Swanson, "Commentary on Luke 20:27–38," *Working Preacher*, November 10, 2013, http://www.workingpreacher.org/preaching.aspx?commentary_id=1852.
21. Culpepper, "Gospel of Luke," 327.
22. Priests for Equality, *The Inclusive Bible: The First Egalitarian Translation* (Lanham, MD: Rowman & Littlefield Publishers, 2009), 693.

Transfiguration Sunday

1. Gale A. Yee, "The Book of Hosea," in *The New Interpreter's Bible Commentary*, vol. 5 (Nashville: Abingdon Press, 2015), 483.
2. Yee, "Book of Hosea," 482.
3. Harold W. Attridge, Wayne A. Meeks, and Jouette M. Bassler, *HarperCollins Study Bible: New Revised Standard Version with the Apocryphal/Deuterocanonical Books* (San Francisco: HarperOne, 2006), 1206.
4. Yee, "Book of Hosea," 483.
5. Beth L. Tanner, "Hosea," in *The New Interpreter's Bible One-Volume Commentary* (Nashville: Abingdon Press, 2010), 498.
6. Yee, "Book of Hosea," 484.
7. Yee, "Book of Hosea," 484.
8. Amy-Jill Levine and Marc Zvi Brettler, *The Jewish Annotated New Testament: New Revised Standard Version Bible Translation* (New York: Oxford University Press, 2017), 80.
9. Attridge, Meeks, and Bassler, *HarperCollins Study Bible*, 1733.
10. Carol Meyers, *Women in Scripture* (Grand Rapids: Wm. B. Eerdmans Publishing Co., 2001), 424.
11. Joel B. Green, ed., *CEB Study Bible* (Nashville: Common English Bible, 2013), 76 NT.

LENT-EASTER-PENTECOST

Ash Wednesday

1. Joel B. Green, ed., *CEB Study Bible* (Nashville: Common English Bible, 2013), 9 OT.
2. Susan Niditch, "Genesis," in *Women's Bible Commentary* (Louisville, KY: Westminster John Knox Press, 2012), 31.
3. Carol Meyers, *Women in Scripture* (Grand Rapids: Wm. B. Eerdmans Publishing Co., 2001), 81.
4. Terence E. Fretheim, "The Book of Genesis," in *The New Interpreter's Bible Commentary*, vol. 1 (Nashville: Abingdon Press, 2015), 53.
5. M. Eugene Boring, "The Gospel of Matthew," in *The New Interpreter's Bible Commentary*, vol. 7 (Nashville: Abingdon Press, 2015), 207–8.
6. Amy-Jill Levine, "Gospel of Matthew," in *Women's Bible Commentary* (Louisville, KY: Westminster John Knox Press, 2012), 476.
7. Harold W. Attridge, Wayne A. Meeks, and Jouette M. Bassler, *HarperCollins Study Bible: New Revised Standard Version with the Apocryphal/Deuterocanonical Books* (San Francisco: HarperOne, 2006), 1712.
8. Levine, "Gospel of Matthew," 476.

9. Boring, "Gospel of Matthew," 234.
10. Boring, "Gospel of Matthew," 234.
11. Green, *CEB Study Bible*, 53 NT.
12. Daniel J. Harrington, *The Gospel of Matthew* (Collegeville, MN: Liturgical Press, 2007), 348.
13. Levine, "Gospel of Matthew," 476.
14. Elisabeth Johnson, "Commentary on Matthew 25:1–13," *Working Preacher*, March 31, 2019, https://www.workingpreacher.org/preaching.aspx?commentary_id=3871.
15. Boring, "Gospel of Matthew," 235.
16. Susan Hylen, "Commentary on Matthew 25:1–13," *Working Preacher*, November 12, 2017, https://www.workingpreacher.org/preaching.aspx?commentary_id=3459.

First Sunday of Lent

1. J. Clinton McCann Jr., "The Book of Psalms," in *The New Interpreter's Bible Commentary*, vol. 3 (Nashville: Abingdon Press: 2015), 347.
2. Nancy L. deClaissé-Walford, "Psalms," in *Women's Bible Commentary* (Louisville, KY: Westminster John Knox Press, 2012), 225.
3. Mark Allan Powell, *HarperCollins Bible Dictionary* (New York: HarperOne, 2011), 926.
4. Elizabeth Struthers Malbon, "Gospel of Mark," in *Women's Bible Commentary* (Louisville, KY: Westminster John Knox Press, 2012), 488.
5. Harold W. Attridge, Wayne A. Meeks, and Jouette M. Bassler, *HarperCollins Study Bible: New Revised Standard Version with the Apocryphal/Deuterocanonical Books* (San Francisco: HarperOne, 2006), 1749.
6. Carol Meyers, *Women in Scripture* (Grand Rapids: Wm. B. Eerdmans Publishing Co., 2001), 432.

Second Sunday of Lent

1. Harold W. Attridge, Wayne A. Meeks, and Jouette M. Bassler, *HarperCollins Study Bible: New Revised Standard Version with the Apocryphal/Deuterocanonical Books* (San Francisco: HarperOne, 2006), 996.
2. Patricia K. Tull, "Isaiah," in *Women's Bible Commentary* (Louisville, KY: Westminster John Knox Press, 2012), 265.
3. Joel B. Green, ed., *CEB Study Bible* (Nashville: Common English Bible, 2013), 1202 OT.
4. Christine Roy Yoder, "Commentary on Isaiah 66:10–14," *Working Preacher*, July 4, 2010, https://www.workingpreacher.org/preaching.aspx?commentary_id=632.
5. Christopher R. Seitz, "The Book of Isaiah 40–66," in *The New Interpreter's Bible Commentary*, vol. 4 (Nashville: Abingdon Press, 2015), 556.
6. Tull, "Isaiah," 265.
7. Green, *CEB Study Bible*, 187 NT.
8. Amy-Jill Levine and Marc Zvi Brettler, *The Jewish Annotated New Testament: New Revised Standard Version Bible Translation* (New York: Oxford University Press, 2017), 193.
9. Gail R. O'Day, "Gospel of John," in *Women's Bible Commentary* (Louisville, KY: Westminster John Knox Press, 2012), 522.
10. Levine and Brettler, *Jewish Annotated New Testament*, 193.
11. Levine and Brettler, *Jewish Annotated New Testament*, 194.

Third Sunday of Lent

1. Susanne Scholz, "Judges," in *Women's Bible Commentary* (Louisville, KY: Westminster John Knox Press, 2012), 121.
2. Harold W. Attridge, Wayne A. Meeks, and Jouette M. Bassler, *HarperCollins Study Bible: New Revised Standard Version with the Apocryphal/Deuterocanonical Books* (San Francisco: HarperOne, 2006), 371.
3. Attridge, Meeks, and Bassler, *HarperCollins Study Bible*, 372.
4. Carol Meyers, *Women in Scripture* (Grand Rapids: Wm. B. Eerdmans Publishing Co., 2001), 69.
5. Attridge, Meeks, and Bassler, *HarperCollins Study Bible*, 372.
6. Jerome F. D. Creach, "Judges," in *The New Interpreter's Bible One-Volume Commentary* (Nashville: Abingdon Press, 2010), 176.
7. Attridge, Meeks, and Bassler, *HarperCollins Study Bible*, 1821.
8. Mark Allan Powell, *HarperCollins Bible Dictionary* (New York: HarperOne, 2011), 912.
9. Amy-Jill Levine and Marc Zvi Brettler, *The Jewish Annotated New Testament: New Revised Standard Version Bible Translation* (New York: Oxford University Press, 2017), 183.
10. Levine and Brettler, *Jewish Annotated New Testament*, 183.
11. Gail R. O'Day, "Gospel of John," in *Women's Bible Commentary* (Louisville, KY: Westminster John Knox Press, 2012), 521.
12. Joel B. Green, ed., *CEB Study Bible* (Nashville: Common English Bible, 2013), 178 NT.
13. O'Day, "Gospel of John," 521.

Fourth Sunday of Lent

1. Carol A. Newsom, "The Book of Job," in *The New Interpreter's Bible Commentary*, vol. 3 (Nashville: Abingdon Press, 2015), 185.
2. Adele Berlin, "Job," in *The New Interpreter's Bible One-Volume Commentary* (Nashville: Abingdon Press, 2010), 298.
3. Berlin, "Job," 298.
4. Newsom, "Book of Job," 186.
5. Sarah Stokes Musser, "Comfort in the Whirlwind? Job, Creation, and Environmental Degradation," *Word & World* 32, no. 3 (Summer 2012): 292.
6. Gail R. O'Day, "Gospel of John," in *Women's Bible Commentary* (Louisville, KY: Westminster John Knox Press, 2012), 523.
7. Gail R. O'Day, "The Gospel of John," in *The New Interpreter's Bible Commentary*, vol. 8 (Nashville: Abingdon Press, 2015), 583; Harold W. Attridge, Wayne A. Meeks, and Jouette M. Bassler, *HarperCollins Study Bible: New Revised Standard Version with the Apocryphal/Deuterocanonical Books* (San Francisco: HarperOne, 2006), 1836.
8. Amy-Jill Levine and Marc Zvi Brettler, *The Jewish Annotated New Testament: New Revised Standard Version Bible Translation* (New York: Oxford University Press, 2017), 201.
9. O'Day, "The Gospel of John," 584.
10. O'Day, "The Gospel of John," 584.
11. O'Day, "The Gospel of John," 585.
12. Joel B. Green, ed., *CEB Study Bible* (Nashville: Common English Bible, 2013), 194 NT.
13. Levine and Brettler, *Jewish Annotated New Testament*, 201.
14. O'Day, "The Gospel of John," 585.

Fifth Sunday of Lent

1. Carol Meyers, *Women in Scripture* (Grand Rapids: Wm. B. Eerdmans Publishing Co., 2001), 549.
2. Joel B. Green, ed., *CEB Study Bible* (Nashville: Common English Bible, 2013), 1008 OT.
3. Harold W. Attridge, Wayne A. Meeks, and Jouette M. Bassler, *HarperCollins Study Bible: New Revised Standard Version with the Apocryphal/Deuterocanonical Books* (San Francisco: HarperOne, 2006), 853.
4. Raymond C. Van Leeuwen, "The Book of Proverbs," in *The New Interpreter's Bible Commentary*, vol. 3 (Nashville: Abingdon Press, 2015), 768.
5. R. Alan Culpepper, "The Gospel of Luke," in *The New Interpreter's Bible Commentary*, vol. 8 (Nashville: Abingdon Press, 2015), 144.
6. Meyers, *Women in Scripture*, 103.
7. Culpepper, "Gospel of Luke," 144.
8. Green, *CEB Study Bible*, 124 NT.
9. Green, *CEB Study Bible*, 124 NT.
10. Jane D. Schaberg and Sharon H. Ringe, "Gospel of Luke," in *Women's Bible Commentary* (Louisville, KY: Westminster John Knox Press, 2012), 507.
11. Amy-Jill Levine and Marc Zvi Brettler, *The Jewish Annotated New Testament: New Revised Standard Version Bible Translation* (New York: Oxford University Press, 2017), 129.
12. Culpepper, "Gospel of Luke," 145.
13. Culpepper, "Gospel of Luke," 146.

Sixth Sunday of Lent

1. Raymond C. Van Leeuwen, "The Book of Proverbs," in *The New Interpreter's Bible Commentary*, vol. 3 (Nashville: Abingdon Press, 2015), 810.
2. Van Leeuwen, "Book of Proverbs," 811.
3. Van Leeuwen, "Book of Proverbs," 811.
4. Judy Fentress-Williams and Melody D. Knowles, "Affirming and Contradicting Gender Stereotypes," in *The Hebrew Bible: Feminist and Intersectional Perspectives* (Minneapolis: Fortress Press, 2018), 149.
5. Glenn D. Pemberton, "Proverbs," in *New Interpreter's Bible One-Volume Commentary* (Nashville: Abingdon Press, 2010), 355.
6. Pemberton, "Proverbs," 355.
7. Joel B. Green, ed., *CEB Study Bible* (Nashville: Common English Bible, 2013), 1018 OT.
8. Christine Roy Yoder, "Proverbs," in *Women's Bible Commentary* (Louisville, KY: Westminster John Knox Press, 2012), 236.
9. Daniel J. Harrington, *The Gospel of Matthew* (Collegeville, MN: Liturgical Press, 2007), 388.
10. Amy-Jill Levine and Marc Zvi Brettler, *The Jewish Annotated New Testament: New Revised Standard Version Bible Translation* (New York: Oxford University Press, 2017), 63.
11. Harrington, *Gospel of Matthew*, 388; M. Eugene Boring, "The Gospel of Matthew," in *The New Interpreter's Bible Commentary*, vol. 7 (Nashville: Abingdon Press, 2015), 361.
12. Boring, "Gospel of Matthew," 361.
13. Boring, "Gospel of Matthew," 361–62.
14. Amy-Jill Levine, "Gospel of Matthew," in *Women's Bible Commentary* (Louisville, KY: Westminster John Knox Press, 2012), 477.

Maundy Thursday

1. Raymond C. Van Leeuwen, "The Book of Proverbs," in *The New Interpreter's Bible Commentary*, vol. 3 (Nashville: Abingdon Press, 2015), 818.
2. Harold W. Attridge, Wayne A. Meeks, and Jouette M. Bassler, *HarperCollins Study Bible: New Revised Standard Version with the Apocryphal/Deuterocanonical Books* (San Francisco: HarperOne, 2006), 863.
3. Van Leeuwen, "Book of Proverbs," 817.
4. Joel B. Green, ed., *CEB Study Bible* (Nashville: Common English Bible, 2013), 1019–20 OT.
5. Carol Meyers, *Women in Scripture* (Grand Rapids: Wm. B. Eerdmans Publishing Co., 2001), 549.
6. Meyers, *Women in Scripture*, 434.
7. C. Clifton Black, "Mark," in *The New Interpreter's Bible One-Volume Commentary* (Nashville: Abingdon Press, 2010), 673.
8. Attridge, Meeks, and Bassler, *HarperCollins Study Bible*, 1752.
9. Amy-Jill Levine and Marc Zvi Brettler, *The Jewish Annotated New Testament: New Revised Standard Version Bible Translation* (New York: Oxford University Press, 2017), 99.
10. Black, "Mark," 673.
11. Pheme Perkins, "The Gospel of Mark," in *The New Interpreter's Bible Commentary*, vol. 7 (Nashville: Abingdon Press, 2015), 530.
12. Perkins, "Gospel of Mark," 530; Attridge, Meeks, and Bassler, *HarperCollins Study Bible*, 1752.
13. Meyers, *Women in Scripture*, 434.
14. Meyers, *Women in Scripture*, 434.
15. Perkins, "Gospel of Mark," 530.
16. Green, *CEB Study Bible*, 96 NT.

Good Friday

1. Harold W. Attridge, Wayne A. Meeks, and Jouette M. Bassler, *HarperCollins Study Bible: New Revised Standard Version with the Apocryphal/Deuterocanonical Books* (San Francisco: HarperOne, 2006), 303.
2. Joel B. Green, ed., *CEB Study Bible* (Nashville: Common English Bible, 2013), 317 OT.
3. Carolyn Pressler, "Deuteronomy," in *Women's Bible Commentary* (Louisville, KY: Westminster John Knox Press, 2012), 102.
4. Gail R. O'Day, "The Gospel of John," in *The New Interpreter's Bible Commentary*, vol. 8 (Nashville: Abingdon Press, 2015), 711.
5. Attridge, Meeks, and Bassler, *HarperCollins Study Bible*, 1850.
6. Green, *CEB Study Bible*, 209 NT.
7. O'Day, "The Gospel of John," 712; Amy-Jill Levine and Marc Zvi Brettler, *The Jewish Annotated New Testament: New Revised Standard Version Bible Translation* (New York: Oxford University Press, 2017), 215.
8. O'Day, "The Gospel of John," 712.
9. Levine and Brettler, *Jewish Annotated New Testament*, 215.
10. Gail R. O'Day, "Gospel of John," in *Women's Bible Commentary* (Louisville, KY: Westminster John Knox Press, 2012), 527.
11. Robert E. Goss, "John," in *Queer Bible Commentary* (London: SCM Press, 2006), 562.
12. Dorothy Ann Lee, "John," in *The New Interpreter's Bible One-Volume Commentary* (Nashville: Abingdon Press, 2010), 731.

Holy Saturday

1. Gale A. Yee, "The Book of Hosea," in *The New Interpreter's Bible Commentary*, vol. 5 (Nashville: Abingdon Press, 2015), 491; Harold W. Attridge, Wayne A. Meeks, and Jouette M. Bassler, *HarperCollins Study Bible: New Revised Standard Version with the Apocryphal/Deuterocanonical Books* (San Francisco: HarperOne, 2006), 1207.
2. Joel B. Green, ed., *CEB Study Bible* (Nashville: Common English Bible, 2013), 1442 OT.
3. Yee, "Book of Hosea," 492.
4. Beth L. Tanner, "Hosea," in *The New Interpreter's Bible One-Volume Commentary* (Nashville: Abingdon Press, 2010), 498.
5. Yee, "Book of Hosea," 493.
6. Amy-Jill Levine and Marc Zvi Brettler, *The Jewish Annotated New Testament: New Revised Standard Version Bible Translation* (New York: Oxford University Press, 2017), 162; John T. Carroll, "Luke," in *The New Interpreter's Bible One-Volume Commentary* (Nashville: Abingdon Press, 2010), 707.
7. Green, *CEB Study Bible*, 163 NT.
8. R. Alan Culpepper, "The Gospel of Luke," in *The New Interpreter's Bible Commentary*, vol. 8 (Nashville: Abingdon Press, 2015), 394.
9. Green, *CEB Study Bible*, 163 NT.
10. Attridge, Meeks, and Bassler, *HarperCollins Study Bible*, 1810.
11. Culpepper, "Gospel of Luke," 395.
12. Luke Timothy Johnson, *The Gospel of Luke* (Collegeville, MN: Liturgical Press, 1991), 385.

Resurrection Sunday

1. Renita J. Weems, "The Song of Songs," in *The New Interpreter's Bible Commentary*, vol. 3 (Nashville: Abingdon Press, 2015), 1024.
2. J. Cheryl Exum, "Song of Songs," in *Women's Bible Commentary* (Louisville, KY: Westminster John Knox Press, 2012), 248.
3. Weems, "Song of Songs," 1024.
4. Weems, "Song of Songs," 1023.
5. Harold W. Attridge, Wayne A. Meeks, and Jouette M. Bassler, *HarperCollins Study Bible: New Revised Standard Version with the Apocryphal/Deuterocanonical Books* (San Francisco: HarperOne, 2006), 1757.
6. Amy-Jill Levine and Marc Zvi Brettler, *The Jewish Annotated New Testament: New Revised Standard Version Bible Translation* (New York: Oxford University Press, 2017), 105.
7. C. Clifton Black, "Mark," in *The New Interpreter's Bible One-Volume Commentary* (Nashville: Abingdon Press, 2010), 677–78.
8. Carol Meyers, *Women in Scripture* (Grand Rapids: Wm. B. Eerdmans Publishing Co., 2001), 123.

Resurrection Evening

1. Fred W. Dobbs-Allsopp, "Song of Songs," in *The New Interpreter's Bible One-Volume Commentary* (Nashville: Abingdon Press, 2010), 379.
2. Renita J. Weems, "The Song of Songs," in *The New Interpreter's Bible Commentary*, vol. 3 (Nashville: Abingdon Press, 2015), 1046.
3. Harold W. Attridge, Wayne A. Meeks, and Jouette M. Bassler, *HarperCollins Study Bible: New Revised Standard Version with the Apocryphal/Deuterocanonical Books* (San Francisco: HarperOne, 2006), 906.

4. Wil Gafney, "Commentary on Song of Solomon 2:8–13," *Working Preacher*, September 2, 2012, https://www.workingpreacher.org/preaching.aspx?commentary_id=1402.
5. Brittany E. Wilson, "Mary Magdalene and Her Interpreters," in *Women's Bible Commentary* (Louisville, KY: Westminster John Knox Press, 2012), 532.
6. Wilson, "Mary Magdalene and Her Interpreters," 532.
7. Mark Allan Powell, *HarperCollins Bible Dictionary*, 3rd ed. (New York: HarperOne, 2011), 607.
8. Carol Meyers, *Women in Scripture* (Grand Rapids: Wm. B. Eerdmans Publishing Co., 2001), 120–21.
9. Attridge, Meeks, and Bassler, *HarperCollins Study Bible*, 1852.
10. Powell, *HarperCollins Bible Dictionary*, 608.

Second Sunday of Easter

1. Nancy Bowen, "Esther," in *The New Interpreter's Bible One-Volume Commentary* (Nashville: Abingdon Press, 2010), 280.
2. Sidnie White Crawford, "The Book of Esther," in *The New Interpreter's Bible Commentary*, vol. 6 (Nashville: Abingdon Press, 2015), 21.
3. Harold W. Attridge, Wayne A. Meeks, and Jouette M. Bassler, *HarperCollins Study Bible: New Revised Standard Version with the Apocryphal/Deuterocanonical Books* (San Francisco: HarperOne, 2006), 682.
4. Crawford, "Book of Esther," 22.
5. Sidnie White Crawford, "Esther," in *Women's Bible Commentary* (Louisville, KY: Westminster John Knox Press, 2012), 204.
6. M. Eugene Boring, "The Gospel of Matthew," in *The New Interpreter's Bible Commentary*, vol. 7 (Nashville: Abingdon Press, 2015), 371.
7. Carol Meyers, *Women in Scripture* (Grand Rapids: Wm. B. Eerdmans Publishing Co., 2001), 123.
8. Boring, "Gospel of Matthew," 372.
9. Boring, "Gospel of Matthew," 372.
10. Stephen Westerholm, "Matthew," in *The New Interpreter's Bible One-Volume Commentary* (Nashville: Abingdon Press, 2010), 656.
11. Attridge, Meeks, and Bassler, *HarperCollins Study Bible*, 1720.
12. Amy-Jill Levine and Marc Zvi Brettler, *The Jewish Annotated New Testament: New Revised Standard Version Bible Translation* (New York: Oxford University Press, 2017), 66.
13. Boring, "Gospel of Matthew," 373.

Third Sunday of Easter

1. Harold W. Attridge, Wayne A. Meeks, and Jouette M. Bassler, *HarperCollins Study Bible: New Revised Standard Version with the Apocryphal/Deuterocanonical Books* (San Francisco: HarperOne, 2006), 683.
2. Mark Allan Powell, *HarperCollins Bible Dictionary* (New York: HarperOne, 2011), 261.
3. Lincoln Blades, "Why You Can't Ever Call an Enslaved Woman a 'Mistress,'" *Teen Vogue*, February 27, 2017, http://www.teenvogue.com/story/the-washington-post-thomas-jefferson-sally-hemings-slavery-mistress.
4. Sidnie White Crawford, "The Book of Esther," in *The New Interpreter's Bible Commentary*, vol. 6 (Nashville: Abingdon Press, 2015), 6.
5. Nancy Bowen, "Esther," in *The New Interpreter's Bible One-Volume Commentary* (Nashville: Abingdon Press, 2010), 281.

6. Joel B. Green, ed., *CEB Study Bible* (Nashville: Common English Bible, 2013), 164 NT.

7. Amy-Jill Levine and Marc Zvi Brettler, *The Jewish Annotated New Testament: New Revised Standard Version Bible Translation* (New York: Oxford University Press, 2017), 166; John T. Carroll, "Luke," in *The New Interpreter's Bible One-Volume Commentary* (Nashville: Abingdon Press, 2010), 707.

8. Robert E. Goss, "Luke," in *Queer Bible Commentary* (London: SCM Press, 2006), 545; R. Alan Culpepper, "The Gospel of Luke," in *The New Interpreter's Bible Commentary*, vol. 8 (Nashville: Abingdon Press, 2015), 405.

9. Luke Timothy Johnson, *The Gospel of Luke* (Collegeville, MN: Liturgical Press, 1991), 393.

10. Culpepper, "Gospel of Luke," 405.

11. Culpepper, "Gospel of Luke," 405.

12. Attridge, Meeks, and Bassler, *HarperCollins Study Bible*, 1811; Levine and Brettler, *Jewish Annotated New Testament*, 166.

13. Culpepper, "Gospel of Luke," 406.

14. Levine and Brettler, *Jewish Annotated New Testament*, 165.

15. Carroll, "Luke," 707; Goss, "Luke," 545.

Fourth Sunday of Easter

1. Mona West, "Esther," in *Queer Bible Commentary* (London: SCM Press, 2006), 282.

2. Nancy Bowen, "Esther," in *The New Interpreter's Bible One-Volume Commentary* (Nashville: Abingdon Press, 2010), 283.

3. Sidnie White Crawford, "The Book of Esther," in *The New Interpreter's Bible Commentary*, vol. 6 (Nashville: Abingdon Press, 2015), 41.

4. Crawford, "Book of Esther," 41.

5. Sidnie White Crawford, "Esther," in *Women's Bible Commentary* (Louisville, KY: Westminster John Knox Press, 2012), 206.

6. Crawford, "Book of Esther," 41.

7. Harold W. Attridge, Wayne A. Meeks, and Jouette M. Bassler, *HarperCollins Study Bible: New Revised Standard Version with the Apocryphal/Deuterocanonical Books* (San Francisco: HarperOne, 2006), 1776.

8. Carol Meyers, *Women in Scripture* (Grand Rapids: Wm. B. Eerdmans Publishing Co., 2001), 440.

9. R. Alan Culpepper, "The Gospel of Luke," in *The New Interpreter's Bible Commentary*, vol. 8 (Nashville: Abingdon Press, 2015), 130.

10. Culpepper, "Gospel of Luke," 129.

11. Joel B. Green, ed., *CEB Study Bible* (Nashville: Common English Bible, 2013), 122 NT.

12. Amy-Jill Levine and Marc Zvi Brettler, *The Jewish Annotated New Testament: New Revised Standard Version Bible Translation* (New York: Oxford University Press, 2017), 127.

Fifth Sunday of Easter

1. Sidnie White Crawford, "Esther," in *Women's Bible Commentary* (Louisville, KY: Westminster John Knox Press, 2012), 206.

2. Brent A. Strawn, "Commentary on Esther 7:1–6, 9–10; 9:20–22," *Working Preacher*, September 27, 2009, https://www.workingpreacher.org/preaching .aspx?commentary_id=389.

3. David Schnasa Jacobsen, "Commentary on Luke 13:10–17," *Working Preacher*, August 21, 2016, https://www.workingpreacher.org/preaching.aspx ?commentary_id=2956.
4. Carol Meyers, *Women in Scripture* (Grand Rapids: Wm. B. Eerdmans Publishing Co., 2001), 446.
5. Ira Brent Driggers, "Commentary on Luke 13:10–17," *Working Preacher*, August 25, 2019, https://www.workingpreacher.org/preaching.aspx?commen tary_id=4144.
6. R. Alan Culpepper, "The Gospel of Luke," in *The New Interpreter's Bible Commentary*, vol. 8 (Nashville: Abingdon Press, 2015), 226.

Sixth Sunday of Easter

1. Carol A. Newsom, "The Book of Job," in *The New Interpreter's Bible Commentary*, vol. 3 (Nashville: Abingdon Press, 2015), 39.
2. Newsom, "Book of Job," 47.
3. Adele Berlin, "Job," in *The New Interpreter's Bible One-Volume Commentary* (Nashville: Abingdon Press, 2010), 290.
4. Newsom, "Book of Job," 47.
5. Newsom, "Book of Job," 47–48.
6. Carol Meyers, *Women in Scripture* (Grand Rapids: Wm. B. Eerdmans Publishing Co., 2001), 293.
7. Luke Timothy Johnson, *The Gospel of Luke* (Collegeville, MN: Liturgical Press, 1991), 218.
8. Harold W. Attridge, Wayne A. Meeks, and Jouette M. Bassler, *HarperCollins Study Bible: New Revised Standard Version with the Apocryphal/Deuterocanonical Books* (San Francisco: HarperOne, 2006), 1792.
9. R. Alan Culpepper, "The Gospel of Luke," in *The New Interpreter's Bible Commentary*, vol. 8 (Nashville: Abingdon Press, 2015), 232.
10. Culpepper, "Gospel of Luke," 233.
11. Amy-Jill Levine and Marc Zvi Brettler, *The Jewish Annotated New Testament: New Revised Standard Version Bible Translation* (New York: Oxford University Press, 2017), 145.
12. Attridge, Meeks, and Bassler, *HarperCollins Study Bible*, 1792.

Ascension (Thursday)

1. Joel B. Green, ed., *CEB Study Bible* (Nashville: Common English Bible, 2013), 980 OT.
2. Carol Meyers, *Women in Scripture* (Grand Rapids: Wm. B. Eerdmans Publishing Co., 2001), 300.
3. Wilda Gafney, *Womanist Midrash: A Reintroduction to the Women of the Torah and the Throne* (Louisville, KY: Westminster John Knox Press, 2017), 75.
4. Nancy L. deClaissé-Walford, "Psalms," in *Women's Bible Commentary* (Louisville, KY: Westminster John Knox Press, 2012), 230.
5. Amy-Jill Levine and Marc Zvi Brettler, *The Jewish Annotated New Testament: New Revised Standard Version Bible Translation* (New York: Oxford University Press, 2017), 117, 147.
6. Levine and Brettler, *Jewish Annotated New Testament*, 146.
7. Green, *CEB Study Bible*, 143 NT.
8. R. Alan Culpepper, "The Gospel of Luke," in *The New Interpreter's Bible Commentary*, vol. 8 (Nashville: Abingdon Press, 2015), 245.
9. Green, *CEB Study Bible*, 143 NT.

10. Culpepper, "Gospel of Luke," 245.
11. Luke Timothy Johnson, *The Gospel of Luke* (Collegeville, MN: Liturgical Press, 1991), 236.
12. Culpepper, "Gospel of Luke," 245.
13. L. Johnson, *Gospel of Luke*, 236.
14. Levine and Brettler, *Jewish Annotated New Testament*, 147.
15. Levine and Brettler, *Jewish Annotated New Testament*, 146.

Seventh Sunday of Easter

1. Christine Roy Yoder, "Proverbs," in *Women's Bible Commentary* (Louisville, KY: Westminster John Knox Press, 2012), 235.
2. Elizabeth Stuart, "Proverbs," in *Queer Bible Commentary* (London: SCM Press, 2006), 330.
3. Yoder, "Proverbs," 235.
4. Raymond C. Van Leeuwen, "The Book of Proverbs," in *The New Interpreter's Bible Commentary*, vol. 3 (Nashville: Abingdon Press, 2015), 805.
5. Harold W. Attridge, Wayne A. Meeks, and Jouette M. Bassler, *HarperCollins Study Bible: New Revised Standard Version with the Apocryphal/Deuterocanonical Books* (San Francisco: HarperOne, 2006), 859.
6. Luke Timothy Johnson, *The Gospel of Luke* (Collegeville, MN: Liturgical Press, 1991), 269.
7. R. Alan Culpepper, "The Gospel of Luke," in *The New Interpreter's Bible Commentary*, vol. 8 (Nashville: Abingdon Press, 2015), 280; Joel B. Green, ed., *CEB Study Bible* (Nashville: Common English Bible, 2013), 148 NT.
8. Carol Meyers, *Women in Scripture* (Grand Rapids: Wm. B. Eerdmans Publishing Co., 2001), 449.
9. Culpepper, "Gospel of Luke," 281.
10. Green, *CEB Study Bible*, 148 NT.
11. Culpepper, "Gospel of Luke," 282.
12. L. Johnson, *Gospel of Luke*, 269.
13. David Lose, "Commentary on Luke 18:1–8," *Working Preacher*, October 17, 2010, http://www.workingpreacher.org/preaching.aspx?commentary_id=810.
14. Brittany E. Wilson, "Commentary on Luke 18:1–8," *Working Preacher*, October 20, 2019, https://www.workingpreacher.org/preaching.aspx?commentary_id=4201.

Pentecost Sunday

1. Wil Gafney, "Commentary on Joel 2:23–32," *Working Preacher*, October 24, 2010, https://www.workingpreacher.org/preaching.aspx?commentary_id=706.
2. Harold W. Attridge, Wayne A. Meeks, and Jouette M. Bassler, *HarperCollins Study Bible: New Revised Standard Version with the Apocryphal/Deuterocanonical Books* (San Francisco: HarperOne, 2006), 1210.
3. L. Juliana M. Claassens, "Joel," in *Women's Bible Commentary* (Louisville, KY: Westminster John Knox Press, 2012), 310.
4. Joel B. Green, ed., *CEB Study Bible* (Nashville: Common English Bible, 2013), 1450 OT.
5. Elizabeth Achtemeier, "The Book of Joel," in *The New Interpreter's Bible Commentary*, vol. 5 (Nashville: Abingdon Press, 2015), 519.
6. Attridge, Meeks, and Bassler, *HarperCollins Study Bible*, 1213.

7. Luke Timothy Johnson, *The Acts of the Apostles* (Collegeville, MN: Liturgical Press, 1992), 34.
8. Robert W. Wall, "The Acts of the Apostles," in *The New Interpreter's Bible Commentary*, vol. 9 (Nashville: Abingdon Press, 2015), 32.
9. L. Johnson, *Acts of the Apostles*, 34.
10. L. Johnson, *Acts of the Apostles*, 34.
11. Attridge, Meeks, and Bassler, *HarperCollins Study Bible*, 1858.
12. Joel B. Green, "Acts," in *The New Interpreter's Bible One-Volume Commentary* (Nashville: Abingdon Press, 2010), 739.
13. Green, "Acts," 739.
14. Margaret Aymer, "Commentary on Acts 2:1–21," *Working Preacher*, June 4, 2017, https://www.workingpreacher.org/preaching.aspx?commentary _id=3282.
15. Thomas Bohache, Robert Goss, Deryn Guest, and Mona West, "Acts of the Apostles," in *Queer Bible Commentary* (London: SCM Press, 2006), 568.
16. Margaret Aymer, "Acts of the Apostles," in *Women's Bible Commentary* (Louisville, KY: Westminster John Knox Press, 2012), 538–39.
17. Green, "Acts," 739.
18. Attridge, Meeks, and Bassler, *HarperCollins Study Bible*, 1859–60.

THE SEASON AFTER PENTECOST

Trinity Sunday

1. Joel B. Green, ed., *CEB Study Bible* (Nashville: Common English Bible, 2013), 4 OT.
2. Harold W. Attridge, Wayne A. Meeks, and Jouette M. Bassler, *HarperCollins Study Bible: New Revised Standard Version with the Apocryphal/Deuterocanonical Books* (San Francisco: HarperOne, 2006), 5.
3. Susan Niditch, "Genesis," in *Women's Bible Commentary* (Louisville, KY: Westminster John Knox Press, 2012), 30.
4. Green, *CEB Study Bible*, 4 OT.
5. "Other ancient authorities read *for as yet the Spirit* (others, *Holy Spirit*) *had not been given*." Attridge, Meeks, and Bassler, *HarperCollins Study Bible*, 1830.

Ninth Sunday in Ordinary Time

1. Terence E. Fretheim, "The Book of Genesis," in *The New Interpreter's Bible Commentary*, vol. 1 (Nashville: Abingdon Press, 2015), 41.
2. Joel B. Green, ed., *CEB Study Bible* (Nashville: Common English Bible, 2013), 7 OT.
3. Michael Carden, "Genesis/Bereshit," in *Queer Bible Commentary* (London: SCM Press, 2006), 26.
4. Green, *CEB Study Bible*, 8 OT.
5. Fretheim, "Book of Genesis," 43.
6. Harold W. Attridge, Wayne A. Meeks, and Jouette M. Bassler, *HarperCollins Study Bible: New Revised Standard Version with the Apocryphal/Deuterocanonical Books* (San Francisco: HarperOne, 2006), 9.
7. Fretheim, "Book of Genesis," 45.
8. Amy-Jill Levine and Marc Zvi Brettler, *The Jewish Annotated New Testament: New Revised Standard Version Bible Translation* (New York: Oxford University Press, 2017), 230.

9. Robert W. Wall, "The Acts of the Apostles," in *The New Interpreter's Bible Commentary*, vol. 9 (Nashville: Abingdon Press, 2015), 77 n. 213.

10. Carol Meyers, *Women in Scripture* (Grand Rapids: Wm. B. Eerdmans Publishing Co., 2001), 150.

11. Margaret Aymer, "Acts of the Apostles," in *Women's Bible Commentary* (Louisville, KY: Westminster John Knox Press, 2012), 539.

Tenth Sunday in Ordinary Time

1. Harold W. Attridge, Wayne A. Meeks, and Jouette M. Bassler, *HarperCollins Study Bible: New Revised Standard Version with the Apocryphal/Deuterocanonical Books* (San Francisco: HarperOne, 2006), 27.

2. Dennis T. Olson, "Genesis," in *The New Interpreter's Bible One-Volume Commentary* (Nashville: Abingdon Press, 2010), 16.

3. Olson, "Genesis," 16.

4. Susan Niditch, "Genesis," in *Women's Bible Commentary* (Louisville, KY: Westminster John Knox Press, 2012), 33.

5. Amy-Jill Levine and Marc Zvi Brettler, *The Jewish Annotated New Testament: New Revised Standard Version Bible Translation* (New York: Oxford University Press, 2017), 243.

6. Attridge, Meeks, and Bassler, *HarperCollins Study Bible*, 1873.

7. Margaret Aymer, "Acts of the Apostles," in *Women's Bible Commentary* (Louisville, KY: Westminster John Knox Press, 2012), 541.

8. Carol Meyers, *Women in Scripture* (Grand Rapids: Wm. B. Eerdmans Publishing Co., 2001), 160.

9. Robert W. Wall, "The Acts of the Apostles," in *The New Interpreter's Bible Commentary*, vol. 9 (Nashville: Abingdon Press, 2015), 133.

10. Susan E. Hylen, *Women in the New Testament World* (New York: Oxford University Press, 2019), 61.

11. Hylen, *Women in the New Testament World*, 61.

Eleventh Sunday in Ordinary Time

1. Joel B. Green, ed., *CEB Study Bible* (Nashville: Common English Bible, 2013), 32 OT.

2. Terence E. Fretheim, "The Book of Genesis," in *The New Interpreter's Bible Commentary*, vol. 1 (Nashville: Abingdon Press, 2015), 138.

3. See Karen D. Scheib, *Pastoral Care: Telling the Stories of Our Lives* (Nashville: Abingdon Press, 2016), 28.

4. Fretheim, "Book of Genesis," 140.

5. Tamar Kadari, "Lot's Wife: Midrash and Aggadah," *Jewish Women's Archive*, https://jwa.org/encyclopedia/article/lots-wife-midrash-and-aggadah.

6. Kadari, "Lot's Wife"; Michael Carden, "Genesis/Bereshit," in *Queer Bible Commentary* (London: SCM Press, 2006), 38.

7. Mark Allan Powell, *HarperCollins Bible Dictionary* (New York: HarperOne, 2011), 908.

8. Amy-Jill Levine and Marc Zvi Brettler, *The Jewish Annotated New Testament: New Revised Standard Version Bible Translation* (New York: Oxford University Press, 2017), 247.

9. Robert W. Wall, "The Acts of the Apostles," in *The New Interpreter's Bible Commentary*, vol. 9 (Nashville: Abingdon Press, 2015), 140.

10. Carol Meyers, *Women in Scripture* (Grand Rapids: Wm. B. Eerdmans Publishing Co., 2001), 123.

11. Margaret Aymer, "Acts of the Apostles," in *Women's Bible Commentary* (Louisville, KY: Westminster John Knox Press, 2012), 542–43.
12. Meyers, *Women in Scripture*, 145.
13. Aymer, "Acts of the Apostles," 543.

Twelfth Sunday in Ordinary Time

1. Carol Meyers, *Women in Scripture* (Grand Rapids: Wm. B. Eerdmans Publishing Co., 2001), 179.
2. Joel B. Green, ed., *CEB Study Bible* (Nashville: Common English Bible, 2013), 32 OT.
3. Terence E. Fretheim, "The Book of Genesis," in *The New Interpreter's Bible Commentary*, vol. 1 (Nashville: Abingdon Press, 2015), 140.
4. Harold W. Attridge, Wayne A. Meeks, and Jouette M. Bassler, *HarperCollins Study Bible: New Revised Standard Version with the Apocryphal/Deuterocanonical Books* (San Francisco: HarperOne, 2006), 30.
5. Mark Allan Powell, *HarperCollins Bible Dictionary* (New York: HarperOne, 2011), 796.
6. Attridge, Meeks, and Bassler, *HarperCollins Study Bible*, 795.
7. Robert W. Wall, "The Acts of the Apostles," in *The New Interpreter's Bible Commentary*, vol. 9 (Nashville: Abingdon Press, 2015), 182.
8. Attridge, Meeks, and Bassler, *HarperCollins Study Bible*, 1886.
9. Joel B. Green, "Acts," in *The New Interpreter's Bible One-Volume Commentary* (Nashville: Abingdon Press, 2010), 755.
10. Susan E. Hylen, *Women in the New Testament World* (New York: Oxford University Press, 2019), 157.
11. Margaret Aymer, "Acts of the Apostles," in *Women's Bible Commentary* (Louisville, KY: Westminster John Knox Press, 2012), 543.

Thirteenth Sunday in Ordinary Time

1. Harold W. Attridge, Wayne A. Meeks, and Jouette M. Bassler, *HarperCollins Study Bible: New Revised Standard Version with the Apocryphal/Deuterocanonical Books* (San Francisco: HarperOne, 2006), 25.
2. Phyllis Trible, *Texts of Terror: Literary-Feminist Readings of Biblical Narratives* (Philadelphia: Fortress Press, 1984), 28–29.
3. Trible, *Texts of Terror*, 27.
4. Susan Niditch, "Genesis," in *Women's Bible Commentary* (Louisville, KY: Westminster John Knox Press, 2012), 34.
5. Wilda Gafney, *Womanist Midrash: A Reintroduction to the Women of the Torah and the Throne* (Louisville, KY: Westminster John Knox Press, 2017), 34.
6. Amy-Jill Levine and Marc Zvi Brettler, *The Jewish Annotated New Testament: New Revised Standard Version Bible Translation* (New York: Oxford University Press, 2017), 260–61.
7. Robert W. Wall, "The Acts of the Apostles," in *The New Interpreter's Bible Commentary*, vol. 9 (Nashville: Abingdon Press, 2015), 200.
8. Wall, "Acts of the Apostles," 200.
9. Margaret Aymer, "Acts of the Apostles," in *Women's Bible Commentary* (Louisville, KY: Westminster John Knox Press, 2012), 544.
10. Miriam Therese Winter, *WomanWord: A Feminist Lectionary and Psalter; Women of the New Testament* (New York: Crossroad, 1990), 234.
11. Carol Meyers, *Women in Scripture* (Grand Rapids: Wm. B. Eerdmans Publishing Co., 2001), 137.

Fourteenth Sunday in Ordinary Time

1. Kathryn M. Schifferdecker, "Commentary on Genesis 24:34–38, 42–49, 58–67," *Working Preacher*, July 9, 2017, https://www.workingpreacher.org /preaching.aspx?commentary_id=3281.
2. Susan Niditch, "Genesis," in *Women's Bible Commentary* (Louisville, KY: Westminster John Knox Press, 2012), 34.
3. Robert W. Wall, "The Acts of the Apostles," in *The New Interpreter's Bible Commentary*, vol. 9 (Nashville: Abingdon Press, 2015), 229.
4. Joel B. Green, "Acts," in *The New Interpreter's Bible One-Volume Commentary* (Nashville: Abingdon Press, 2010), 760; Luke Timothy Johnson, *The Acts of the Apostles* (Collegeville, MN: Liturgical Press, 1992), 369.
5. Carol Meyers, *Women in Scripture* (Grand Rapids: Wm. B. Eerdmans Publishing Co., 2001), 467.
6. Harold W. Attridge, Wayne A. Meeks, and Jouette M. Bassler, *HarperCollins Study Bible: New Revised Standard Version with the Apocryphal/Deuterocanonical Books* (San Francisco: HarperOne, 2006), 1895.
7. Margaret Aymer, "Acts of the Apostles," in *Women's Bible Commentary* (Louisville, KY: Westminster John Knox Press, 2012), 544.
8. Wall, "Acts of the Apostles," 229.
9. Attridge, Meeks, and Bassler, *HarperCollins Study Bible*, 1895.
10. Wall, "Acts of the Apostles," 230.
11. Meyers, *Women in Scripture*, 467–68.
12. Meyers, *Women in Scripture*, 468.

Fifteenth Sunday in Ordinary Time

1. Terence E. Fretheim, "The Book of Genesis," in *The New Interpreter's Bible Commentary*, vol. 1 (Nashville: Abingdon Press, 2015), 174.
2. Wilda Gafney, *Womanist Midrash: A Reintroduction to the Women of the Torah and the Throne* (Louisville, KY: Westminster John Knox Press, 2017), 49.
3. Fretheim, "Book of Genesis," 175.
4. Carol Meyers, *Women in Scripture* (Grand Rapids: Wm. B. Eerdmans Publishing Co., 2001), 143.
5. Harold W. Attridge, Wayne A. Meeks, and Jouette M. Bassler, *HarperCollins Study Bible: New Revised Standard Version with the Apocryphal/Deuterocanonical Books* (San Francisco: HarperOne, 2006), 40; Michael Carden, "Genesis/Bereshit," in *Queer Bible Commentary* (London: SCM Press, 2006), 47.
6. Susan Niditch, "Genesis," in *Women's Bible Commentary* (Louisville, KY: Westminster John Knox Press, 2012), 37.
7. Joel B. Green, ed., *CEB Study Bible* (Nashville: Common English Bible, 2013), 300 NT.
8. N. T. Wright, "The Letter to the Romans," in *The New Interpreter's Bible Commentary*, vol. 9 (Nashville: Abingdon Press, 2015), 661.
9. Charles Cousar, "Romans," in *The New Interpreter's Bible One-Volume Commentary* (Nashville: Abingdon Press, 2010), 786; Green, *CEB Study Bible*, 300 NT.
10. Green, *CEB Study Bible*, 300 NT.
11. Meyers, *Women in Scripture*, 135.
12. Meyers, *Women in Scripture*, 135; Wright, "Letter to the Romans," 657.
13. Wright, "Letter to the Romans," 658.
14. Cousar, "Romans," 786.

15. Attridge, Meeks, and Bassler, *HarperCollins Study Bible*, 1931.
16. Wright, "Letter to the Romans," 658.
17. Cousar, "Romans," 786; Meyers, *Women in Scripture*, 107.
18. Cousar, "Romans," 786.
19. Thomas Hanks, "Romans," in *Queer Bible Commentary* (London: SCM Press, 2006), 604.
20. Beverly Roberts Gaventa, "Romans," in *Women's Bible Commentary* (Louisville, KY: Westminster John Knox Press, 2012), 555–56.

Sixteenth Sunday in Ordinary Time

1. Harold W. Attridge, Wayne A. Meeks, and Jouette M. Bassler, *HarperCollins Study Bible: New Revised Standard Version with the Apocryphal/Deuterocanonical Books* (San Francisco: HarperOne, 2006), 46.
2. Joel B. Green, ed., *CEB Study Bible* (Nashville: Common English Bible, 2013), 40 OT.
3. Wilda Gafney, *Womanist Midrash: A Reintroduction to the Women of the Torah and the Throne* (Louisville, KY: Westminster John Knox Press, 2017), 56.
4. Terence E. Fretheim, "The Book of Genesis," in *The New Interpreter's Bible Commentary*, vol. 1 (Nashville: Abingdon Press, 2015), 192.
5. Carol Meyers, *Women in Scripture* (Grand Rapids: Wm. B. Eerdmans Publishing Co., 2001), 62.
6. Meyers, *Women in Scripture*, 62–63.
7. J. Paul Sampley, "The First Letter to the Corinthians," in *The New Interpreter's Bible Commentary*, vol. 9 (Nashville: Abingdon Press, 2015), 688.
8. Green, *CEB Study Bible*, 306 NT.
9. Holly E. Hearon, "1 and 2 Corinthians," in *Queer Bible Commentary* (London: SCM Press, 2006), 608.
10. Attridge, Meeks, and Bassler, *HarperCollins Study Bible*, 1935.
11. Suzanne Watts Henderson, "1 Corinthians," in *The New Interpreter's Bible One-Volume Commentary* (Nashville: Abingdon Press, 2010), 790.
12. Sampley, "First Letter to the Corinthians," 691.
13. Henderson, "1 Corinthians," 790.
14. Sampley, "First Letter to the Corinthians," 693.

Seventeenth Sunday in Ordinary Time

1. Terence E. Fretheim, "The Book of Genesis," in *The New Interpreter's Bible Commentary*, vol. 1 (Nashville: Abingdon Press, 2015), 196.
2. Susan Niditch, "Genesis," in *Women's Bible Commentary* (Louisville, KY: Westminster John Knox Press, 2012), 39.
3. Niditch, "Genesis," 40.
4. Priests for Equality, *The Inclusive Bible: The First Egalitarian Translation* (Lanham, MD: Rowman & Littlefield Publishers, 2009).
5. Harold W. Attridge, Wayne A. Meeks, and Jouette M. Bassler, *HarperCollins Study Bible: New Revised Standard Version with the Apocryphal/Deuterocanonical Books* (San Francisco: HarperOne, 2006), 50.
6. Amy-Jill Levine and Marc Zvi Brettler, *The Jewish Annotated New Testament: New Revised Standard Version Bible Translation* (New York: Oxford University Press, 2017), 335.
7. Levine and Brettler, *Jewish Annotated New Testament*, 335.
8. Jouette M. Bassler, "1 Corinthians," in *Women's Bible Commentary* (Louisville, KY: Westminster John Knox Press, 2012), 561.

9. Joel B. Green, ed., *CEB Study Bible* (Nashville: Common English Bible, 2013), 316 NT.

10. Holly E. Hearon, "1 and 2 Corinthians," in *Queer Bible Commentary* (London: SCM Press, 2006), 615.

11. Attridge, Meeks, and Bassler, *HarperCollins Study Bible*, 1942.

12. Green, *CEB Study Bible*, 316 NT.

13. J. Paul Sampley, "The First Letter to the Corinthians," in *The New Interpreter's Bible Commentary*, vol. 9 (Nashville: Abingdon Press, 2015), 763–64.

Eighteenth Sunday in Ordinary Time

1. Carol Meyers, *Women in Scripture* (Grand Rapids: Wm. B. Eerdmans Publishing Co., 2001), 70.

2. Joel B. Green, ed., *CEB Study Bible* (Nashville: Common English Bible, 2013), 56 OT.

3. Harold W. Attridge, Wayne A. Meeks, and Jouette M. Bassler, *HarperCollins Study Bible: New Revised Standard Version with the Apocryphal/Deuterocanonical Books* (San Francisco: HarperOne, 2006), 55.

4. Amanda Hess, "Elizabeth Smart Says Pro-Abstinence Sex Ed Harms Victims of Rape," *Slate*, May 6, 2013, https://slate.com/human-interest/2013/05/eliza beth-smart-abstinence-only-sex-education-hurts-victims-of-rape-and-human -trafficking.html.

5. Terence E. Fretheim, "The Book of Genesis," in *The New Interpreter's Bible Commentary*, vol. 1 (Nashville: Abingdon Press, 2015), 213.

6. Green, *CEB Study Bible*, 329 NT.

7. Jouette M. Bassler, "1 Corinthians," in *Women's Bible Commentary* (Louisville, KY: Westminster John Knox Press, 2012), 565.

8. Suzanne Watts Henderson, "1 Corinthians," in *The New Interpreter's Bible One-Volume Commentary* (Nashville: Abingdon Press, 2010), 805.

9. Green, *CEB Study Bible*, 328 NT.

10. Green, *CEB Study Bible*, 328 NT.

11. J. Paul Sampley, "The First Letter to the Corinthians," in *The New Interpreter's Bible Commentary*, vol. 9 (Nashville: Abingdon Press, 2015), 834.

12. Sampley, "First Letter to the Corinthians," 835.

13. Holly E. Hearon, "1 and 2 Corinthians," in *Queer Bible Commentary* (London: SCM Press, 2006), 617.

Nineteenth Sunday in Ordinary Time

1. Susan Niditch, "Genesis," in *Women's Bible Commentary* (Louisville, KY: Westminster John Knox Press, 2012), 44.

2. Harold W. Attridge, Wayne A. Meeks, and Jouette M. Bassler, *HarperCollins Study Bible: New Revised Standard Version with the Apocryphal/Deuterocanonical Books* (San Francisco: HarperOne, 2006), 64.

3. Wilda Gafney, *Womanist Midrash: A Reintroduction to the Women of the Torah and the Throne* (Louisville, KY: Westminster John Knox Press, 2017), 124 n. 19.

4. Attridge, Meeks, and Bassler, *HarperCollins Study Bible*, 1743.

5. Pheme Perkins, "The Gospel of Mark," in *The New Interpreter's Bible Commentary*, vol. 7 (Nashville: Abingdon Press, 2015), 487.

6. Joel B. Green, ed., *CEB Study Bible* (Nashville: Common English Bible, 2013), 87 NT.

7. Elizabeth Struthers Malbon, "Gospel of Mark," in *Women's Bible Commentary* (Louisville, KY: Westminster John Knox Press, 2012), 487.

8. Perkins, "Gospel of Mark," 489.
9. Perkins, "Gospel of Mark," 489.

Twentieth Sunday in Ordinary Time

1. Nyasha Junior, "Exodus," in *Women's Bible Commentary* (Louisville, KY: Westminster John Knox Press, 2012), 58.
2. Carol Meyers, *Women in Scripture* (Grand Rapids: Wm. B. Eerdmans Publishing Co., 2001), 138.
3. Harold W. Attridge, Wayne A. Meeks, and Jouette M. Bassler, *HarperCollins Study Bible: New Revised Standard Version with the Apocryphal/Deuterocanonical Books* (San Francisco: HarperOne, 2006), 85.
4. Attridge, Meeks, and Bassler, *HarperCollins Study Bible*, 85.
5. Joel B. Green, ed., *CEB Study Bible* (Nashville: Common English Bible, 2013), 84 OT.
6. Walter Brueggemann, "The Book of Exodus," in *The New Interpreter's Bible Commentary*, vol. 1 (Nashville: Abingdon Press, 2015), 295.
7. Richard B. Hayes, "The Letter to the Galatians," in *The New Interpreter's Bible Commentary*, vol. 9 (Nashville: Abingdon Press, 2015), 1126.
8. Hayes, "Letter to the Galatians," 1127.
9. Susan Eastman, "Galatians," in *The New Interpreter's Bible One-Volume Commentary* (Nashville: Abingdon Press, 2010), 830.
10. Hayes, "Letter to the Galatians," 1132.
11. Brigitte Kahl, "Hagar's Babylonian Captivity: A Roman Re-imagination of Galatians 4:21–31," *Interpretation* 68, no. 3 (July 2014): 257–69, esp. 258.
12. Kahl, "Hagar's Babylonian Captivity," 257–69, esp. 258.
13. Meyers, *Women in Scripture*, 88.
14. Meyers, *Women in Scripture*, 88.

Twenty-First Sunday in Ordinary Time

1. Carol Meyers, *Women in Scripture* (Grand Rapids: Wm. B. Eerdmans Publishing Co., 2001), 171.
2. Walter Brueggemann, "The Book of Exodus," in *The New Interpreter's Bible Commentary*, vol. 1 (Nashville: Abingdon Press, 2015), 310.
3. Harold W. Attridge, Wayne A. Meeks, and Jouette M. Bassler, *HarperCollins Study Bible: New Revised Standard Version with the Apocryphal/Deuterocanonical Books* (San Francisco: HarperOne, 2006), 91.
4. Nyasha Junior, "Exodus," in *Women's Bible Commentary* (Louisville, KY: Westminster John Knox Press, 2012), 60.
5. Meyers, *Women in Scripture*, 171.
6. Attridge, Meeks, and Bassler, *HarperCollins Study Bible*, 91.
7. Junior, "Exodus," 60.
8. Pheme Perkins, "The Letter to the Ephesians," in *The New Interpreter's Bible Commentary*, vol. 10 (Nashville: Abingdon Press, 2015), 84.
9. E. Elizabeth Johnson, "Ephesians," in *Women's Bible Commentary* (Louisville, KY: Westminster John Knox Press, 2012), 578; Joel B. Green, ed., *CEB Study Bible* (Nashville: Common English Bible, 2013), 370 NT.
10. E. Johnson, "Ephesians," 579; Green, *CEB Study Bible*, 370 NT.
11. Meyers, *Women in Scripture*, 481.
12. Amy-Jill Levine and Marc Zvi Brettler, *The Jewish Annotated New Testament: New Revised Standard Version Bible Translation* (New York: Oxford University Press, 2017), 396.

13. E. Johnson, "Ephesians," 579.
14. Attridge, Meeks, and Bassler, *HarperCollins Study Bible*, 1989.
15. E. Johnson, "Ephesians," 576.
16. Margaret Y. McDonald, "Ephesians," in *The New Interpreter's Bible One-Volume Commentary* (Nashville: Abingdon Press, 2010), 840.
17. Robert E. Goss, "Ephesians," in *Queer Bible Commentary* (London: SCM Press, 2006), 635.
18. Levine and Brettler, *Jewish Annotated New Testament*, 395.
19. E. Johnson, "Ephesians," 579.

Twenty-Second Sunday in Ordinary Time

1. Carol Meyers, *Women in Scripture* (Grand Rapids: Wm. B. Eerdmans Publishing Co., 2001), 127.
2. Brent A. Strawn, "Exodus," in *The New Interpreter's Bible One-Volume Commentary* (Nashville: Abingdon Press, 2010), 45.
3. Harold W. Attridge, Wayne A. Meeks, and Jouette M. Bassler, *HarperCollins Study Bible: New Revised Standard Version with the Apocryphal/Deuterocanonical Books* (San Francisco: HarperOne, 2006), 86.
4. Nyasha Junior, "Exodus," in *Women's Bible Commentary* (Louisville, KY: Westminster John Knox Press, 2012), 62.
5. Bruce C. Birch, Walter Brueggemann, Terence E. Fretheim, and David L. Petersen, *A Theological Introduction to the Old Testament* (Nashville: Abingdon Press, 2005), 115.
6. Morna D. Hooker, "The Letter to the Philippians," in *The New Interpreter's Bible Commentary*, vol. 10 (Nashville: Abingdon Press, 2015), 169.
7. Amy-Jill Levine and Marc Zvi Brettler, *The Jewish Annotated New Testament: New Revised Standard Version Bible Translation* (New York: Oxford University Press, 2017), 405.
8. Hooker, "Letter to the Philippians," 169; Attridge, Meeks, and Bassler, *HarperCollins Study Bible*, 1996.
9. Hooker, "Letter to the Philippians," 169.
10. Meyers, *Women in Scripture*, 79.
11. Hooker, "Letter to the Philippians," 170.
12. Levine and Brettler, *Jewish Annotated New Testament*, 405.
13. Hooker, "Letter to the Philippians," 169.
14. Carla Swafford Works, "Philippians," in *Women's Bible Commentary* (Louisville, KY: Westminster John Knox Press, 2012), 584.
15. Meyers, *Women in Scripture*, 159.
16. Meyers, *Women in Scripture*, 159.
17. Meyers, *Women in Scripture*, 79.

Twenty-Third Sunday in Ordinary Time

1. Wilda Gafney, *Womanist Midrash: A Reintroduction to the Women of the Torah and the Throne* (Louisville, KY: Westminster John Knox Press, 2017), 156.
2. Katharine Doob Sakenfeld, "Numbers," in *Women's Bible Commentary* (Louisville, KY: Westminster John Knox Press, 2012), 85.
3. Carol Meyers, *Women in Scripture* (Grand Rapids: Wm. B. Eerdmans Publishing Co., 2001), 234.
4. Thomas B. Dozeman, "The Book of Numbers," in *The New Interpreter's Bible Commentary*, vol. 1 (Nashville: Abingdon Press, 2015), 815.
5. Dozeman, "Book of Numbers," 816.

6. Stephen Fowl, "Colossians," in *The New Interpreter's Bible One-Volume Commentary* (Nashville: Abingdon Press, 2010), 851.
7. Amy-Jill Levine and Marc Zvi Brettler, *The Jewish Annotated New Testament: New Revised Standard Version Bible Translation* (New York: Oxford University Press, 2017), 417; Harold W. Attridge, Wayne A. Meeks, and Jouette M. Bassler, *HarperCollins Study Bible: New Revised Standard Version with the Apocryphal/Deuterocanonical Books* (San Francisco: HarperOne, 2006), 2004.
8. Fowl, "Colossians," 851.
9. Andrew T. Lincoln, "The Letter to the Colossians," in *The New Interpreter's Bible Commentary*, vol. 10 (Nashville: Abingdon Press, 2015), 275.
10. Lincoln, "Letter to the Colossians," 274.
11. Fowl, "Colossians," 856.
12. Levine and Brettler, *Jewish Annotated New Testament*, 418.
13. Joel B. Green, ed., *CEB Study Bible* (Nashville: Common English Bible, 2013), 387 NT.
14. Meyers, *Women in Scripture*, 133.
15. Meyers, *Women in Scripture*, 133.
16. Lincoln, "Letter to the Colossians," 279.
17. Meyers, *Women in Scripture*, 133.
18. Meyers, *Women in Scripture*, 133.

Twenty-Fourth Sunday in Ordinary Time

1. Jerome F. D. Creach, "Judges," in *The New Interpreter's Bible One-Volume Commentary* (Nashville: Abingdon Press, 2010), 166.
2. Harold W. Attridge, Wayne A. Meeks, and Jouette M. Bassler, *HarperCollins Study Bible: New Revised Standard Version with the Apocryphal/Deuterocanonical Books* (San Francisco: HarperOne, 2006), 346.
3. Carol Meyers, *Women in Scripture* (Grand Rapids: Wm. B. Eerdmans Publishing Co., 2001), 66.
4. Meyers, *Women in Scripture*, 66.
5. Sara Koenig, "Commentary on Judges 4:1–7," *Working Preacher*, November 16, 2014, https://www.workingpreacher.org/preaching.aspx?commentary_id =2216.
6. Attridge, Meeks, and Bassler, *HarperCollins Study Bible*, 2015; Joel B. Green, ed., *CEB Study Bible* (Nashville: Common English Bible, 2013), 403 NT.
7. Attridge, Meeks, and Bassler, *HarperCollins Study Bible*, 2015.
8. Joanna Dewey, "1 Timothy," in *Women's Bible Commentary* (Louisville, KY: Westminster John Knox Press, 2012), 596.
9. Dewey, "1 Timothy," 596.
10. Dewey, "1 Timothy," 596.
11. Green, *CEB Study Bible*, 407 NT.
12. James D. G. Dunn, "The First and Second Letters to Timothy and the Letter to Titus," in *The New Interpreter's Bible Commentary*, vol. 10 (Nashville: Abingdon Press, 2015), 393.
13. Dunn, "First and Second Letters to Timothy and the Letter to Titus," 392; Green, *CEB Study Bible*, 409 NT.
14. Dewey, "1 Timothy," 596; Green, *CEB Study Bible*, 408 NT.
15. Attridge, Meeks, and Bassler, *HarperCollins Study Bible*, 2018.
16. Dewey, "1 Timothy," 599.
17. Dunn, "First and Second Letters to Timothy and the Letter to Titus," 393.
18. Dewey, "1 Timothy," 596.

Twenty-Fifth Sunday in Ordinary Time

1. Jerome F. D. Creach, "Judges," in *The New Interpreter's Bible One-Volume Commentary* (Nashville: Abingdon Press, 2010), 167.

2. Harold W. Attridge, Wayne A. Meeks, and Jouette M. Bassler, *HarperCollins Study Bible: New Revised Standard Version with the Apocryphal/Deuterocanonical Books* (San Francisco: HarperOne, 2006), 355.

3. Carol Meyers, *Women in Scripture* (Grand Rapids: Wm. B. Eerdmans Publishing Co., 2001), 98.

4. Dennis T. Olson, "The Book of Judges," in *The New Interpreter's Bible Commentary*, vol. 2 (Nashville: Abingdon Press, 2015), 191.

5. Meyers, *Women in Scripture*, 492.

6. Susan E. Hylen, "Widows in the New Testament Period," *The Bible and Interpretation*, February 2019, https://bibleinterp.arizona.edu/articles/widows-new -testament-period?sfns=ncl.

7. Amy-Jill Levine and Marc Zvi Brettler, *The Jewish Annotated New Testament: New Revised Standard Version Bible Translation* (New York: Oxford University Press, 2017), 438; Joel B. Green, ed., *CEB Study Bible* (Nashville: Common English Bible, 2013), 410 NT.

8. Attridge, Meeks, and Bassler, *HarperCollins Study Bible*, 2021.

9. Green, *CEB Study Bible*, 411 NT.

10. Matthew Skinner, "1–2 Timothy," in *The New Interpreter's Bible One-Volume Commentary* (Nashville: Abingdon Press, 2010), 871.

11. Joanna Dewey, "1 Timothy," in *Women's Bible Commentary* (Louisville, KY: Westminster John Knox Press, 2012), 600.

12. Dewey, "1 Timothy," 600; Meyers, *Women in Scripture*, 492–93.

13. Dewey, "1 Timothy," 600.

14. Meyers, *Women in Scripture*, 493.

15. Levine and Brettler, *Jewish Annotated New Testament*, 438.

16. Attridge, Meeks, and Bassler, *HarperCollins Study Bible*, 2021.

17. Attridge, Meeks, and Bassler, *HarperCollins Study Bible*, 2021.

Twenty-Sixth Sunday in Ordinary Time

1. Phyllis Trible, *Texts of Terror: Literary-Feminist Readings of Biblical Narratives* (Philadelphia: Fortress Press, 1984), 97.

2. Joel B. Green, ed., *CEB Study Bible* (Nashville: Common English Bible, 2013), 390 OT.

3. Jerome F. D. Creach, "Judges," in *The New Interpreter's Bible One-Volume Commentary* (Nashville: Abingdon Press, 2010), 173.

4. Harold W. Attridge, Wayne A. Meeks, and Jouette M. Bassler, *HarperCollins Study Bible: New Revised Standard Version with the Apocryphal/Deuterocanonical Books* (San Francisco: HarperOne, 2006), 367.

5. Creach, "Judges," 173.

6. Carol Meyers, *Women in Scripture* (Grand Rapids: Wm. B. Eerdmans Publishing Co., 2001), 110.

7. Attridge, Meeks, and Bassler, *HarperCollins Study Bible*, 2023.

8. Green, *CEB Study Bible*, 404 NT.

9. Attridge, Meeks, and Bassler, *HarperCollins Study Bible*, 2024.

10. James D. G. Dunn, "The First and Second Letters to Timothy and the Letter to Titus," in *The New Interpreter's Bible Commentary*, vol. 10 (Nashville: Abingdon Press, 2015), 419.

11. Attridge, Meeks, and Bassler, *HarperCollins Study Bible*, 2024.

12. Meyers, *Women in Scripture*, 110.

13. Amy-Jill Levine and Marc Zvi Brettler, *The Jewish Annotated New Testament: New Revised Standard Version Bible Translation* (New York: Oxford University Press, 2017), 442.

14. Dunn, "First and Second Letters to Timothy and the Letter to Titus," 420.

15. Meyers, *Women in Scripture*, 110.

16. Meyers, *Women in Scripture*, 78–79.

17. Dunn, "First and Second Letters to Timothy and the Letter to Titus," 420.

18. Dunn, "First and Second Letters to Timothy and the Letter to Titus," 420.

Twenty-Seventh Sunday in Ordinary Time

1. Mona West, "Ruth," in *Queer Bible Commentary* (London: SCM Press, 2006), 191.

2. Eunny P. Lee, "Ruth," in *Women's Bible Commentary* (Louisville, KY: Westminster John Knox Press, 2012), 142.

3. Katharine D. Sakenfeld, "Ruth," in *The New Interpreter's Bible One-Volume Commentary* (Nashville: Abingdon Press, 2010), 182.

4. Kirsten Nielson, *Ruth: A Commentary*, trans. E. Broadbridge (Louisville, KY: Westminster John Knox Press, 1997), 50.

5. James D. G. Dunn, "The First and Second Letters to Timothy and the Letter to Titus," in *The New Interpreter's Bible Commentary*, vol. 10 (Nashville: Abingdon Press, 2015), 432–33.

6. Dunn, "First and Second Letters to Timothy and the Letter to Titus," 432.

7. Harold W. Attridge, Wayne A. Meeks, and Jouette M. Bassler, *HarperCollins Study Bible: New Revised Standard Version with the Apocryphal/Deuterocanonical Books* (San Francisco: HarperOne, 2006), 2025.

8. Amy-Jill Levine and Marc Zvi Brettler, *The Jewish Annotated New Testament: New Revised Standard Version Bible Translation* (New York: Oxford University Press, 2017), 445.

9. Carol Meyers, *Women in Scripture* (Grand Rapids: Wm. B. Eerdmans Publishing Co., 2001), 494; Dunn, "First and Second Letters to Timothy and the Letter to Titus," 433.

10. Matthew Skinner, "1–2 Timothy," in *The New Interpreter's Bible One-Volume Commentary* (Nashville: Abingdon Press, 2010), 873.

11. Attridge, Meeks, and Bassler, *HarperCollins Study Bible*, 2026; Levine and Brettler, *Jewish Annotated New Testament*, 446.

12. Skinner, "1–2 Timothy," 873; Meyers, *Women in Scripture*, 494.

13. Dunn, "First and Second Letters to Timothy and the Letter to Titus," 433.

14. Dunn, "First and Second Letters to Timothy and the Letter to Titus," 433.

Twenty-Eighth Sunday in Ordinary Time

1. Harold W. Attridge, Wayne A. Meeks, and Jouette M. Bassler, *HarperCollins Study Bible: New Revised Standard Version with the Apocryphal/Deuterocanonical Books* (San Francisco: HarperOne, 2006), 393.

2. Jo Ann Hackett, "1 and 2 Samuel," in *Women's Bible Commentary* (Louisville, KY: Westminster John Knox Press, 2012), 155.

3. Steve McKenzie, "1 Samuel," in *The New Interpreter's Bible One-Volume Commentary* (Nashville: Abingdon Press, 2010), 189.

4. Matthew Skinner, "1–2 Timothy," in *The New Interpreter's Bible One-Volume Commentary* (Nashville: Abingdon Press, 2010), 873.

5. James D. G. Dunn, "The First and Second Letters to Timothy and the Letter to Titus," in *The New Interpreter's Bible Commentary*, vol. 10 (Nashville: Abingdon Press, 2015), 439.

6. Dunn, "First and Second Letters to Timothy and the Letter to Titus," 439.

7. Attridge, Meeks, and Bassler, *HarperCollins Study Bible*, 2027.

8. Dunn, "First and Second Letters to Timothy and the Letter to Titus," 439.

9. Amy-Jill Levine and Marc Zvi Brettler, *The Jewish Annotated New Testament: New Revised Standard Version Bible Translation* (New York: Oxford University Press, 2017), 447; Dunn, "First and Second Letters to Timothy and the Letter to Titus," 441.

10. Joel B. Green, ed., *CEB Study Bible* (Nashville: Common English Bible, 2013), 420 NT.

11. Dunn, "First and Second Letters to Timothy and the Letter to Titus," 440.

12. Joanna Dewey, "2 Timothy," in *Women's Bible Commentary* (Louisville, KY: Westminster John Knox Press, 2012), 603.

13. Dunn, "First and Second Letters to Timothy and the Letter to Titus," 441.

14. Carol Meyers, *Women in Scripture* (Grand Rapids: Wm. B. Eerdmans Publishing Co., 2001), 63.

15. Meyers, *Women in Scripture*, 63.

Twenty-Ninth Sunday in Ordinary Time

1. Carol Meyers, *Women in Scripture* (Grand Rapids: Wm. B. Eerdmans Publishing Co., 2001), 126.

2. Steve McKenzie, "1 Samuel," in *The New Interpreter's Bible One-Volume Commentary* (Nashville: Abingdon Press, 2010), 196.

3. Wilda Gafney, *Womanist Midrash: A Reintroduction to the Women of the Torah and the Throne* (Louisville, KY: Westminster John Knox Press, 2017), 193.

4. Joel B. Green, ed., *CEB Study Bible* (Nashville: Common English Bible, 2013), 451 OT.

5. Bruce C. Birch, "The First and Second Books of Samuel," in *The New Interpreter's Bible Commentary*, vol. 2 (Nashville: Abingdon Press, 2015), 536.

6. Meyers, *Women in Scripture*, 495.

7. James D. G. Dunn, "The First and Second Letters to Timothy and the Letter to Titus," in *The New Interpreter's Bible Commentary*, vol. 10 (Nashville: Abingdon Press, 2015), 450.

8. Meyers, *Women in Scripture*, 495.

9. Joanna Dewey, "Titus," in *Women's Bible Commentary* (Louisville, KY: Westminster John Knox Press, 2012), 604.

10. Dunn, "First and Second Letters to Timothy and the Letter to Titus," 451.

11. Meyers, *Women in Scripture*, 495.

12. Amy-Jill Levine and Marc Zvi Brettler, *The Jewish Annotated New Testament: New Revised Standard Version Bible Translation* (New York: Oxford University Press, 2017), 453.

13. Green, *CEB Study Bible*, 426 NT.

Thirtieth Sunday in Ordinary Time

1. Bruce C. Birch, "The First and Second Books of Samuel," in *The New Interpreter's Bible Commentary*, vol. 2 (Nashville: Abingdon Press, 2015), 471.

2. Steve McKenzie, "1 Samuel," in *The New Interpreter's Bible One-Volume Commentary* (Nashville: Abingdon Press, 2010), 198–99.

3. Birch, "First and Second Books of Samuel," 472.

4. Harold W. Attridge, Wayne A. Meeks, and Jouette M. Bassler, *HarperCollins Study Bible: New Revised Standard Version with the Apocryphal/Deuterocanonical Books* (San Francisco: HarperOne, 2006), 427.
5. Birch, "First and Second Books of Samuel," 469.
6. Birch, "First and Second Books of Samuel," 470.
7. Amy-Jill Levine and Marc Zvi Brettler, *The Jewish Annotated New Testament: New Revised Standard Version Bible Translation* (New York: Oxford University Press, 2017), 455.
8. Joel B. Green, ed., *CEB Study Bible* (Nashville: Common English Bible, 2013), 432 NT.
9. Green, *CEB Study Bible*, 432 NT.
10. Cain Hope Felder, "The Letter to Philemon," in *The New Interpreter's Bible Commentary*, vol. 10 (Nashville: Abingdon Press, 2015), 469.
11. Felder, "Letter to Philemon," 468.
12. Carol Meyers, *Women in Scripture* (Grand Rapids: Wm. B. Eerdmans Publishing Co., 2001), 52–53.
13. Felder, "Letter to Philemon," 468.
14. Meyers, *Women in Scripture*, 53.
15. Emerson Powery, "Philemon," in *The New Interpreter's Bible One-Volume Commentary* (Nashville: Abingdon Press, 2010), 878; Mitzi J. Smith, "Philemon," in *Women's Bible Commentary* (Louisville, KY: Westminster John Knox Press, 2012), 606.
16. Smith, "Philemon," 605.

All Saints' Day

1. Glenn D. Pemberton, "Proverbs," in *The New Interpreter's Bible One-Volume Commentary* (Nashville: Abingdon Press, 2010), 367.
2. Christine Roy Yoder, "Proverbs," in *Women's Bible Commentary* (Louisville, KY: Westminster John Knox Press, 2012), 241.
3. Amy G. Oden, "Commentary on Proverbs 31:10–31," *Working Preacher*, September 23, 2012, https://www.workingpreacher.org/preaching.aspx?commentary_id=1377.
4. Raymond C. Van Leeuwen, "The Book of Proverbs," in *The New Interpreter's Bible Commentary*, vol. 3 (Nashville: Abingdon Press, 2015), 941.
5. Joel B. Green, ed., *CEB Study Bible* (Nashville: Common English Bible, 2013), 1051 OT.
6. Green, *CEB Study Bible*, 941–42 OT.
7. Luke Timothy Johnson, "The Letter of James," in *The New Interpreter's Bible Commentary*, vol. 10 (Nashville: Abingdon Press, 2015), 648.
8. L. Johnson, "Letter of James," 648–49.
9. Harold W. Attridge, Wayne A. Meeks, and Jouette M. Bassler, *HarperCollins Study Bible: New Revised Standard Version with the Apocryphal/Deuterocanonical Books* (San Francisco: HarperOne, 2006), 2055.
10. Green, *CEB Study Bible*, 457 NT; L. Johnson, "Letter of James," 648.
11. Amy-Jill Levine and Marc Zvi Brettler, *The Jewish Annotated New Testament: New Revised Standard Version Bible Translation* (New York: Oxford University Press, 2017), 489.
12. Levine and Brettler, *Jewish Annotated New Testament*, 494.
13. Gay L. Byron, "James," in *Women's Bible Commentary* (Louisville, KY: Westminster John Knox Press, 2012), 613; L. William Countryman, "James," in *Queer Bible Commentary* (London: SCM Press, 2006), 719.

14. L. Johnson, "Letter of James," 649.
15. L. Johnson, "Letter of James," 650.
16. Jerome F. D. Creach, "Judges," in *The New Interpreter's Bible One-Volume Commentary* (Nashville: Abingdon Press, 2010), 147.

Thirty-First Sunday in Ordinary Time

1. Bruce C. Birch, "The First and Second Books of Samuel," in *The New Interpreter's Bible Commentary*, vol. 2 (Nashville: Abingdon Press, 2015), 578.
2. Phyllis Trible, *Texts of Terror: Literary-Feminist Readings of Biblical Narratives* (Philadelphia: Fortress Press, 1984), 41.
3. Harold W. Attridge, Wayne A. Meeks, and Jouette M. Bassler, *HarperCollins Study Bible: New Revised Standard Version with the Apocryphal/Deuterocanonical Books* (San Francisco: HarperOne, 2006), 453–54.
4. Jo Ann Hackett, "1 and 2 Samuel," in *Women's Bible Commentary* (Louisville, KY: Westminster John Knox Press, 2012), 160.
5. Carol Meyers, *Women in Scripture* (Grand Rapids: Wm. B. Eerdmans Publishing Co., 2001), 164.
6. Birch, "First and Second Books of Samuel," 575.
7. Attridge, Meeks, and Bassler, *HarperCollins Study Bible*, 2101.
8. Attridge, Meeks, and Bassler, *HarperCollins Study Bible*, 2101; Judith L. Kovacs, "The Revelation to John," in *The New Interpreter's Bible One-Volume Commentary* (Nashville: Abingdon Press, 2010), 931.
9. Amy-Jill Levine and Marc Zvi Brettler, *The Jewish Annotated New Testament: New Revised Standard Version Bible Translation* (New York: Oxford University Press, 2017), 557; Kovacs, "Revelation to John," 931.
10. Meyers, *Women in Scripture*, 544.
11. Levine and Brettler, *Jewish Annotated New Testament*, 558.
12. Joel B. Green, ed., *CEB Study Bible* (Nashville: Common English Bible, 2013), 512 NT.
13. Attridge, Meeks, and Bassler, *HarperCollins Study Bible*, 2101–2.
14. Attridge, Meeks, and Bassler, *HarperCollins Study Bible*, 2102; Levine and Brettler, *Jewish Annotated New Testament*, 558.
15. Levine and Brettler, *Jewish Annotated New Testament*, 559.
16. Green, *CEB Study Bible*, 513 NT.
17. Christopher C. Rowland, "The Book of Revelation," in *The New Interpreter's Bible Commentary*, vol. 10 (Nashville: Abingdon Press, 2015), 1036.

Thirty-Second Sunday in Ordinary Time

1. Harold W. Attridge, Wayne A. Meeks, and Jouette M. Bassler, *HarperCollins Study Bible: New Revised Standard Version with the Apocryphal/Deuterocanonical Books* (San Francisco: HarperOne, 2006), 495.
2. Priests for Equality, *The Inclusive Bible: The First Egalitarian Translation* (Lanham, MD: Rowman & Littlefield Publishers, 2009), 195.
3. Attridge, Meeks, and Bassler, *HarperCollins Study Bible*, 495.
4. Attridge, Meeks, and Bassler, *HarperCollins Study Bible*, 495.
5. Choon-Leong Seow, "The First and Second Books of Kings," in *The New Interpreter's Bible Commentary*, vol. 2 (Nashville: Abingdon Press, 2015), 683–84.
6. Seow, "First and Second Books of Kings," 684.
7. Seow, "First and Second Books of Kings," 683–84.
8. Priests for Equality, *The Inclusive Bible*, 195.

9. Cameron B. R. Howard, "1 and 2 Kings," in *Women's Bible Commentary* (Louisville, KY: Westminster John Knox Press, 2012), 168.

10. Carol Meyers, *Women in Scripture* (Grand Rapids: Wm. B. Eerdmans Publishing Co., 2001), 270–71.

11. Howard, "1 and 2 Kings," 168.

12. Attridge, Meeks, and Bassler, *HarperCollins Study Bible*, 2106.

13. Judith L. Kovacs, "The Revelation to John," in *The New Interpreter's Bible One-Volume Commentary* (Nashville: Abingdon Press, 2010), 917.

14. Kovacs, "Revelation to John," 917.

15. Meyers, *Women in Scripture*, 528.

16. Attridge, Meeks, and Bassler, *HarperCollins Study Bible*, 2106.

17. Amy-Jill Levine and Marc Zvi Brettler, *The Jewish Annotated New Testament: New Revised Standard Version Bible Translation* (New York: Oxford University Press, 2017), 565–66.

18. Tina Pippin, "Revelation/Apocalypse of John," in *Women's Bible Commentary* (Louisville, KY: Westminster John Knox Press, 2012), 630.

Thirty-Third Sunday in Ordinary Time

1. Cameron B. R. Howard, "1 and 2 Kings," in *Women's Bible Commentary* (Louisville, KY: Westminster John Knox Press, 2012), 172.

2. Carol Meyers, *Women in Scripture* (Grand Rapids: Wm. B. Eerdmans Publishing Co., 2001), 101.

3. Ken Stone, "1 and 2 Kings," in *Queer Bible Commentary* (London: SCM Press, 2006), 238.

4. Wilda Gafney, *Womanist Midrash: A Reintroduction to the Women of the Torah and the Throne* (Louisville, KY: Westminster John Knox Press, 2017), 243.

5. Gafney, *Womanist Midrash*, 244.

6. Gafney, *Womanist Midrash*, 246.

7. Meyers, *Women in Scripture*, 100.

8. Joel B. Green, ed., *CEB Study Bible* (Nashville: Common English Bible, 2013), 503 NT; Amy-Jill Levine and Marc Zvi Brettler, *The Jewish Annotated New Testament: New Revised Standard Version Bible Translation* (New York: Oxford University Press, 2017), 544.

9. Christopher C. Rowland, "The Book of Revelation," in *The New Interpreter's Bible Commentary*, vol. 10 (Nashville: Abingdon Press, 2015), 969.

10. Meyers, *Women in Scripture*, 102.

11. Rowland, "Book of Revelation," 975.

12. Meyers, *Women in Scripture*, 102.

13. Judith L. Kovacs, "The Revelation to John," in *The New Interpreter's Bible One-Volume Commentary* (Nashville: Abingdon Press, 2010), 923.

14. Meyers, *Women in Scripture*, 102.

15. Levine and Brettler, *Jewish Annotated New Testament*, 544; Rowland, "Book of Revelation," 975.

16. Meyers, *Women in Scripture*, 102.

17. Tina Pippin, "Revelation/Apocalypse of John," in *Women's Bible Commentary* (Louisville, KY: Westminster John Knox Press, 2012), 629.

Christ the King Sunday

1. Harold W. Attridge, Wayne A. Meeks, and Jouette M. Bassler, *HarperCollins Study Bible: New Revised Standard Version with the Apocryphal/Deuterocanonical Books* (San Francisco: HarperOne, 2006), 554.

2. Wilda Gafney, *Womanist Midrash: A Reintroduction to the Women of the Torah and the Throne* (Louisville, KY: Westminster John Knox Press, 2017), 264.

3. Ken Stone, "1 and 2 Kings," in *Queer Bible Commentary* (London: SCM Press, 2006), 245: also possibly the woman named in Isa. 8:3, though she may be the wife of a prophet.

4. Carol Meyers, *Women in Scripture* (Grand Rapids: Wm. B. Eerdmans Publishing Co., 2001), 96.

5. Cameron B. R. Howard, "1 and 2 Kings," in *Women's Bible Commentary* (Louisville, KY: Westminster John Knox Press, 2012), 178.

6. Meyers, *Women in Scripture*, 515.

7. Amy-Jill Levine and Marc Zvi Brettler, *The Jewish Annotated New Testament: New Revised Standard Version Bible Translation* (New York: Oxford University Press, 2017), 569; Christopher C. Rowland, "The Book of Revelation," in *The New Interpreter's Bible Commentary*, vol. 10 (Nashville: Abingdon Press, 2015), 1068.

8. Attridge, Meeks, and Bassler, *HarperCollins Study Bible*, 2110; Joel B. Green, ed., *CEB Study Bible* (Nashville: Common English Bible, 2013), 521 NT.

9. Rowland, "Book of Revelation," 1068.

10. Rowland, "Book of Revelation," 1068.

11. Tina Pippin, "Revelation/Apocalypse of John," in *Women's Bible Commentary* (Louisville, KY: Westminster John Knox Press, 2012), 631.

12. Meyers, *Women in Scripture*, 515.

Index of Lectionary Passages

Texts in bold include passages from the Revised Common Lectionary.

CPSIA information can be obtained
at www.ICGtesting.com
Printed in the USA
BVHW062319180222
629436BV00016B/216